Feminists Under Fire

Feminists Under Fire
Exchanges across War Zones

Wenona Giles, Malathi de Alwis,
Edith Klein, Neluka Silva
(Co-Editors)

with
Maja Korač, Djurdja Knežević, Žarana Papić
(Advisory Editors)

Between the Lines
Toronto, Canada

Feminists Under Fire

© 2003 by Wenona Giles, Malathi de Alwis, Edith Klein, and Neluka Silva

First published in Canada in 2003 by
Between the Lines
720 Bathurst Street, Suite #404
Toronto, Ontario
M5S 2R4
http://www.btlbooks.com

Every reasonable effort has been made to identify copyright holders. Between the Lines would be pleased to have any errors or omissions brought to its attention.

National Library of Canada Cataloguing in Publication

Main entry under title:
    Feminists under fire : exchanges across war zones / edited by Wenona Giles . . . [et al.].
Includes bibliographical references and index.
ISBN 1-896357-78-4

1. Women and war – Former Yugoslav republics. 2. Women and war – Sri Lanka.
3. Nationalism and feminism – Former Soviet republics. 4. Nationalism and feminism – Sri Lanka. 5. Former Yugoslav republics – Ethnic relations. 6. Sri Lanka – Ethnic relations. I. Giles, Wenona, 1949-
HQ1233.F42 2003   303.6'6'08209497   C2003-901770-2

Cover design by Jennifer Tiberio
Text design and page preparation by Steve Izma
Printed in Canada by union labour

Between the Lines gratefully acknowledges assistance for its publishing activities from the Canada Council for the Arts, the Ontario Arts Council, the Government of Ontario through the Ontario Book Publishers Tax Credit program and through the Ontario Book Initiative, and the Government of Canada through the Book Publishing Industry Development Program.

Canada

We dedicate this book
to the women of the former Yugoslavia and of Sri Lanka
who are courageous activists, scholars, and peace builders,
and in particular to

Žarana Papić

who was an inspiration to so many of us.

Table of Contents

The Federal Republic of Yugoslavia
and surrounding countries

Ljubljana

Slovenia

Zagreb

Croatia

Romania

Vojvodina
Novi Sad

Belgrad

Banja Luka

Bosnia &
Herzegonia

Yugoslavia

Sarajevo

Serbia

Mostar

Adriatic Sea

Montenegro

Pristina

Podgorica

Kosova/o

Italy

Albania

0   500   1000 km

Macedonia

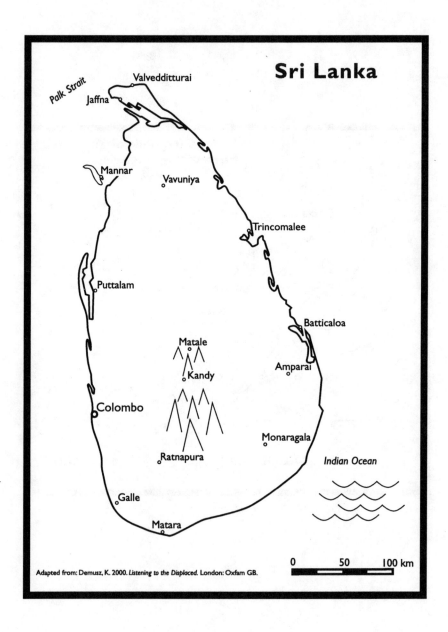

Sri Lanka

Polk Strait

Valvedditturai

Jaffna

Mannar

Vavuniya

Trincomalee

Puttalam

Batticaloa

Matale

Kandy

Amparai

Colombo

Monaragala

Ratnapura

Indian Ocean

Galle

Matara

0   50   100 km

Adapted from: Demusz, K. 2000. *Listening to the Displaced*. London: Oxfam GB.

Preface

This book is a collaborative endeavour derived from the Women in Conflict Zones Network (WICZNET), a multi-year research relationship that began in 1996 and that evolved into a comparative project between Sri Lanka and the region of the former Yugoslavia in 1998-99. The project enabled the Network participants to assess the various positions of women vis-à-vis specific forms and constructions of nationalism and its accompanying social and geopolitical relations, as well as to make cross-cultural comparisons regarding women's status and roles. In this respect our debate has, to a large extent, addressed the issue of difference as well as simultaneously exploring the contradictory positions of women and their varied and complex social realities. The first working meeting of the project was held in Hendela, Sri Lanka, in December 1998. It was originally planned that our second meeting would be held in Sarajevo, Bosnia, but because of the NATO bombings, we met in Budapest in October 1999.

The two sites of Sri Lanka and the region of the former Yugoslavia were chosen for particular reasons. First, several members of the Women in Conflict Zones Network live in each of the two regions and work in activist and/or academic institutions there. Thus, the project was conceived both by and with members of the Network who were already situated in those two regions in the late 1990s. Our work, therefore, evolved very much from within the two regions, while still being linked to the international Network. It was crucial to the development of the project that participants were rooted in each geopolitical location, while also in constant contact with those Network members located throughout the world. It was equally important that the Network expand to include participants across as many ethnic-national boundaries of the conflict as possible in each region of Sri Lanka (e.g., Sinhalese, Tamil, Moslem) and the former Yugoslavia (e.g., Bosnian, Croatian, Kosovar, Serbian). All of the participants in the project were feminists who were committed to challenging and crossing nationalist boundaries in their activism and their research.

Second, the two regions of Sri Lanka and the former Yugoslavia pose very different geopolitical histories. In Sri Lanka, a nationalist struggle with the British colonialists has been followed by two decades of internal ethnic-nationalist struggles. The region of the former Yugoslavia has been affected by ethnic-nationalist struggles that accompanied the transformation of a socialist society to a market-based democracy. International interventions in both regions (i.e., India in Sri Lanka, and UN and NATO forces in the region of the former Yugoslavia) have either exacerbated the internal conflicts or have been inadequate to end them. Similarities across the two very different regions, including some of the ways in which nationalism, violence, citizenship, and the refugee experience are gendered, have contributed to our commitment to the comparative study. Feminist scholars and activists in both regions insisted on examining the differences and the similarities in the two regions in order to understand and inform their politics of resistance at the local and international levels.

The Women in Conflict Zones Network, from its inception, included a broad range of people from distinct geographical locations, political backgrounds, and experiences. The interdisciplinary character of the Network has ensured varied understandings of feminist issues, and the Network never sought consensus on a specific brand of feminist thinking or politics. If categories can be deployed here, solely as a heuristic device, we can say that socialist feminists sat next to anti-nationalist feminists employing post-structuralist perspectives, who sat next to feminists whose approaches were primarily quantitative, who sat across the table from feminist activists dealing directly with the aftermath of violence invoked by war. Having said this, the Network and its projects have illustrated a common commitment to combatting violence against women (and men) and the conflict that perpetrates such violence.[1]

Certainly the recent NATO-Balkan war deepened our understanding of this form of communication and of comparative research, as well as challenged, in a very poignant way, our attempts to define a "conflict zone."[2] As we organized our second meeting with our colleagues in the region of the former Yugoslavia, NATO bombings began in Serbia and Kosova/o (see Lepa Mladjenović in chapter 3, and Žarana Papić in chapter 4). The conflict in this region had spread to Western Europe and North America and many people who might have considered themselves to be outside of a "conflict zone" now began to sense that they were very much inside the boundaries of war. The impacts on the WICZNET were immediate: in the spring of 1999, we temporarily abandoned attempts to organize a meeting to discuss our collaborative research with Network members inside the war zone. For those outside, it was difficult to deal with the fact that our colleagues were being targeted not only by nationalists in their own regions, but also by bombs dropped by the armies of our own countries. Notwithstanding the difficulties (both practical and emotional) of doing so, Network members succeeded in maintaining constant and often terrifying contact. Our solidarity with one another and with other anti-nationalist feminists around the world at that time was a form of defiance against NATO aggression. It was also a means by which we assisted Network members in the region of the former Yugoslavia to reach the rest of the world with information and requests for assistance.[3]

We are grateful to many steadfast supporters, without whom this project could not have happened. Thanks are due to the Social Scientists' Association in Colombo, the International Centre for Ethnic Studies, the Kerepesi Conference Centre in Budapest; the Centre for Refugee Studies, the Centre for Feminist Research, and the York Centre for International and Security Studies at York University, Toronto – all of which have hosted the Network, its workshops, and activities. We would also like to thank the contributors to this volume from Bosnia-Herzegovina, Croatia, Serbia, and Sri Lanka who overcame serious obstacles in order to be present at our meetings and to share their insights about gender and conflict in their regions. We also owe a debt of gratitude to the scores of unnamed activists and survivors in the regions whose experiences figure so prominently in the words of our authors. Their work and their struggles have been a source of inspiration. We would especially like to acknowledge the role of Žarana Papić. Žarana was a powerful voice for feminists in Serbia and beyond, an activist and a scholar who played an immensely significant role in the women's movement and in women's studies in Belgrade. Her death in September 2002 came as a deep shock to all her colleagues, friends, and students.

The following people provided invaluable assistance with research and fundraising related to the WICZNET and the comparative project, as well as with the organization of the meetings over the years. In Sri Lanka: Kumari Jayawardena, along with her staff at the Social Scientists' Association, worked tirelessly over a period of several months to organize the 1998 WICZNET conference at the Pegasus Hotel, Hendela, which was attended by forty international participants and over seventy local participants. In the region of the former Yugoslavia: Nada Ler Sofronić of the Soros Foundation (Sarejevo), assisted by York University staff and research assistants, organized the 1999 Budapest meeting of forty-eight international participants from Sri Lanka, several states in the region of the former Yugoslavia, and other parts of the world, including Britain, Canada, Guatemala, India, Switzerland, France, and the USA. In Canada: Maja Korać, Joan Broussard, Alison Crosby, Vanessa Farr, Steve Mataija, Alex Neve, Alejandra Park, Sharmini Peries, Barbara Treviranus, and Kim Ward provided a wide range of research and administrative assistance. This project could not have happened without the wisdom and energy of all of these wonderful individuals.

National and international non-governmental organizations (NGOs) that assisted in establishing the WICZNET and helped us with the development of the comparative project include the Gender Caucus of the Canadian Council on Refugees, in particular Janet Dench, Jetty Chakkalakal, and Afsaneh Hojabri; the International Centre for Human Rights and Democratic Development in Ottawa, specifically Ariane Brunet and Isabelle Solon Helal; the Ford Foundation, in particular Mahnaz Ispahani and Cathy Feingold; Oxfam (Colombo), in particular Simon Harris; Amnesty International (London), in particular Leanne MacMillan; UNICEF headquarters in New York, Ottawa, Tehran, and Islamabad, in particular Silvia Luciani, Niloufar Pourzand, Angela Raven-Roberts, and Sherrill Whittington; the Office of the UN High Commissioner for Refugees (UNHCR) Senior Co-ordinator for Women's Issues in Geneva, in particular Rita Reddy; and the UN Special Rapporteur on Violence Against Women, Radhika Coomaraswamy.

Paul Eprile of Between the Lines has provided excellent guidance, encouragement, and support throughout the development of this book. We are also grateful to Beth McAuley for her careful editorial work; Jennifer Tiberio and and Steve Izma for their very competent and creative design and layout; Martin Boyne who skilfully and quickly completed the index; and Nadine Schuurman for the maps that she researched and carefully crafted.

Funding from the Ford Foundation (New York, USA), Open Society Soros Foundation (Budapest, Hungary), Oxfam (Colombo, Sri Lanka), and the Social Sciences and Humanities Research Council of Canada was essential to the development of this comparative project. In addition to their financial assistance, we are grateful to these organizations for their valuable advice and support along the way, as well as their patience and flexibility when our timelines were affected by the unpredictable effects of war in the regions under study.

Notes

1 See Wenona Giles and Jennifer Hyndman, "New Directions for Feminist Research and Politics in Conflict Zones," in Wenona Giles and Jennifer Hyndman, eds., *Sites of Violence: Gender and Conflict Zones* (Berkeley: University of California Press, 2003).

2 Edith Klein, "Multilateralism and Its Consequences for Women in the Balkans: Intervention, Reconstruction, and Globalization," in Giles and Hyndman, eds., *Sites of Violence*.

3 However, while feminist activists have relied on the Internet during the height of militarized conflict, so have nationalists, such as the Slobodan Milošević regime (see Djurdja Knežević in chapter 6). Indeed, workshop participants in both regions pointed out that it is also important not to ignore other, more established forms of communication and information sharing, such as various media outlets, as they are frequently appropriated by ethnic-nationalist forces and authoritarian states.

Wenona Giles

Introduction

Feminist Exchanges and Comparative Perspectives across Conflict Zones

War is an ambivalent process for women. While on the one hand they suffer acutely from its violence, on the other, those living in traditional patriarchal societies may find that war is a time of release from the constricting hierarchies of peacetime existence. But such a gain can rarely be sustained in the aftermath of war. Different kinds of wars permit different kinds of female participation, and women's lives are affected in a variety of ways by the resolution of war. Women are seldom simply victimized or empowered by war: their experiences are more complicated. And yet, there are commonalities among women across sites of conflict.

In many places, women are primary witnesses of wartime atrocities and violence while at the same time they are pushed to take on greater responsibilities within the home and beyond as household heads and breadwinners (see Selvy Thiruchandran in chapter 10). Patterns of victimization may range from sexual violence to more subtle methods of abuse. For example, the spatial planning of a refugee camp may ignore the culturally and socially constructed roles of women as caregivers and caretakers; or the insensitivity of planners towards the gendered division of labour and customs in different cultures may cause the daily humiliation of women who are forced to perform various tasks related to their caregiving role in ways that are not accepted in their cultures.[1]

As well, the mental anguish and stress suffered by displaced women in response to intensely frightening experiences are often delegitimized and pathologized. In chapter 9, Ananda Galappatti calls for a reconceptualization of blanket forms of labelling such as "post-traumatic stress disorder" (PTSD) that medicalize and psychologize. It is particularly important to

1

produce feminist analyses that mobilize and support sensitive feminist practices in counselling women survivors of violence. In this regard, the innovative work of the feminist organization Medica Zenica in Bosnia-Herzegovina is particularly instructive (see Duška Andrić-Ružičić in chapter 8).

The contributors to this book have all been part of an international research network called the Women in Conflict Zones Network (WICZNET or the Network), established in 1996. It is comprised of feminist scholars, activists, and staff working in humanitarian and human rights agencies, all of whom are interested in ethnic-nationalism and gender relations, violence and women's rights, women's empowerment in war, and gender and citizenship. In order to contextualize nationalism, and explore its various forms and meanings in different societies, we engaged in the project "A Comparative Study of the Issues Faced by Women as a Result of Armed Conflict: Sri Lanka and the Post-Yugoslav States" from 1998-99. That project and this book address the causes of war and the ways in which militarized conflict and violence have affected women's lives in Sri Lanka and the former Yugoslavia. An analysis and comparison of the gender relations of war in these two sites raises questions about the causes and consequences of geopolitical conflicts worldwide. In this volume, academics and activists bring into focus their different approaches to understanding the conflict in both Sri Lanka and the former Yugoslavia. Speaking across geopolitical and methodological borders and boundaries, they address nationalism, militarization, gender violence, and resistance in the context of war.

The extent to which women may be empowered by nationalist movements, militarization, or their experiences of armed conflict has been raised by a number of participants in this project. This issue, as the chapters in this book reveal, has theoretical and practical/political ramifications for gender-sensitive analyses as well as for national and international feminist politics. While it is emphasized that it is theoretically and politically important not to view women in zones of armed conflict solely as victims, it is also stressed that the empowerment of women has to be considered more widely, in a context which examines the gendered relations of power both locally and in the broader international realm (see Radhika Coomaraswamy in chapter 7). Thus, to take Sri Lanka as an example, while some younger war widows might openly acknowledge the relief they feel from the responsibilities of constricting marriages, the clutches of abusive husbands or tyrannical and exploitative in-laws, they still have to negotiate larger and similarly oppressive patriarchal, capitalistic, or militaristic structures as they confront government bureaucracies, work in the fields, or pass military checkpoints (see Selvy Thiruchandran in chapter 10). The issue of women's empowerment becomes central in addressing processes of militarization and the roles of women within militaries and militant movements.

We need focused theoretical debates concerning women's participation in the military and its relation to the empowerment of women. The importance of such debates is indicated by our knowledge of the subordination of women in the military. Many women activists argue that women's participation in the military cannot be viewed as an avenue towards equality or peace. A further complication is the role that women play within supposedly "liberationary" organizations in Sri Lanka, such as the Liberation Tigers of Tamil Eelam (LTTE) or Janatha Vimukthi Peramuna (JVP). Even as the woman militant "transcends the bounds of traditional female identity," as Neloufer de Mel questions in chapter 5, "is there a price, other than death, of course, to be paid for such 'freedom'?" Her response is that women militants do experience significant losses "within the domain of gender constructs and, in particular, the forms of female sexuality and reproduction that are valued within it." Feminist research should include a more extensive analysis of the military.

We identified a range of ways in which women are marginalized, expropriated, and disempowered during and in the aftermath of forced migration. As Malathi de Alwis has pointed out, the refugee woman is "frequently produced as a cipher for all that was (temporarily) lost as well as what must be preserved for the future; the purity of displacement [is] imbricated in her moral purity,"[2] thus legitimizing even stricter surveillance and disciplining of her dress and bodily practices by her family, community, and society at large. Women's very "out of placeness" in contexts of displacement increases their vulnerability to domestic and sexual violence as their usual safeguards and means of redress are disrupted in such situations. As Jennifer Hyndman and I argue elsewhere:

> The public/private distinctions between battlefield and home, soldier and civilian, state security and human security have broken down. Feminist analyses of conflict elucidate the intimate connections between war, political economy, nationalism, and human displacement, and their various impacts across scale. The body, household, nation, state, and economy all represent sites at which violence can be invoked against people in highly gendered ways.[3]

Transnational feminist practices have provided the basis for our comparative analyses in the WICZNET. The concept of "transnational feminism" is characterized by Jacqui Alexander and Chandra Mohanty as a kind of global alliance that is a critique of and response to earlier models of "global sisterhood" that were built on "center-periphery" or "first world/Third world" models. While they do not deny the necessity for "national democracy," they call for a "feminist democracy" that is global – a "transborder participatory democracy."[4] Although the definition of the "national" or the "nation" in theories of the "transnational" requires further analysis,[5] the manner in which this concept challenges the notion of borders and boundaries for feminist politics warrants our attention. An approach towards comparative work as linked to "relational and historically based conceptions of feminisms"[6] begins to address the dangers of comparative work as being limited and mechanistic. However, our discussions about transnational feminist practices were prefaced by and interwoven with other debates about a "code of conduct" and definitions of "conflict zones." It is these concepts that I must first address before returning to a discussion of transnationalist feminist practices.

From Where We Speak:
Defining Codes of Conduct and "Conflict Zones"

Before beginning the comparative project, we discussed the use of a "code of conduct" for research,[7] policy development, and practice, which we later referred to as "aspirations of research relationships." One of the participants described this as

> a framework through which to realize a common ethic and shared principles which can be used to evaluate what is being proposed and implemented in both peacekeeping/making and humanitarian agendas with respect to the issue of women in conflict. We need to find ways to ensure accountability and to demonstrate commitment.[8]

By the end of our second Network meeting, and as we began to plan the comparative project, we were not only addressing the ethics of doing research in conflict zones but also addressing how to work across our own differences within the WICZNET. Some of the ways in which these two discursive levels are interwoven are revealed in these points that the Network developed:

- We are not all in equal positions in the research relationship, or in the WICZNET.
- We should not deny our politics in doing research, i.e., while we don't have to take on the politics of the "other," we should have a political commitment towards the research/policy/practice that we do and to the country/region we write about or work in.
- The Network needs to live with some tensions that cultural politics

poses (i.e., human rights versus culture in particular), rather than resolve or "fix" them.

- Can academics find ways of presenting theory that are useful to activists and policy-makers? How can abstraction, generalization, and theory, which can be valuable, be inserted into debates among activists without being destructive?
- How do we deal with the potentially detrimental involvement of "outsiders" in conflict zones?

At one of our meetings, Sharmini Pereis read us a quote about incarcerated Arabic women. It reflected the research methodology issues with which we were grappling:

> Don't claim to "speak for" or worse to "speak on" barely speaking next to, and if possible *very close to*: these are the first of the solidarities to be taken on by the few Arabic women who obtain or acquire freedom of movement, of body and of mind. And don't forget that those who are incarcerated, no matter what their age or class, may have imprisoned bodies, but have souls that move more freely than ever before.[9]

Another concern for all of us in both the broader context of the Network and the more narrow focus of the comparative project has been how to define a "conflict zone." One of the early commentaries from Network member Valerie Preston concerning this issue proposed that we define "a conflict zone" as "a series of relative locations" that are subject to redefinition:

> Dislocated by acts of violence, unable to return to their previous homes, women's relative locations change. As a result, locations that were nearby become far away, i.e., a place where help is available can become a location where acts of violence occur.[10]

Preston argued that "place" is crucial in enabling women to move past their experiences in conflict zones, to transform places, and that conflicts are maintained at multiple spatial scales: local, national, and international. She cited the example of the "Madres de Mayo" of Argentina, a group of mothers whose sons had been "disappeared" during the Dirty Wars in that country. By seizing and occupying the space of the Plaza de Mayo, one of the most important public spaces in Buenos Aires, they transformed many Argentinians' views about women's "place" in political participation.[11] Cynthia Cockburn has described "democracy" as related to "the way we cross the space between us, the choices we make about speaking, listening, waiting, acting, deciding" which she pointed out, can also be "peace in process."[12]

Extending this discussion, the workshop participants later argued that we must be constantly vigilant regarding "space," particularly when cultural ideologies of peace are used by the military and the state to reinforce ethnic-nationalism. For example, during the seventy-seven days of the NATO bombings of Belgrade, Republic Square – a regular site of the vigils by the Women in Black against the Serbian regime – was taken over by the Serbian regime itself for official "peace concerts in the piazza" (see Lepa Mladjenović in chapter 3). This brief discussion of multiple spatial scales of the local, the national, and the international forms the basis for our discussion of transnationalism, which is located in feminist practices across these scales.

Transnational Feminist Practices

Linking "transnationalism" to a comparative framework decreases the danger of the latter being characterized by a static essentialism and provides a way for grounding theories of transnationalism.[13] A major focus of feminist transnational research has been the articulation of gender in relation to the dominant discourses of globalization, nationalism, and the state. Nationality, gender, religion, class, caste, and cultural context situate people unevenly within a web of relationships that transcend political borders. Thus, as Daiva Stasiulis elaborates, an understanding of "relational positionality" to feminist politics is important for us to understand. She refers to "the multiple relations of power that intersect in complex ways to position individuals and collectivities in shifting and often contradictory locations within geopolitical spaces, historical narratives, and movement politics."[14] Feminists do need to be concerned "with mapping the complex societal relationships which construct dominance and subjugation,"[15] as well as identifying ways to address the material effects of such dominance and subjugation. The two are inseparable.[16]

Alexander and Mohanty argue for a theorization of feminism, central to which is a comparative analysis of feminist organizing, criticism, and self-reflection. This is associated with a "comparative, relational feminist praxis that is transnational in its response to and engagement with global processes of colonization."[17] In a related way, Hyndman argues for "transnational feminist practices: political action which conceives of differences as linked, if unequal, and which upsets commonplace markers of social, cultural and political identity." She (along with Inderpal Grewal and Caren Kaplan) regards feminist transnational practices as challenging purely locational politics and as engaging and connecting rather than distinguishing and distancing people of different locations: "Women whose bodies, families and communities bear the violent inscriptions of war and hate are neither universal subjects, nor unrelated individual subjects, in their different locations."[18]

Indeed, while comparative research work is vulnerable to a static essentialism that denies difference and divergent histories of domination and dominance, we argue that it is also potentially an activist approach that incorporates social change towards the elimination of inequality and oppression. In our view, one of the outcomes of comparison can be to demonstrate difference, but this is not the central, nor the sole, focus of an approach that is oriented towards activism. Avtar Brah's work on "diaspora space" can facilitate an understanding of how comparison can incorporate both a comprehension of common ground as well as differentiation. She uses the concepts of diaspora, border, and the politics of location as a "conceptual grid" for historically analyzing "trans/national movements of people, information, cultures, commodities and capital":

> Diaspora space is the intersectionality of diaspora, border and dis/location as a point of confluence of economic, political, cultural and psychic processes . . . [and] is "inhabited" not only by those who have migrated and their descendants but equally by those who are constructed and represented as indigenous.[19]

Brah's ideas have important implications for analyses of forced migration and gendered violence in the context of war. The concept of "diaspora space" allows us to connect locations of violent conflict with people living "in peace" elsewhere. Likewise, gender relations are not fixed but are produced unevenly across sites of violence and relative calm. The production and trade in military weapons, as well as resistance to banning land mines and other weapons of destruction, can no longer be viewed as issues that are located elsewhere, that is, in a "war zone."[20] Rather, "feminist work tends to represent war as a continuum of violence from the bedroom to the battlefield, traversing our bodies and our sense of self."[21]

Anannya Bhattacharjee's work on home also provides a basis on which it is possible to think about the relationship between comparative analysis and activism. The three levels that she defines as the cornerstones for definitions of home among immigrants (the domestic sphere, the ethnic community, and the nation of origin) are interrelated in such a way that immigrants define and are defined through all three levels. She states that activism requires challenging the status quo in all three "homes."[22] For example, in her discussion of domestic violence she states:

> It is not enough to fight the abuse in the family home alone. It is also necessary to fight the violence inherent in the community's use of the

figure of the woman to construct its identity, and in its summoning up of essentialist and elitist national culture. It is important to fight the way definitions of the immigrant family, the immigrant community, and immigrants' national heritage conveniently work toward creating a privatized U.S. nation-state based on oppression.[23]

Forms of activism that parallel or are interwoven with these different notions of "home" can be envisaged as activisms that are rooted in local feminist politics and that inform and connect to national and global forms of feminist politics. Malathi de Alwis's reflections on comparison are pertinent and speak to the inclusion of a class analysis. She writes that class difference in the country of origin as well as in the country of resettlement is another level that must be addressed in defining home. Indeed, the various ways in which global restructuring affects homes and communities differently, depending on their class status, need constant monitoring. De Alwis has commented that comparative analytical frameworks can occur either at the level of global structures of power – such as capitalism, imperialism, and international aid – or with reference to particular conceptual categories – such as nationalism, ethnicity, motherhood, or home.[24] These approaches are important for understanding any particular location and its similarities to and differences from another location. The challenge arises when combining two scales of analysis in order to compare specific regions. It is also crucial to understand how larger-scale processes, such as colonialism, capitalism, and nationalism affect the local level of community, household, and home; and it is important that we are able to compare these across regions involved in conflict.

The participants in the WICZNET project agree that a comparative approach helps us understand what a low-level war (i.e., of domestic violence) against women in a country like Canada has in common with a high-level war against women in a more militarized conflict zone.[25] (Such an approach can help those researching a completely different area of the world to think differently about their own work.) But we are equally concerned about what is to be done in the face of a transformation that shifts the management of the political processes of democratization from the state to the market. What kinds of comparative research will assist us in understanding processes of economic globalization in a transnational context? In what follows, I trace some of the discussions and questions that were raised and that contributed to our struggles to work together to build "transnational feminism" into our comparative project.

The WICZNET Comparative Project

There are two key catalysts that have inspired our discussions and subsequently the writing of this book. First, the point of entry into the discussion on women in ethnic-national conflict zones intended to build a debate on the issues of "universality in diversity."[26] That is, we are acknowledging difference, but beyond this, we are acknowledging the need to examine issues of commonality. In this respect, our discussions have addressed the material, historical, and political realities of women in ethnic-national conflict zones, including state and class relations, as well as systems of production and culture. We believe that this type of discussion can provide a basis for what Yuval-Davis refers to as "empowered knowledge," which can lead to some "common denominators"[27] regarding women's roles and status in ethnic-national conflict zones, and help prevent falling into uncritical universalism.

Related to these conceptual and practical or political challenges has been the issue of women's solidarity. The complex and sometimes contradictory dynamic of solidarity among women is associated with the conceptualization of identity as "open, fluid and inclusive."[28] At issue here is a debate on the situation of women which, while it recognizes differences among women, does so without fixing the boundaries between them. This conceptual approach, we believe, could open up space for dialogue across differences and provide an avenue to define politics and policies that can appropriately address the situation and needs of women in ethnic-national conflict zones.[29]

A consideration of difference also addresses the way in which the culture and histories of international institutions lead to particular ways of defining difference and commonalities in these conflict zones. Our purpose in the Network and in undertaking the comparative project has been to find ways of reaching across institutional-academic boundaries to develop "spaces" that will allow for dialogue concerning theory, empirical research, and policy development. From the beginning of the Network, a central issue has been whether it is possible to discuss gender, which is marked or sharpened by differing particularities, without losing a feminist and humanist edge. In this respect, we planned that our debates should address how ethnic-nationalism as a gendered social phenomenon is both general and always already concretely specific.

The second catalyst has been to understand the usefulness, limitations, and sometimes dangers of comparative research. On the one hand, we have been wary of traditional forms of comparative analysis based on static and homogeneous definitions that do not address difference within and across communities or groups, and we have argued that these are not appropriate to a feminist analysis. On the other hand, most of us agree about the importance of extending comparative work to other regions of the world as a way of moving towards a deeper understanding of differences and commonalities, thus laying the groundwork for transnational forms of feminist activisms.

Exchanges across Conflict Zones

This book arises out of the papers, discussions, and meetings before, during, and after workshops in Hendela, Sri Lanka, and in Budapest, Hungary. Following this Introduction, chapters 1 and 2 set the historical and theoretical contexts in Sri Lanka and in the region of the former Yugoslavia. Both chapters are sensitive to the problematic relationship between nationalisms and the creation of histories for political purposes.

In chapter 1, Malathi de Alwis examines South Asian feminist scholarship on nationalism and ethnicity from the late 1970s to the 1990s. She questions why a disjuncture exists in the literature between feminist practice and analysis on ethnicity/communalism, challenging the ways in which these two latter concepts have been used in the WICZNET and beyond. In chapter 2, Maja Korać gives a historical chronology of events leading up to the wars in the region of the former Yugoslavia. She also raises the issue of feminist praxis vis-à-vis ethnic-national identity and its relationship to women's struggles for women's rights. Korać describes the evolution of a split between the "patriotic" and "disloyal" women and feminists and the difficulties of working across differences. She states that "the acute, everyday problems of these women became the 'spaces' of their productive co-operation and exchange," as many of the chapters in this book demonstrate.

The book is then divided into three parts that reflect the topics and discussions associated with the two workshops: ethnic nationalism and the militarization of women (Part 1); gendered forms of militarized violence (Part 2); and politics and cultures of resistance in conflict zones (Part 3).

Neluka Silva's commentary, which introduces Part 1, draws our attention to the possibilities of, as well as the very real limitations on, women's participation in nationalist movements. Her reflections on the various forms of resistance by women and feminists in Serbia, Sri Lanka, and Croatia is followed by Lepa Mladjenović's description of the evolution and politics of Women in Black Against War (Belgrade) in chapter 3. In chapter 4, Žarana Papić looks at two feminist documents to analyze ethnic struggle and feminist resistance to the war in Serbia: the "I Confess" document created in 1998 by the Women in Black, and the *Activity*

Report during the Wartime (25 March to 24 April) of the Autonomous Women's Centre Against Sexual Violence (Belgrade). She argues that the work of these anti-nationalist feminist organizations are "the building blocks towards an anti-fascist future in the region of the former Yugoslavia." Neloufer de Mel continues this conversation in chapter 5 by turning to an analysis of women in the military. She argues that the interregnum, when a Tamil woman might feel most empowered through armed battle, is in fact a time when a woman's freedom is controlled through the repression of her sexuality. Although an armed woman warrior might enjoy a degree of liberty, having transcended the prescribed female role, her freedom is diminished through the patriarchal enforcement of discipline and chastity. Tamil women who have refused to conform to such prescriptions have been murdered by the LTTE.

In chapter 6, Djurdja Knežević describes another group of "activists" – a segment of the Croatian female population who actively engaged in the "national project" during the recent war (1991-95) in Croatia. These women accepted (and, in some cases, still accept) nationalism as an ideological base that offers them opportunities to enter into the political sphere and to be recognized as active participants in public life and civil society. Knežević discusses the attitudes and behaviours of women and women's groups who openly advocate nationalist ideologies in support of state projects.

Part 2 analyses gendered forms of militarized violence. In her commentary, Malathi de Alwis points out that all women living under patriarchal structures are vulnerable to sexual violence, whether in wartime or not. She links the various ways in which women have struggled against violence in the different sites and times described in the four chapters that comprise this section. In chapter 7, Radhika Coomaraswamy – who writes from her position as Special Rapporteur on Violence Against Women to the United Nations Human Rights Commission – discusses the relationship between sexual violence and nationalism, describing the range of ways in which women experience violence in conflict zones, particularly as victims of cultural codes of honour. Lauding the establishment of international normative standards concerning violence against women, Coomaraswamy expresses concern about the implementation of these standards. Pursuing this exchange in chapter 8, as it pertains to war rape in Bosnia-Herzegovina, Duska Andrić-Ružičić argues that rape is used as a strategy of war by the "other." In her experience, non-governmental organizations are the only institutions that have prioritized the treatment of women victims of violence.

There are many similarities between the findings of Andrić-Ružičić and Ananda Galappatti (chapter 9) concerning the treatment of gender violence in wartime Bosnia-Herzegovina and Sri Lanka. In particular, Galappatti explores the legitimacy and utility of the notion of trauma as it is used to describe the psychological suffering of women in Sri Lanka's conflict zones. Instead, he argues that a "self-actualization" approach may bring more benefits to women, although it will affect women differently. He argues for a movement beyond a "passive understanding of women's suffering."

In chapter 10, Selvy Thiruchandran brings a household analysis of refugee women to the issue of gendered violence. Analyzing the experiences of these women and the difficulties and responsibilities they confront in the fulfilment of dual roles, Thiruchandran records how they have managed the lives of their children and themselves through developing coping strategies to deal with economic disadvantages and problems in health delivery.

Part 3 addresses issues of resistance in the lives of women in militarized conflict zones. In her opening reflections, Edith Klein points out that a central concern for all the authors in this section is the effectiveness of women's organizing strategies. She argues, however, that women's struggles have not effectively broadened the democratic space in all these cases. In chapter 11, Neluka Silva addresses one of the most contentious issues in ethnic-national conflict: mixed marriages; in this case, those of Sinhalese and Tamils. These unions pose a threat to nationalisms while at the same time are a form of resistance to nationalist essentialisms. Lepa Mladjenović extends the discussion of resistance to feminist politics in Belgrade in chapter 12, complicating perspectives on feminist pacificism in Serbia. Her analysis of the NATO bombings and the ethnic cleansing of the Albanian nationals of Kosovo/a by the Serbian regime raises further questions for feminists as to whether to accept military intervention or not.

Another approach to resistance is examined in chapter 13 by Kumudini Samuel who discusses the problematic and contradictory uses of "motherhood" by both Sinhalese and Tamil women. She argues that such a construct prevents a critical re-examination of the position of women in Sri Lankan society. In chapter 14, Elissa Helms continues Samuel's discussion of women's activism and motherhood and examines how NGOs in Bosnia-Herzegovina use the gender ideologies imposed on them in their roles as anti-nationalist, non-violent peacemakers trying to rebuild a multi-ethnic Bosnian state and to campaign for gender equality. Helms and Mladjenović both discuss the routes taken by feminist activists: Helms describing how women make use of gender essentialist roles to get what they want and Mladjenović arguing that there is no one form of feminist pacifist resistance in the former Yugoslavia.

Kumari Jayawardena's reflections on the women's movement in Sri Lanka (chapter 15) is very much a commentary on the methodology of transnational feminist practice that has framed the WICZNET project and on which this book is based. She does not perceive a division between the work of activists and academics and argues that women's cross-country alliances and transnational forms of feminist activism are not new phenomena in Sri Lanka. In the Afterword, the co-editors update the events in both Sri Lanka and the post-Yugoslav states and discuss some areas for future research.

Notes

1 Malathi de Alwis, "The 'Purity' of Displacement and the Re-territorialization of Longing: Muslim Women Refugees in North-Western Sri Lanka," and Jennifer Hyndman, "Refugee Camps as Conflict Zones: The Politics of Gender," in Wenona Giles and Jennifer Hyndman, eds., *Sites of Violence: Gender and Conflict Zones* (Berkeley: University of California Press, forthcoming).

2 De Alwis, "The 'Purity' of Displacement and the Re-territorialization of Longing."

3 Wenona Giles and Jennifer Hyndman, "New Directions for Feminist Research and Politics in Conflict Zones," in Giles and Hyndman, eds., *Sites of Violence*.

4 Jacqui C. Alexander and Chandra Talpade Mohanty, "Introduction: Genealogies, Legacies and Movements," in Jacqui C. Alexander and Chandra T. Mohanty, eds., *Feminist Genealogies, Colonial Legacies, Democratic Futures* (New York: Routledge, 1997), pp.xxix, xli.

5 One such issue is the extent to which self-defined nations and/or women associated with these nations retain the possibility of engaging in a global alliance of transnational feminism – for example, Taliban women who are sequestered in purdah, as well as Kurdish and Burmese women whose nations are formally unrecognized.

6 Alexander and Mohanty, "Introduction: Genealogies, Legacies and Movements," p.xvi.

7 Martha Muzychka, Carmen Poulin, Barbara Cottrell, Baukje Miedema, and Barbara Roberts, *Feminist Research Ethics: A Process*, 2d ed. (Ottawa: The Canadian Research Institute for the Advancement of Women, 1996).

8 Angela Raven-Roberts, e-mail communication to the WICZNET, 1997.

9 Assia Djebar, *Women of Algiers in their Apartments* (Charlottesville, VA: Caraf Books, 1992), p.xx. Cynthia Cockburn suggested that, if we rephrased "incarcerated" as "pinned down by violence," the quote would seem to speak about our relationship with all those women with whom we are working in conflict zones.

10 Valerie Preston, Commentary on WICZNET Workshop, York University, November 1996.

11 Ibid.
12 Cynthia Cockburn, e-mail communication to the WICZNET, October 22, 1999.
13 Preston, Commentary.
14 Daiva Stasiulis, "Relational Positionalities of Nationalisms, Racisms, and Feminisms," in C. Kaplan, N. Alarcón, and M. Moallem, eds., *Between Woman and Nation: Nationalisms, Transnational Feminisms, and the State* (Durham, NC: Duke University Press, 1999), p.194.
15 J.P. Sharp, "Gendering Nationhood: A Feminist Engagement with National Identity," in N. Duncan, ed., *Bodyspace: Destabilising Geographies of Gender and Sexuality* (New York: Routledge, 1996), p.107.
16 Giles and Hyndman, "New Directions for Feminist Research and Politics in Conflict Zones."
17 Alexander and Mohanty, "Introduction: Genealogies, Legacies and Movements," p.xx.
18 Jennifer Hyndman, "Organizing Women: UN Approaches to Gender and Culture Among the Displaced" (paper presented at the Women in Conflict Zones Network Meeting, York University, Toronto, November 1996), pp.17-18. See also Inderpal Grewal and Caren Kaplan, "Introduction: Transnational Feminist Practices and Questions of Postmodernity," in Inderpal Grewal and Caren Kaplan, eds., *Scattered Hegemonies: Postmodernity and Transnational Feminist Practices* (Minneapolis: Minnesota University Press, 1994), pp.1-33.
19 Avtar Brah, *Cartographies of Diaspora: Contesting Identities* (New York: Routledge, 1996), p.181.
20 Giles and Hyndman, "New Directions for Feminist Research and Politics in Conflict Zones."
21 Cynthia Cockburn, *The Space Between Us: Negotiating Gender and National Identities in Conflict* (London: Zed Books, 1998), p.4.
22 Anannya Bhattacharjee, "The Public/Private Mirage: Mapping Homes and Undomesticating Violence Work in the South Asian Immigrant Community," in Alexander and Mohanty, eds., *Feminist Genealogies, Colonial Legacies, Democratic Futures*, p.327.
23 Ibid., p.324.
24 Malathi de Alwis, WICZNET, e-mail communication, June 23, 1997.
25 However, this statement was challenged by those Network members who argued that the Canadian state has been involved in a long-term war against Aboriginal women and men, one that is frequently militarized.
26 Nira Yuval-Davis, "Identity Politics and Women's Ethnicity," Valentine Moghadam, ed., *Identity Politics and Women: Cultural Reassertions and Feminisms in International Perspective* (Boulder, CO: Westview Press, 1994), p.422.
27 Nira Yuval-Davis, "Women, Ethnicity and Empowerment," *Feminist Psychology* 4,1 (1994), p.192.
28 Kum Kum Bhavnani, "Towards a Multicultural Europe: Race, Nation and Identity in 1992 and Beyond," *Feminist Review* 45 (1993), p.35.
29 Cockburn, *The Space Between Us*; Alexander and Mohanty, "Introduction: Genealogies, Legacies and Movements."

Malathi de Alwis

Chapter 1

Reflections on Gender and Ethnicity in Sri Lanka

Thinking back on the discussions that have taken place within the Women in Conflict Zones Network (WICZNET) these past few years, it would not be an exaggeration to note that two key categories that came up over and over again were gender and ethnicity. Indeed in an intellectual universe where the category "race" usually predominates, it is rather unusual that the category "ethnicity" has been and continues to be mobilized in both Sri Lanka and the former Yugoslavia. In hindsight, this has sometimes enabled rather sad and ironic comparisons, such as when the Yugoslavian ambassador to Sri Lanka shared his views in July 1987 (under the auspices of the International Centre for Ethnic Studies in Colombo) on how successfully the Yugoslavian nation-state was managing its various ethnic groups, in the hope that there might be some lessons to be learned by the Sri Lankan state.

In fact, the last decade of the twentieth century has seen a proliferation of South Asian and South Asian(ist) feminist work on gender and ethnicity/communalism. I want especially to highlight here the crucial contribution that the Delhi-based feminist press Kali for Women has made to this field of scholarship through the publication of landmark collections such as *Recasting Women: Essays in Colonial History* edited by Kumkum Sangari and Sudesh Vaid (1989); *Forging Identities: Gender, Communities and the State* edited by Zoya Hasan (1994); *Embodied Violence: Communalising Women's Sexuality in South Asia* edited by Kumari Jayawardena and Malathi de Alwis (1996); and *Borders and Boundaries: Women in India's Partition* by Ritu Menon and Kamla Bhasin (1998).

Recasting Women sought to denaturalize the link between "nation" and

15

"woman" and to problematize nationalism and communalism, particularly its reinscription and reification of "culture" and "tradition" upon women's bodies. *Forging Identities* concentrated on interrogating the category "Muslim" and delineating the multiplicities and contradictions that it encompasses while also highlighting the subordination of women's rights under minority politics. *Embodied Violence* and *Borders and Boundaries* introduced violence into this now denaturalized equation between ethnicity and gender, nation and woman, and specifically focused on how women were both survivors as well as perpetrators of communal(ized) violence.

What I want to think about in these brief notes, however, is the conceptual labour that has produced the contemporary theorization of gender and ethnicity in South Asia and more specifically in Sri Lanka. The particular question I wish to pose is, Why has it taken so long for South Asian(ist) feminists to theorize the conjuncture between "ethnicity" and "gender"? I wish to explore here some of the possible reasons for this by focusing on some Indian and Sri Lankan examples. These will be rather tentative arguments presented in a somewhat schematic fashion. But my task here is not so much to convince as to provoke debate.

If one could conceptualize nationalism as providing an intellectual and political space to talk about "ethnicity," and feminism as providing a similar space to talk about "gender," one could then go a step further and posit that nationalism and feminism have both been conceived and perceived as liberatory discourses and practices. While nationalism has historically functioned as one of the most powerful weapons against colonialism and provided a crucial space for the construction of post-colonial identities, feminism has and continues to function as the most powerful weapon against patriarchal structures of power that seek to oppress, exploit, and subordinate women. It is thus not a mere coincidence that one of the earliest and now landmark books on feminism that was to come out of South Asia was Kumari Jayawardena's *Feminism and Nationalism in the Third World*. As Jayawardena notes in her Preface to that book, the "struggle for women's emancipation [during colonialism] was necessarily bound up with the fight for national liberation and formed an essential part of the democratic struggles of the period."[1]

Jayawardena primarily describes nationalist struggles as being successful in "achieving political independence," "asserting national identity," and "modernizing society" while simultaneously enabling the emergence of an "educated and enlightened new woman" who participated in anticolonial struggles alongside her male peers. Yet she also acknowledges that this is not the "total picture."[2] The "new woman could not be a total negation of traditional culture"; women still had to "act as guardians of national culture, indigenous religion and family traditions – in other words, to be both 'modern' and 'traditional.'"[3] Nevertheless, Jayawardena's central task in this book is to "uncover" the role played by women in nationalist struggles rather than highlight their subordination within them. Such a trajectory was very much tied to Jayawardena's project of insisting that feminism in the Third World could not be brushed off as a mere "importation" from the "West"; rather, feminism had to be understood as being an organic part of the concerns of and struggles for nationhood and political and economic emancipation.

This project was also linked to a broader, more global feminist concern, which, in Joan Scott's words, was to "make women a focus of enquiry, a subject of the story, an agent of the narrative."[4] The early issues of *Voice of Women*, the first feminist journal in Sri Lanka, were published in English, Sinhala, and Tamil from the 1980s onward and are excellent examples of this kind of "retrieval" – of women in the past as well as the present – that was taking place during this period. Many articles concentrated on analyzing the representation of women in the local media, literary texts, and school textbooks, while others sought to highlight the hitherto hidden inequalities and forms of violence that existed within society such as cultural constraints imposed on women, domestic violence, sexual discrimination in the workplace, unequal pay, the exploitation of women in the plantation sector, and hazardous working conditions in the Free Trade Zone. The journal also ran a series of articles that focused on contemporary women heroines from the working classes and the peasantry.

The primary objective of South Asian feminists was thus to "retrieve" and "restore" the South Asian woman to her rightful place while simultaneously unmasking and struggling against the patriarchal structures of power that sought to continue to hide, ignore, and subordinate her. This was a project, then, that united women across classes, religions, languages, and ethnicities. The common enemy was patriarchy and the emphasis was on sexual difference.

But it was also during the 1980s that South Asia experienced some of the most brutal and bloody ethnic riots and conflicts – the anti-Tamil riots in Sri Lanka in 1983 and the anti-Sikh riots in India in 1984, for example. While many groups of South Asian feminists were at the forefront of movements that called for a cessation of violence and immediately dedicated themselves to working with survivors of riots (the majority of whom were women), it was clear that they did not have a set of conceptual tools with which they could even begin to grasp and analyze this ugly underbelly of nationalism that had suddenly brought itself into the foreground. If one looks at South Asian(ist) feminist scholarship in the mid-1980s, one notices that, frequently, an analysis of the "ethnic question" as opposed to the "woman question" is either deferred or taken up in other intellectual spaces.

Take, for example, one of the key texts on the contemporary women's movement in India written by Nandita Shah and Nandita Gandhi. Entitled *The Issues at Stake*, Shah and Gandhi carefully go through some of the central issues that animated the feminist movement in India in the 1970s and 1980s – various forms of violence against women, health and reproductive issues, low wages and unequal treatment in the workplace and home, and legal battles about personal and custodial law. In their conclusion, the two feminists are rather apologetic that they have not been able to "come to grips with the complex issues of religion, fundamentalism and communalism."[5] Even the brief discussion that follows this statement is taken up by considering the strategic purchase of religious symbolism and mobilization rather than confronting the violent effects of such mobilizations.

In Sri Lanka in the 1980s, some feminists did participate in discussing and writing about the "ethnic question," but such debates usually took place in other intellectual and political spaces. One such space was the Left movement, or at least certain circles within the Left. As Pradeep Jeganathan notes, "Left scholars, who had been theorizing the crisis of the nation as a problem in nationalism and national liberation, turned to ethnicity as a categorical name for the new crisis of the nation" when the question of Tamil separatism came to the fore in the late 1970s and when the Left movement was decimated in the national elections of 1977.[6] *Ethnicity and Social Change in Sri Lanka* was the first publication to result from these debates, which spanned several years. In the opening article, archaeologist Senake Bandaranayake makes a strong argument for the mobilization of the category of "ethnicity" in future Sri Lankan scholarship:

> It is as common an error in day to day discourse as in the rhetoric of communal discord, to use the term "race," with clear biological connotations, when what is meant is an "an ethnic group." What "ethnic group" signifies is a historically defined, self-conscious community, which has its own distinctive history and culture, of which language and religion often constitute important aspects, and which has or had definite territorial affiliations, in the present and/or the past.[7]

Similarly, Leslie Gunawardena's landmark paper, "The People of the Lion," cautions against projecting modern conceptions of "ethnic con-

sciousness" into the past and provides an extensive analysis and histori-
cization of the ethnic(ized) label "Sinhala."[8] Many of the other articles in
this collection engage with terms such as "cultural and linguistic consciousness," "ethnic identity and representation," and "communalism."

What I am most interested in considering here, however, is the sole
contribution that was made to this publication (*Facets of Ethnicity*) by a
woman and a feminist, Kumari Jayawardena. In her essay "Ethnic Consciousness in Sri Lanka," Jayawardena argues that "communalism" was a
modern ideological formation and provides a careful analysis of its rise in
conjunction with merchant capitalism in the late nineteenth and early
twentieth centuries. Surprisingly, while the article engages with the categories of class and communalism/ethnicity, it makes no effort to engage
with the category of gender or, for that matter, even discuss women's
positioning vis-à-vis these categories.[9]

A similar trajectory was followed by Jayawardena along with two
other feminists, Serena Tennekoon and Radhika Coomaraswamy, who
contributed articles to the sequel that was published two years later, *Facets
of Ethnicity in Sri Lanka*. While Coomaraswamy and Tennekoon were
concerned with the contemporary re-constitution of ethnic identity
among the Sinhalese and Tamils,[10] Jayawardena sought to explore why
there had been no serious theoretical debate within the Left in Sri Lanka
on the existence of a "national question" – defined by Marxists as "the
totality of political, ideological, economic and legal relations between
national communities."[11]

What is particularly interesting is that at the same time that feminists
like Jayawardena were focused on theorizing "ethnicity" and "class," they
were also actively involved in several feminist organizations in the country. In 1978, Jayawardena was a founding member of the first feminist
organization in the country, which was a multi-ethnic, socialist women's
collective called the Voice of Women. She was also, along with
Coomaraswamy and Tennekoon, a founding member of another multi-
ethnic group called Women for Peace, founded in 1984 in the aftermath
of the anti-Tamil riots of July 1983. The primary objective of the latter
group was to protest against the increased militarization of Sri Lankan
society and to agitate for a peaceful and politically negotiated settlement
to the ethnic conflict. How, then, do we understand the discontinuity
between these women's feminist practices and their non-articulation of a
feminist analysis in their writings on ethnicity?

I have alluded so far to several possibilities for such a discontinuity. At
the level of praxis, South Asian feminists' primary objective, which
Amrita Chhachhi describes as the first phase of the women's movement

in South Asia, was to emphasize sexual difference rather than ethnic, religious, or class difference and to highlight patriarchal structures that impinged on all women.[12] In fact, one of the most significant and unfortunate splits that occurred within the feminist movement in Sri Lanka had to do with the "ethnic question." After the anti-Tamil riots of 1983, feminists who sought to question the pervasiveness of Sinhala hegemony within Sri Lankan society and who began to critique Sinhala nationalism and militarism diverged drastically from those who refused to perceive these issues as being central to the conflict between Sinhalese and Tamils. Much of this work, however, was produced in the wake of prior theorizing on "ethnicity," which had taken place in other fora. As Radhika Coomaraswamy noted in her 1984 article on the politics of ethnicity, a discussion of ethnic conflict automatically raises the issue of nationalism and calls for a re-evaluation of the oft repeated argument that "cultural nationalism based on a collective ethnic consciousness of groups, has moved third world countries a step beyond feudalism and colonialism."[13] Recall, also, Jayawardena's 1986 shift towards such a cautionary note.

This discontinuity between praxis and theory was also a symptom of the patriarchal hegemony that pervaded scholarship in and on South Asia. As I noted earlier, the late 1970s and early 1980s were mainly taken up with South Asian(ist) feminists trying to retrieve women's histories and lay bare patriarchal biases and prejudices not just in the production of knowledge about South Asia but within South Asian society and culture as well. The fruition of such conceptual labour is especially well articulated in the later work of Jayawardena:

> Gender can be viewed as a core element of the ethnic issue . . . It is true that women within the ethnic group are segmented in various ways and that they will participate in the religious and ethnic processes differently as determined by their class, age or status in the family (Anthias and Yuval-Davis, 1983). Yet what is crucial is that the ethnic identity of each group is frequently expressed in terms of its womanhood and its vision of the ideal woman. She symbolizes the purity, continuity and exclusivity of the ethnic group and is therefore central to ethnic discourse.[14]

One of the central contributions of contemporary feminist scholarship in South Asia has been to prise ethnicity loose from the nationalist framework. However, such a move has frequently failed to make a clear distinction between ethnicity and communalism, the two categories often being used coterminously, as I have demonstrated above and been guilty of doing myself. This distinction is particularly crucial in light of Gyan

Pandey's pathbreaking theorization of "communalism" aptly described as "nationalism-gone-awry."[15] In Pandey's argument, notes Jeganathan, "communalism is both the other of colonialism and nationalism, a name for the pathologization of socio-political projects that are no longer different in structure from the nationalism that seeks to rise above it."[16] In juxtaposition to such a conceptualization, Jeganathan's formulation of ethnicity as a "conceptual bridge" between nationalism and communalism is indeed persuasive: "It prises us out of both colonial and anthropological knowledge, and a political location within the first flush of nationalism to a more mature, complex analytical location."[17]

"'Communalism' today means the advocacy of violence," Gyan Pandey has also noted, and the central project of a book such as *Embodied Violence* was to pursue the question of how communalism, operating within patriarchal structures of power, often implies the advocacy of sexual violence towards women. Yet violence, as Jeganathan rightly reminds us, is not simply an expression of an already existing political project but is itself constitutive.[18] It is thus at the cusp of "gender," "ethnicity," and "violence" that our future theorizations must be located.

Acknowledgements

An earlier version of this paper was presented during the Afro-Asia Consultation at the CODESRIA conference in Dakar, Senegal, in December 1998, and at the ICES/SSA/Social Science Research Council Forum in Colombo, Sri Lanka, in January 1999. It was published in *Identity, Culture & Politics* 1,1 (January 2000). For their questions and comments regarding this earlier version, I am grateful to Nicholas Dirks, Kumari Jayawardena, and the late Neelan Tiruchelvam. For extensive long-distance conversations and arguments about several versions of this chapter, I am indebted to Pradeep Jeganathan.

Notes

1 Kumari Jayawardena, *Feminism and Nationalism in the Third World* (London: Zed Press, 1986), pp.ix-x.

2 Ibid., pp.3, 12-14.

3 Ibid., p.14.

4 Joan Wallach Scott, "Women's History and the Rewriting of History," in Christie Farnham, ed., *Impact of Feminist Research in the Academy* (Bloomington: Indiana University Press, 1987), p.36.

5 Nandita Shah and Nandita Gandhi, *The Issues at Stake: Theory and Practice in the Contemporary Women's Movement in India* (New Delhi: Kali for Women, 1992), p.325.

6 Pradeep Jeganathan, "Violence as an Anthropological Problem," *Nethra: Journal of the International Centre for Ethnic Studies* 2,2 (1998), p.35.

7 Senake Bandaranayake, "The Peopling of Sri Lanka: The National Question and Some Problems of History and Ethnicity," in Charles Abeysekera and Newton Gunasinghe, eds., *Facets of Ethnicity in Sri Lanka* (Colombo: Social Scientists' Association, 1987), p.4. A similar definition is given in the short essay "Why Ethnic Studies," in the brochure published by the International Centre for Ethnic Studies, Colombo, which was yet another important space within which the category of "ethnicity" was debated and continues to be debated since the institution's founding in 1982 to grapple with the changing political and social climate in the country. For a thoughtful critique of the definition of "ethnicity" that appears in this text, see Natalie Pickering, "Cartographies of the Body and Being: Deconstructing the Biology of Identity," in Radhika Coomaraswamy and Nira Wickremasinghe, eds., *Introduction to Social Theory* (New Delhi: Konark Publishers, 1994), pp.139-40. Other important spaces within which debates on "ethnicity" took place were the Centre for Society and Religion, the Movement for Inter-Racial Justice and Equality, and the Committee for Rational Development.

8 R.A.L.H. Gunawardena, "The People of the Lion: Sinhala Consciousness in History and Historiography," in Abeysekera and Gunasinghe, eds., *Facets of Ethnicity in Sri Lanka*.

9 Kumari Jayawardena, "The National Question and the Left Movement in Sri Lanka," in Abeysekera and Gunasinghe, eds., *Facets of Ethnicity in Sri Lanka*. The only instance where Jayawardena even mentions women is in conjunction with what she terms "racist" attitudes of the Sinhalese towards their women marrying those perceived to be non-Aryans (migrant workers from Kerala), in the 1930s. She refers to an article in a Sinhala newspaper that specifically condoned Hitler's anti-Semitic policies of prohibiting similar kinds of marriages between Aryan and non-Aryan Germans. See Jayawardena, "Ethnic Consciousness in Sri Lanka: Continuity and Change," in Committee for Rational Development, ed., *Sri Lanka, The Ethnic Conflict: Myths, Realities and Perspectives* (New Delhi: Navrang, 1984), pp.137-8.

10 Radhika Coomaraswamy, "Myths Without Conscience: Tamil and Sinhalese Nationalist Writings of the 1980s," and Serena Tennekoon, "Symbolic Refractions of the Ethnic Crisis: The *Divaina* Debates on Sinhala Identity," in Abeysekera and Gunasinghe, eds., *Facets of Ethnicity in Sri Lanka*.

11 Nimni quoted in Jayawardena, "The National Question and the Left Movement in Sri Lanka," p.230.

12 Amrita Chhachhi, "Identity Politics, Secularism and Women: A South Asian Perspective," in Zoya Hasan, ed., *Forging Identities: Gender, Communities and the State* (New Delhi: Kali for Women, 1994).

13 Radhika Coomaraswamy, "'Through the Looking Glass Darkly': Politics of Ethnicity," in Committee for Rational Development, ed., *Sri Lanka, The Ethnic Conflict*, p.191.

14 Kumari Jayawardena, "Some Aspects of Religious and Cultural Identity and the Construction of Sinhala Buddhist Womanhood," in Douglas Allen, ed., *Religion and Political Conflict in South Asia* (New Delhi: Oxford University Press, 1993), pp.161-2. Reference to Anthias and Yuval-Davis is from Floya Anthias and Nira Yuval-Davis, "Contextualizing Feminism: Gender, Ethnic and Class Divisions," *Feminist Review* 24 (1983), pp.62-75.

15 Pradeep Jeganathan, "Theorizing 'Ethnicity' and 'Violence'" (paper presented

at the Afro-Asia Consultation at CODESRIA, Dakar, Senegal, December 1998), p.2.
16 Ibid., pp.2-3.
17 Ibid., p.3. Jeganathan's formulation here builds on Mahmood Mamdani's remarks on the changing vocabulary of African Social Science from tribalism to ethnicity to identity. Each succeeding term, Mamdani writes, "gives the phenomenon increasing respectability by casting it within a more acceptable human universal frame. Whereas the sound of tribalism was undeniably pathological, ethnicity is more placid, part of a value free vocabulary on the way to reconciling itself with the object it claims to describe; but identity has more the ring of a personal quest, if not quite the sound of a battle cry" (quoted in Jeganathan, "Theorizing 'Ethnicity,'" pp.2-3). Note here how Jeganathan completely overturns Mamdani's presentation of "ethnicity" as "part of a value free vocabulary" by marking it as both political and analytical.
18 Ibid., p.4.

Maja Korač

Chapter 2

Women Organizing against Ethnic Nationalism and War in the Post-Yugoslav States

The opposition of women to the war, violence, and politics of ethnic nationalism in Southeastern Europe represents a unique struggle to regain and reconfirm social inclusion and social integration in the region. Their efforts to build relationships among women across ethnic-national divisions and to advocate new forms of solidarity despite their own differences have gone against the tide of the exclusionary politics of ethnic nationalism. Further, women's anti-war and anti-nationalist political protests during the recent wars represent genuinely autonomous women's initiatives. By making their resistance to war and all forms of control over women visible, local women activists have refused to assume the role of passive victims of militaristic and nationalistic politics in the post-Yugoslav states. In so doing, feminists and activists have sought to denaturalize the link between "nation" and "woman."

The nationalistic discourse of the late 1980s in Yugoslavia was constructed in opposition to the socialist ideology. Its exponents successfully manipulated the millions of citizens who felt socially insecure and rootless as a result of the economic, social, and political changes that accompanied the dismantling of state socialism. After the end of the Second World War, socialist Yugoslavia experienced "one of the most rapid processes of urbanization in history."[1]

Before the war, 80 per cent of the population in Yugoslavia was rural; as of 1978, however, more than 70 per cent of the population lived in urban settings. The millions of people who had moved from rural to urban areas within the time span of a single generation never fully integrated into the urban milieu. They belonged to neither a rural nor an urban life, but somewhere in between. For many Yugoslavs, rapid industrialization and urbanization increased the importance of wider social connections and social identifiers, which were linked to the ideology of a "workers' society" and, consequently, weakened the significance of extended family ties. But because an equally rapid process of social and political development did not accompany these changes, a considerable proportion of the population remained rootless, with poorly defined social status and identity.

Such rootlessness bred a sense of insecurity – a condition that was effectively exploited by the socialist state in its efforts to forge a collective identity and provide millions of people with a sense of belonging. During the years following the fall of the Berlin Wall (post-1989), this rootlessness was also fertile ground for the revival of ethnic nationalism. The dismantling of state socialism triggered the onset of a personal and collective identity crisis for the population in the region; it also heightened people's sense of economic and social insecurity, because they were no longer protected by the shield of the socialist state.

The first signs of this insecurity emerged in the 1980s, a time when many Central and East European states confronted deep economic and/or political crises.[2] In Yugoslavia, the economic crisis, which began at the end of the 1970s, resulted in a drastic fall of all economic indicators after 1982 and in an increase in the percentage of the population living below the poverty line, from 17 to 25 per cent.[3] The impact of the economic crisis on people's lives was visible and demoralizing. In such circumstances, ethnic nationalism – which promised millions of people a sense of belonging and security as well as a compelling antidote for the difficulties society would have to confront during the process of economic, political, and social restructuring – had a powerful appeal.

The first order of the day for the post-socialist nationalist governments was to create a base for an ethnic-national identity that would support their projects of ethnically exclusive states. By seeking political power over subfederal territories, politicians aggressively sought to alter the voters' ambivalence towards recognition of difference among the various ethnic-national collectivities. Employing an ethnic-nationalistic discourse of "common blood" and "common destiny," the political elite generated the notion of essentialist difference among ethnic-nations. In so doing, they successfully manipulated millions of rural-urban migrants who felt socially insecure and rootless. As Woodward points out in commenting on the results of the first multi-party elections in Yugoslavia in

1990: "The voters did not make a clear choice for nationalists and independence. They did push the nationalist momentum further, not because of the voting results themselves, but because of the use politicians made of them."[4]

These voters became the first targets of war propaganda engineered by neo-nationalist political leaders. In their rhetoric, they claimed that the "unnatural" socialist regime had replaced religion, tradition, shared blood, and kin for the emancipation of the working class, women, and proletarian internationalism. The nationalistic discourse, for its part, offered a set of values constructed as traditional, which could easily be perceived as "natural." According to these "new" values, men were assigned the role of the "real warrior," while women were assigned the responsibilities for the reproduction of the group, as well as the custody of cultural values and cultural identity. These proscriptions became the basis for the "new" society and the nationalist family in the region.

Rural-urban migrants were the initial group from whom the "real warriors" were recruited, and they eagerly mobilized behind their leaders' ethnic-national projects. A mini-survey that profiled fifty volunteers in the Serbian paramilitary forces, who were members of the Serbian Radical Party (SRS),[5] illustrates this point. Undertaken by the then Serbian independent newspaper *Borba* at the end of 1991, the survey demonstrates that most of the volunteers were of a rural background but with a permanent residence in one of the regional urban centres in Serbia.[6] Feeling economic, social, and political pressures, these men began to engage in military combat, and some committed incomprehensibly cruel crimes. Yet behind the brutal images of these male perpetrators and the inhumanity and destruction that raged throughout the region, there were many thousands of tragic examples of men psychologically destroyed by pressures to take part in these wars.

Miroslav Milenković, born in 1951, a construction worker and reservist from the Serbian town Gornji Milanovac, was among those who could not give themselves up to violence and hate. He could not accept that he must pick up a gun and kill in order to prove himself a worthy representative of his ethnic-nation, a patriot, and, above all, a real man. Milenković, like many others, was drafted as a reservist in the army. On September 20, 1991, when he reached Šid, a town on the border of Serbia and Croatia, Milenković killed himself. Standing between two groups of reservists in the town square – on the one side were men who refused to take up weapons and thus faced incarceration, and on the other side were men who had chosen to take up arms in preparation for the war front in Croatia – he shot himself.[7]

Milenković thus represents the extreme contradiction faced by these men who could not see themselves fighting and perhaps killing others, nor wanting to be stigmatized as traitors to their country. It is difficult to provide an accurate and reliable figure of the number of deserters and draft evaders from the conflict in the post-Yugoslav states. However, according to a petition of the European Civic Forum intended to protect the rights of men who fled the region as deserters and draft evaders, there were hundreds of thousands of these men within Europe alone.[8]

Indeed, militarization and war in the region were not straightforward processes of change. Political leaders and elites had to deploy different types of manipulation and control over the population in order to achieve their nationalistic goals. With respect to women, for example, the high rates of women's unemployment, which resulted from economic restructuring, were justified and embraced by nationalists as women's long overdue return to their sacred and natural family and household duties. In order to secure this natural order, nationalists established different ways of controlling women through state mechanisms, which violated their basic rights. The first instances of such control were the restrictions placed on women's reproductive freedoms and the introduction of pro-life policies.

Between 1988 and 1991, feminists in the region focused more attention on preventing the manipulation of women's reproductive rights for nationalistic purposes. Before the revival of ethnic nationalism, feminist activists in socialist Yugoslavia had voiced concern mainly about the "woman question" as defined under state socialism.[9] This group of urban, educated, predominantly young, middle-class women publicly challenged the socialist patriarchy and the assumption that the struggle for the equality of women was synonymous with class struggle. The changing social and political context altered the character of their activism. It became a more explicitly political form of protest against the specific violation of concrete women's rights. As a result, the first autonomous women's groups, established in the late 1970s, were transformed in the early 1990s into women's lobbies, women's parliaments, and umbrella organizations. These new feminist initiatives linked women across republic/ethnic-national boundaries. Among other achievements, their campaigns succeeded in preventing the republican parliaments from prohibiting abortion, although pro-life aspirations remained one of the important social and political goals of the governments.

The outbreak of war and the violent destruction of the country and the lives of its peoples brought women face to face with new forms of oppression and victimization. Feminists reacted to the new political crisis by shifting their activism to anti-war politics. Feminist groups issued protest statements to the governments and the public, expressing their disagreement with militarization and with the warmongering tendencies of the political elite. Gradually, they were joined by some of the women who had been previously engaged in the "Mothers' Movement," which had emerged throughout the region at the beginning of the wars. These spontaneous protests by mothers first began in Serbia, in the summer of 1991, in reaction to the federal army's intervention in Slovenia, after the latter declared unilateral independence. Hundreds of women stormed the Serbian Parliament during its session, demanding a peaceful solution to the crisis and the immediate return of their sons involved in the military intervention in Slovenia.[10] This protest was followed by similar protests in Ljubljana (Slovenia), Zagreb (Croatia), and Sarajevo (Bosnia-Herzegovina), which were also organized across ethnic-national lines and which were joined by feminist and peace groups.[11]

The nationalistic oligarchies reacted immediately with repressive measures, including arrests and police interrogations, to stop the protests. Simultaneously, they mobilized the media propaganda machine to prevent further development of the women's resistance to war. The media manipulation of the Mothers' Movement was not particularly difficult, because this massive grassroots protest, though highly political in essence, had no clear strategy or well-articulated message. Nevertheless, the protests rejected the role of the "patriotic mother" as constructed by nationalists. Gradually, however, the protests were politically marginalized and, with the escalation of the armed conflict, the role of woman was transformed into a stereotype of "the mother of the nation, the martyr, and the heroine." The escalation of the war's violence intensified the importance of differences among women rooted in their ethnic origin.

Partly as a result of the failure of the anti-war protests of women/mothers, and partly as a consequence of the invisibility of women's voices in the peace movements, some feminists began to organize anti-war centres. Women involved in anti-war activism continued their commitment to communicate across ethnic boundaries and borders. However, the effort to maintain communication among women who were divided by the new political circumstances was often a painful experience of broken trust, friendships, and co-operation. During the first years of the conflict, feminists had found some of these experiences almost impossible to bear. The political climate tended to force a major division among feminists that created a distinction between the aggressors and the victims. The mass rape of women in Bosnia-Herzegovina intensified this divide.

The polarization originated within feminists' different conceptualizations of the intersection of gender and ethnic nationalism in determining the character of these rapes. Feminists who stressed that women raped in the war had been subjected to this form of abuse first and foremost because of their gender and not because of their ethnic nationality have been severely attacked as traitors to their ethnic-nations. Feminists who became supporters of the ethnic-national projects and the exclusionary politics of their governments could not accept any notion of a more broadly defined category of "women," namely, one that would cut across ethnic-national divisions. Consequently, they have labelled the approach taken by the former group of feminists as a betrayal of the ethnic-national collective.

As numerous historical and sociological analyses have demonstrated, rape during war, and ethnic-national war in particular, becomes a powerful symbolic weapon against the "enemy."[12] The very logic of rape as a symbolic weapon, as Mežnarić explains, rests upon "the use of gender as a means to control communication and to sharpen the boundaries between two opposed ethnicities."[13] The rape of the "enemy's" women carries an important symbolic message for the men. As Seifert points out, it communicates to them that they have been unable to protect "their" women.[14] I would add that this, in turn, functions as an important mobilizing element in further militarizing ethnic-national collectives.

Women's groups that supported their endangered ethnic-nations and their respective states-in-the-making were the groups which Benderly describes as "[t]hose who conflated 'women as victim' and 'nation as victim,'" and who "moved toward a sort of feminist nationalism, the patriotism of the victimized."[15] The central questions in this dispute have been whether ethnic-national identity or belonging has been a demarcation line between women and what its effect has been on the struggle for women's rights. Because of the political circumstances in which feminists have had to function, the initial divide among women along ethnic-national lines, between "the women aggressors" and "the women victims," has been transformed into a split between the "patriotic" and "disloyal" women and feminists.

"Patriotic" and "disloyal" women's groups have disagreed over the meaning of rape in these wars and the protection of the rights of abused women. The realization by "disloyal" feminists of a common patriarchal male opponent has helped them to discern a continuum of violence and the consequent relation between domestic violence and war violence. They responded rapidly to the threat of further victimization of women survivors of rape in these wars by pointing to how these crimes against women are used for political purposes and to aggravate ethnic-national hatred. These "disloyal" women argued that government reports focused almost exclusively on the crimes of the "other" side in which the ethnic-national identity of the rapist and a possible fetus are the exclusive concern, dismissing both the raped women and the crime committed against them. This, in turn, further victimizes abused women.

Inasmuch as the wars have been victimizing women, they have also given some new directions for women's organizing to deal with issues that were specifically part of women's experiences resulting from the conflicts, such as the adaptation problems faced by women refugees and the trauma that results from sexual and other forms of abuse committed against women in the wars, and so on. It can be argued that the conflict has, in fact, contributed to the emergence of a number of new women's groups in the post-Yugoslav states. Women who joined these new groups as volunteers had not necessarily ever considered themselves to be feminists. Their awareness about particularities of the position of women and of gender dimensions of war and violence grew out of their work with women in need.

The establishment and work of the women's groups would have not been possible without the generous help of women and feminists worldwide. Along with financial support, international feminists helped to establish women's self-help groups and offered seminars and training sessions that focused on feminist therapy and conflict-resolution techniques. The presence of feminists from abroad was an important path of communication through which these women – who were otherwise isolated by war – had an opportunity to contrast their experiences with women internationally. Feminists and other women activists in the post-Yugoslav states, empowered by their own experiences of organizing in the first year of the wars and by the involvement of feminists worldwide, embarked on more organized work with women in the region.

The years of war brought together those "disloyal" women with other women in the region. Relief work in multi-ethnic self-help groups for women victims of war violence, organized by "disloyal" feminists, brought their politics closer to the experiences of refugee women, who came from diverse socio-economic and ethnic-national backgrounds. The encounter between refugee women and feminist activists was a two-way communication because the experiences of the former affected and shaped the work and activism of the latter group of women. Through encounters with the pain and loss experienced by refugee women, feminist activists gained a better understanding of the relationship between victimization and empowerment. Further, the experiences of multi-ethnic self-help groups for women demonstrated that women of different ethnic backgrounds and with diverse experiences of victimization could establish and maintain relationships of mutual respect.[16] The work of such groups helped women victims not only to regain their self-respect and gradually re-establish their lives but also to create a less hostile environment, facilitating the re-establishment of links across the current ethnic-national divide and fostering a reconciliation culture among local populations.

Positive and constructive approaches to crises, which had been learned over the course of the wars through work with women of diverse backgrounds and life histories, became one of the elements influencing feminist approaches to the concept of solidarity among women. This history opened up spaces for a redefinition of women's solidarity and for new forms of alliances among women in the region. Feminist activists' work with the everyday problems of women refugees and women survivors of war violence created the spaces for mutual understanding and ongoing productive exchange; spaces in which women were positioned in a compatible way and where the patriarchal hierarchy of right and wrong did not exist. Through this kind of communication they were able to accept their diverse positionings as sites of "unfinished knowledge" – knowledge that is continuously redefined in relation to the different life situations of women and their differentiated relations to power.[17]

The contributions of women from Bosnia, Croatia, and Serbia in this volume reveal that women's organizing represents a foundation for the creation of alliances among women in the region and that women's organizing is an important force in reconstructing the social fabric of life in these war-torn societies. Their chapters emphasize that the most important parameters of the reconciliation process may lie in a communication that acknowledges different experiences of pain and loss and, thus, differentiated positionings of individuals and groups of women in this conflict. Their continuous engagement in negotiations with others across the ethnic-national divide is an important contribution to a non-violent political culture.

Notes

1 B. Jancar, "The New Feminism in Yugoslavia," in P. Ramet, ed., *Yugoslavia in the 1980s* (Boulder, CO: Westview Press, 1985), p.204.

2 Chris Corrin, ed., *Super Women and the Double Burden: Women's Experience of Change in Central and Eastern Europe and the Former Soviet Union* (Toronto: Second Story Press, 1992; now available from Sumach Press, Toronto); Barbara Einhorn, *Cinderella Goes to Market: Citizenship, Gender and Women's Movements in East and Central Europe* (London: Verso, 1993).

3 S. Woodward, *Balkan Tragedy: Chaos and Dissolution After the Cold War* (Washington, DC: The Brookings Institution, 1995), p.52.

4 Ibid., p.118.

5 The leader of the SRS is Voislav Seselj, who is allegedly responsible for war crimes in Croatia and Bosnia-Herzegovina.

6 N. Ćetković, "Feministička alternativa nacionalizmu i ratu" (Feminist Alternative to Nationalism and War), *S.O.S. Bulletin* 6-7 (1993), pp.70-3. *S.O.S.* is published by the Hotline for Women and Children Vicitims of Violence.

7 D. Aleksov, ed., *Deserters from the War in Former Yugoslavia* (Belgrade: Women in Black, 1994), p.21.

8 Ibid., p.50.

9 For more on the history of feminism in Yugoslavia before the conflict, see Jill Benderly, "Rape, Feminism, and Nationalism in the War in Yugoslav Successor States," in L.A. West, ed., *Feminist Nationalism* (New York: Routledge, 1997), and Žarana Papić, "Women's Movement in Former Yugoslavia: 1970s and 1980s," in M. Blagojević, D. Duhaček, and J. Lukić, eds., *What Can We Do for Ourselves? East European Conference* (Belgrade: Centre for Women's Studies, Research and Communication, 1995).

10 S. Zajović, "Militarism and Women in Serbia," in S. Zajović, ed., *Women for Peace* (Belgrade: Women in Black, 1993), p.7.

11 S. Drakulić, "Women and the New Democracy in the Former Yugoslavia," in N. Funk and M. Mueller, eds., *Gender Policy and Post-Communism* (New York: Routledge, 1993).

12 S. Brownmiller, "Making Female Bodies the Battlefield," in A. Stiglmayer, ed., *Mass Rape: The War against Women in Bosnia-Herzegovina* (Lincoln: University of Nebraska Press, 1994); Z. Eisenstein, *Hatreds: Racialized and Sexualized Conflicts in the Twenty-first Century* (New York: Routledge, 1996); S. Mežnarić, "Gender as an Ethno-marker: Rape, War and Identity Politics in the Former Yugoslavia," in V. Moghadam, ed., *Identity Politics and Women* (Boulder, CO: Westview Press, 1994); R. Seifert, "War and Rape: A Preliminary Analysis," in Stiglmayer, ed., *Mass Rape*.

13 Mežnarić, "Gender as an Ethno-marker," p.79.

14 Seifert "War and Rape," p.58.

15 Benderly, "Rape, Feminism, and Nationalism in the War in Yugoslav Successor States," p.71.

16 M. Belić and V. Kesić, "Report on Work Done between August 1993 and February 1994," in R. Borić, ed., *Edited Volume: Centre for Women War Victims* (Zagreb: Women's Information and Documentation Centre – Centre for Women War Victims, 1994), p.28.

17 Nira Yuval-Davis, "Women, Ethnicity and Empowerment," in K-K. Bhavnani and A. Phoenix, eds., *Shifting Identities – Shifting Racisms* (New Delhi: Sage Publications, 1994), pp.179-99.

Part 1

Ethnic Nationalism and the Militarization of Women

Neluka Silva

Introduction

"**N**ational" metanarratives reveal how gender informs the dominant imagery of the nation. Indeed, Elleke Boehmer has pointed out that, "in its iconographies of power, nationalism may be characterised as a *male* drama."[1] The disjuncture between representation and practice is that, while feminized images define the *iconography* of the nation, the *practice* of nationalism is reserved for the masculine. Significantly, even the most insightful critiques of nationalism are imbued with terms like "fraternity" and "brotherhood," which mark these gender hierarchies.[2] Such linguistic constructions subsume the participatory role foisted upon or undertaken by women in nationalist movements. A further disjuncture is also evident between the abstract idealization of woman as homemaker and her lived experiences which take her out of the domestic sphere. Partha Chatterjee argues that

> [t]he figure of woman often acts as a sign in discursive formations, standing for concepts or entities that have little to do with women in actuality. Each signification of this kind also implies a corresponding sign in which the figure of the man is made to stand for concepts or entities.[3]

Thus, co-opting women into the front lines of nationalist struggle by interpellating them as "national actors" and foisting a "nationalist" label on them as mothers, daughters, educators, workers, and even fighters is not necessarily empowering if it merely reaffirms the boundaries of culturally acceptable feminine conduct and exerts pressure on them to articulate their gender interests solely within the terms of reference set by nationalist discourse.[4] Women, therefore, have often had to confront the symbolic significations assigned to them and position themselves in the public male domain by demanding an active role in combat or resistance.

The four chapters in this section illustrate how moments of ethnic nationalism can provide a space for the militarization of women. Each writer discusses forms of resistance displayed by women during conflict. The geographical contexts highlight the impulses of women who attempt to transcend the boundaries of tradition and devise strategies "to overcome their fear" and to survive the terrors of conflict, as well as find agency through active involvement in the gambit of conflict.

In their individual chapters Lepa Mladjenović and Žarana Papić discuss the situation in Serbia. Mladjenović describes the rise of the Women in Black, Belgrade, as an activist feminist group grounded in the resistance politics in Serbia and linked in its creation to feminist activism in other parts of Europe at the time. Papić notes that during the Milošević regime, women politicians and some feminist and pacifist groups were the only ones who dared to challenge the destructive effects of the ethnic struggle. Her analysis of two important documents link ethnic struggle and feminist resistance to nationalism in two moments of the war in the former Yugoslavia: the October 1998 "I Confess" document of the Women in Black, and the *Activity Report during the Wartime (25 March to 24 April 1999)* of the Autonomous Women's Centre Against Sexual Violence (Belgrade). Her analysis forcefully charts the politics of resistance and the practical initiatives that women adopted.

What is significant in Papić's essay is the way in which she unveils the inadequacy of the "male drama" of nationalism. She shows how the masculinist terms that are associated with the nation – here the slogan "Brotherhood and Unity" of Tito's Yugoslavia – had to be ultimately challenged by the women's groups. Their document "I Confess," which is written "in the form of an extraordinary political public/private narration, testifies to the complex interplay of the continuity of the violent culture against the 'other' in Serbia, and the urgency for the mobilization of individuals and political subjects." This document intertwines the personal and political/historical and is a form of resistance, which in a crisis becomes an articulate feminist political action, although very marginal, but with a powerful symbolic potential. Papić also describes how the process of Active Phone Counselling became a strategy of resistance. The phone work was based on the feminist principles of psychological counselling as well as on women's experiences working with the fear expressed by women during the war in Bosnia when they collaborated with therapists in the Women's Therapy Centre of Medica Zenica in Bosnia-Herzegovina (see Duška Andrić-Ružičić in chapter 8).

In chapter 5, through the situation of the women LTTE and JVP militants in Sri Lanka, Neloufer de Mel poses a series of questions relating to the militarization of women. Moments of national crisis lead to the erosion or destabilization of traditional values and hitherto-accepted certitudes, thus enabling the participation of women in militant armed struggle. However, this participation does not ensure full agency. Just because women are recruited, their autonomy is not guaranteed. She explores whether radical women militants have been able to transform their societies to ensure greater social justice and gender equality. In the interregnum, as they engage in armed struggle towards the anticipated state, there is a containment within the LTTE and JVP of women even at the moment of their most innovative empowerment, since women are often used as adjuncts to the male fighters, not as active participants in their own right. Therefore, to use the participation of women in armed combat as a recognition of their rights and a stride in "liberatory politics" is to ignore the male-centred underpinnings of ethnic-nationalist ideologies.

Although women militants are also circumscribed by patriarchal structures that determine the revolutionary apparatus, Djurdja Knežević argues in chapter 6 that for many women, even a limited and subordinated form of participation in the nationalist project appears to be the easiest and shortest route towards the realization of citizenship; they may, in fact, perceive it as the only route. What this also illustrates is that nationalist concepts of the state do not recognize the human being as an individual; such recognition comes through service to the nation.

During the Bosnian crisis, some Croatian women embraced nationalism as their ideological basis and as the most articulate expression of an irrational sense of belonging to a community. Nationalism offered a sense of inclusion for women that gave them an opportunity to enter politics and the public sphere. Thus they could be recognized as active participants in the social life – but only in a bounded way, limited in both social and political respects. The roles conferred on women in the nationalist space are often limited to a display of suffering, as the basis for the condemnation of the "enemy" (that is, every nationalist community legitimizes itself through images of its own victimization), or to acting as caretakers, and even this is often attractive to them. Women may be allowed to fulfil these roles if they never take an active part in leading the politics of the nation. Yet even these limitations have appeal in a context where they have been denied any form of public recognition or participation. While critiquing the structures of the hegemony of ethnic nationalism and the illusions of feminist transformations, we must also be aware of the potential forms of participation, albeit limited, offered to women within the situation of nationalist conflict.

Notes

1 Elleke Boehmer, "Motherlands, Mothers and Nationalist Sons: Representations of Nationalism and Women in African Literature," in A. Rutherford, ed., *From Commonwealth to Post-Colonial* (Aarhus: Dangaroo Press), p.233. Emphasis added.

2 Benedict Anderson, *Imagined Communities: Reflections on the Origins and Spread of Nationalism* (London: Verso [1983], 1991), p.7. Even now discussions of the Nation are male-centred: see Stein Tønnesson and Hans Antlöv, "Asia in Theories of Nationalism and National Identity," in Stein Tønnesson and Hans Antlöv, eds., *Asian Forms of the Nation* (Surrey, UK: Curzon, 1996), pp.1-40, for an example of this phenomenon. Anne McClintock has also provided several examples of "the very definition of nationhood which rests on the *male* recognition of identity" in *Imperial Leather: Race, Gender, and Sexuality in the Colonial Contest* (New York: Routledge, 1995), p.353.

3 Partha Chatterjee, *The Nation and Its Fragments: Colonial and Post-Colonial Histories* (Princeton, NJ: Princeton University Press, 1993), p.68.

4 D. Kandiyoti, "Identity and Its Discontents: Women and the Nation," in P. Williams and L. Chrisman, eds., *Colonial Discourse and Post-Colonial Theory* (London: Harvester, 1993), p.380.

Lepa Mladjenović

Chapter 3

Women in Black Against War (Belgrade)

In September 1991, the Peace Caravan – an initiative launched by the Helsinki Citizens Assembly – arrived in Belgrade from Zagreb and Ljubljana. These four busloads of pacifists from Europe finished their journey by joining hands with thousands of people in the streets of Sarajevo. Belgrade feminists organized a small session to meet the women from the Caravan who were peace activists from Germany and Italy. We heard for the first time that Women in Black had established groups in Italy to protest the Italian government's involvement in the Gulf War, and that they were supporting Women in Black initiatives in Israel. For three years, Women in Black in Israel had been protesting against their own government's occupation of Palestine. The first vigil of Women in Black in Belgrade was held on 9 October 1991. In the months that followed, one-hour candlelight vigils "for all victims of war" were publicly organized by anti-war intellectuals in front of the Serbian Parliament. During the next two years there were many peace protests. By 1993, however, they had ceased and were transformed into opposition demonstrations against the regime. Women in Black has remained the only permanent anti-war public protest until this day.

In the years that followed, the Belgrade women's movement and the peace movement were barely connected, except by individual women. However, I would argue that Belgrade women made up the majority in the early peace initiatives for three reasons: (1) their experience of doing unpaid work in the household was linked to engagement in unpaid volunteer work; (2) their knowledge of "making do with less" facilitated their engagement in horizontal, non-competitive activities; and (3) their gendered position made it safer for them to act against the regime – men were under threat of forced mobilizations.

41

Almost all the peace initiatives, then, during the first year of such protests in 1991 were initiated by women:

- the Anti-War Centre by Vesna Pešić, Jelena Santić, Zorica Trifunović, Sonja Biserko
- the Candlelight Vigils by Biljana Jovanović, Nataša Kandić, and Nadezda Gace
- the Peace Caravan by Sonja Liht, Janja Beć, and Gordana Šuša
- Women in Black by Staša Zajović, Neda Božinović, and Lepa Mladjenović

As the peace initiatives were transformed into party demonstrations, men entered the stage, and women, apart from Vesna Pešić, slowly disappeared from the protesters for peace scene. Some decided that they did not want to be on the streets any more and set up non-governmental feminist and social justice organizations. For example, the Humanitarian Law Fund, founded by Nataša Kandić, and the Helsinki Committee for Human Rights, founded by Sonja Biserko, were non-governmental organizations that monitored state-based violations of human rights. In Belgrade alone, more than twenty-five small non-governmental organizations have been founded since 1991.

Women in Black Against War (Belgrade) Founded in 1991

Founding team

The founders of the Women in Black were mostly feminists who were active in the feminist group "Women in Society," which was the first such group in Belgrade from 1981 to 1990. Very soon other women joined who were not necessarily feminists but who strongly opposed the Serbian regime, war, and nationalism. Soon, men joined as well.

Aims

- protest against the Serbian government / war / militarism / nationalism / male violence
- support solidarity of women across the "enemy lines" and internationally
- support deserters
- create a women's culture of peace

Activities

- weekly vigils
- peace protests on 10 December, 24 May; participation in other peace and anti-government protests

- public statements
- annual international meeting: "Women's Solidarity against War"
- publishing women's peace history (we have published eleven different books, printing one to three thousand copies each)
- women's peace workshops (1997-99)
- working in refugee camps (1994-96)
- theoretical analysis of the position of women in war and militarism
- weekly meetings and workshops on all related issues: fear, militarism, violence, war

Vigils
Weekly vigils are one of the key activities of the group: Wednesdays on the main square in Belgrade. Women wear black and stand in silence with banners, for one hour.

Political principles
- support national differences
- support all other kinds of differences due to class, age, social status, hetero/gay status, marital status, ableness
- solidarity
- non-violence
- society free of militarism, male violence, and patriarchy

Relation to the state
The group is registered. Every street protest is announced to the police. Every one of the five founders has been interviewed and investigated one or more times by the police. None of the activists has been arrested. The police have banned the protests a few times. Two local police officers are usually sent to "protect" the women during the weekly vigils.

Žarana Papić

Chapter 4

"Bosnian, Albanian, and Roma Women Are Our Sisters": Feminist Politics in Serbia

D uring the most difficult times of the Milošević regime, the only political subjects in Serbia who dared to challenge the deadly game of ethnic struggle were a handful of women politicians and a number of feminist and pacifist groups. In 1991, as described in the previous chapter, the Belgrade Women in Black began to raise their voices against a culture that was ignoring, excluding, and hatefully eliminating the "other." They were among the few who cared enough to oppose the masculinist hate-politics of their former "brothers" by stating, "Bosnian, Albanian, and Roma women are our sisters." In this chapter, I analyze ethnic struggle and feminist resistance to nationalism in two recent moments of war in the region of the former Yugoslavia: the October 1998 creation of the "I Confess" document by the Women in Black, and the *Activity Report during the Wartime (25 March to 24 April 1999)* of the Autonomous Women's Centre Against Sexual Violence (Belgrade). In the pages that follow, I briefly contextualize these two periods, beginning with the transition from "brotherhood and unity" to ethnic hatred and struggle in the late 1980s and early 1990s, followed by the involvement of NATO in the war in Kosovo in 1999.

From "Brotherhood and Unity" to Disillusionment and Hatred

Tito's Yugoslavia laid all its hopes on a multinational and multi-ethnic federation that was based on an exclusive male-dominated identity united under the slogan "Brotherhood and Unity." All the recent wars fought on the territory of the former Yugoslavia were grounded in a transition from this totalitarian communist heritage of "class struggle" to "ethnic struggle." The mutation of class struggle into a more lethal ethnic struggle was based on nourishing cultural, historical, ethnic, national, and racist antagonisms among Serbs, Croats, Slovenes, Bosnians, and Albanians. This process is embedded in the politically and culturally constructed racist antagonisms between nations and ethnic groups that were launched when Slobodan Milošević took over the Serbian Communist Party in 1987. Milošević's system of power was based on producing and transforming hatred for its own ends and, above all, among its own men. Put another way, the wars in the former Yugoslavia have been a series of ill-fated, unsuccessful, and mortally vengeful "broken brotherhoods."

After more than a decade of "brotherly" killings, it was obvious that the former Yugoslav "brothers" had themselves become the most effective tool of the destructive politics of what was by then ethnic struggle. By encouraging a Serbian nationalism that was fascist in form, Milošević (ab)used the legacy of the Serbian "trauma" associated with Tito and the Serbian experience in the Second World War to turn the alleged destruction of Serbian nationhood into a *causus beli*. He also claimed shamelessly to be the only authentic defender of the "Yugoslavian Idea." This form of Serbian nationalism became Milošević's most lethal instrument against all other nations in the region of the former Yugoslavia. Instead of a slow democratic process of disillusionment that would have led Serbs out of their Shangri-La of ideological brotherhood and unity, their awakening was uncontrolled and violent. Since 1987, Serbs have not known exactly *who* they are, but they have been absolutely prepared to discover themselves through a hatred of the "other." Prior to and during the last decade of the twentieth century, Serbia can be defined as a specific historical process – a "transition" from pro-Yugoslav Communism into a politically autistic, aggressive, and pro-fascist collectivism.[1] Until recently and for the above reasons, among others, there have not been significant democratic alternatives to Milošević's war-politics that are based on "ethnic struggle" against all. Even the so-called oppositional men-leaders took part in the game of "I don't mind if you are cleansed."

I understand the principle of ethnic struggle to be based on a politically and culturally constructed racist antagonism. Race/ethnicity/nationality in the region of the former Yugoslavia has been used instrumentally as a political category to define the "other," with whom it was no longer possible to share life. The Kosovo crisis was at the heart of this decade-long drama. As Milošević began to encourage and legitimize a hatred of

Albanians by Serbs as a fundamental component of Serbian national identity, the destiny of the former Yugoslavia became tied to a series of wars in Slovenia, Croatia, and Bosnia-Herzegovina.

As the cycle of war reached Kosovo in 1999 and culminated in the NATO bombings, pro-fascist collectives of Serbs expanded and extended their reach into groups of previously declared democrats, anti-nationalists, and pacifists. Indifference to the destruction of the "other" became the most dominant political, cultural, public, and private fact of Serbia. Martial law (or the "happy to persecute traitors" law) was introduced to make sure that fear would be thoroughly internalized and would thus paralyze any significant resistance to the final act of fascistization of Serbia. The media legitimated a denial of ethnic cleansing in Kosovo. There was an explicit "taboo" against even the mute recognition that Albanians, who were citizens of the Federal Republic of Yugoslavia (FRY), were being brutally cleansed from Kosovo. The real picture of Serbia's political evolution was shown through seductive Serbian narcissism over (finally) becoming a victim of NATO bombings.

The systematic production of what I define as "inevitable barbarity" demonstrates the extent to which the wars in the ex-Yugoslavia were a result of the systematic cultural production of violent representations/narrations before and during the actual militarized violence. The social world in Serbia was constructed through a discourse of exclusion of the "other," which involved exteriorization of the "other"; erasure of empathy; denial of tolerance; and amnesia of a history of living together. In order to be effective, the overall practice of "otherness" and the tolerated destruction of the "other body" had to be prepared through a systematic (discursive, symbolic, and iconic) cultural production. From the cultural production of various levels of identity,[2] a consensus on fascist politics arose as a specific "culture of normality." In Serbia, some of the most effective features of this fascist culture of normality have been legitimated through the dominant political/cultural discourse since 1988 and show signs of persisting even into the post-Milošević era:

- the designation of all "others" as "impossible" as well as suspicious and treacherous conspirators against "Serbianhood"; as the very negation of humanity; as unworthy animals; and as automatic and obedient collective agents;
- radical (media-generated) inversions leading to taboos against the "other": against peace and tolerance; against contacts with the "other body"; against empathy, cross-connections, multi-ethnic friendships, mixed neighbourhoods, interethnic marriages, and personal emotional interactions;

- the depersonalization of social life and reduction to a violent collectivity of the nation, territory, origin, tradition, culture; and
- women cast as the unrepresentative "other" in one's own nation and the representative "other" and the target of violence of the enemy nation; this includes the over-sexualization of the "other" nation and the emasculation of the "warrior's" male body as an obedient servant.

Feminist Anti-War Documents

Women in Black: "I Confess"

The extent to which the pro-fascist cultural, political, and psychological (public and private) *état d'esprit* dominated the political life of Serbia for more than a decade is demonstrated in the document entitled "I Confess," published by Women in Black (Belgrade), in October 1998, on the occasion of the seventh year of their anti-war activity.

Women in Black Against War (Belgrade)
7 Years of Women in Black
We Are Still on the Streets
9 October 1991 to 9 October 1998

I CONFESS:
- to my longtime anti-war activity;
- that I did not agree with the severe beating of people of other ethnicities and nationalities, faiths, race, sexual orientation;
- that I was not present at the ceremonial act of throwing flowers on the tanks headed for Vukovar, 1991, and Priština, 1998;
- that I opposed the politics of repression, apartheid, massacres, and wars of the Serbian regime against the Albanian population on Kosovo;
- that I fed women and children in refugee camps, schools, churches, mosques;
- that for the entire war I crossed the walls of Balkan ethno-states, because solidarity is the politics that interests me;
- that I understood democracy as support to anti-war activists/friends/sisters: Albanian women, Croat women, Roma women, stateless women;
- that I first challenged the murderers from the state where I live and then those from other states, because I consider this to be responsible political behaviour of a woman-citizen;
- that throughout all the seasons of the year I insisted that there be an end to the slaughter, destruction, ethnic cleansing, forced evacuation of people, rape;

- that I took care of others while the patriots took care of themselves.

On 9 October 1998 at 6:30 p.m. on Republic Square we will make visible our non-violent resistance to war.

We Are All Women In Black!

Women in Black
Belgrade

* * *

This singular document, in the form of an extraordinary political public/ private narration, testifies to the complex interplay of the continuity of the violent culture against the "other" in Serbia and to the urgency for the mobilization of individuals and political subjects. The exclusivity of "I Confess" lies in what I call its "discursive loneliness." It is one of the rare public statements that so strongly opposed a culture of exclusion. Moreover, it shows transparently that for years the dominant taboo in political/ social life in Serbia was against respecting the "other." Thus, exclusion of the "other" has been defined as a "virtue," and inclusion of the "other" as a "crime." This discursive loneliness reveals the hidden effects of tolerated violence against the "other" and points out the invisibility of the destruction of the personal and social fabric in Serbia.

The expression "I Confess" marks the fundamental inversion of a dominant pro-fascist social code and, at the same time, the articulation of a political sensibility that demands individual responsibility and public counteraction. It demonstrates how the basic intertwining of the personal and political/historical in traumatic times can become an articulate feminist political action, which, although very marginal, has powerful symbolic potential. Finally, it makes us aware that, in times when a culture of violence and exclusion becomes the "legitimate narrative," there is an exceptional need for the ethical mobilization of the subject and for continuous self-reflection and self-narration.

The Autonomous Women's Centre Against Sexual Violence (Belgrade)

The *Activity Report* of Belgrade's Autonomous Women's Centre Against Sexual Violence, made during the NATO bombings of the former Yugoslavia, is another example of feminist resistance. Not only is it a testimony to the political and psychological effects of the NATO bombings, it is also, and even more so, evidence of the reality under martial law that Milošević promptly introduced the day the bombings began. Using this law, the state aimed to paralyze every possible resistance to its politics of ethnic cleansing. The *Activity Report* demonstrates resistance to such internal fascistization processes as

- the "new" oblivion to the "other" and indifference to the fate of Kosovo's Albanians;
- the "narcissistic homogenization" of many Serbs under NATO bombs;
- the denial of organized crime against Kosovo's Albanians before and during the NATO bombings; and
- the final domination of the vandalist culture, aggressive towards anything that was taken as foreign, Western, un-Orthodox, non-Serb, mixed, civil, or civilian.

This *Activity Report* speaks to the women's ability to organize a rapid response to crisis – an ability acquired through necessity and willingness to take enormous political risks. It also underscores the bridging of distance and ethnicity that took place in the name of mutual support and assistance, without any thought given to the consequences for individual activists. Roma, Serb, Albanian, Muslim – indeed, all were sisters in times of crisis not only in supporting each other but also in forging resistance against a fascist political order.

Autonomous Women's Centre Against Sexual Violence (Belgrade) Activity Report during the Wartime (25 March to 24 April 1999)

Active Support in Overcoming Women's Fear

On 24 March, after the first night of (NATO) bombings, the law of war (martial law) was ordered. Fear had become a fact of life overnight. . . . Activists of the Women's Centre decided to start calling women on the phone to ask them how they were and to offer them some space to overcome their fears. For six years, the work of the Autonomous Women's Centre had been based on the ethical principle that they would serve women when women asked for assistance, when they called for help, or when they came to the Centre. Fear in wartime shifts the borders of private and public space and therefore we transgressed our former work principles. Every woman became a potential client, at least for that time. Connecting with each other, calling on the phone, asking women how they felt – these became legitimate activities of the Women's Centre. And once again, women's solidarity inspired many more women. That is how we started an active telephone support for women to overcome their fear.

Active Phone Counselling

Our counselling phone work was based on the feminist principles of psychological counselling as well as on our experiences in working with the fears expressed by women during the war in Bosnia when we collaborated with therapists in the Women's Therapy Centre of Medica Zenica in Bosnia-Herzegovina.

The Fear Counselling Team chose the approach of telephoning women directly for a variety of reasons. First, in situations of war, women are less mobile and often cannot leave their homes. Second, women often regard their homes as the only safe place. In the majority of cases, the Women's Centre paid the telephone bill – a very important factor in times of war, when poverty increases and women cannot relax enough to talk about themselves if they know they cannot pay the telephone bill.

Documenting the Feelings of Fear

The Autonomous Women's Centre Against Sexual Violence, from its foundation in 1993, believed in anti-war and anti-military politics, multi-nationality, as well as in establishing solidarity with women from the other side of the front line. The Women's Centre documented the responses of women who were afraid of the NATO bombings and the entire war situation, as well as the feelings of women in Priština and other parts of Kosovo who were experiencing other specific processes of fear, terror, and pain.

Documenting Calls

In the first twenty-five working days during the NATO bombings, five counsellors gave 378 telephone counselling sessions to women from thirty-four towns in the Federal Republic of Yugoslavia. The statistics of the Women's Centre indicate that 232 counselling phone sessions were done with women in Belgrade, and other counselling phone sessions were done with women in other towns in the regions of Vojvodina, Sandžak, Montenegro, and Kosovo. Of the total number of calls, 87 per cent were initiated from the Centre.

Documenting Statements of Fear

The Women's Centre documented all types of fears and the forms in which fear was manifested . . . in the body, in dreams, in behaviours, in thoughts. . . . From the statements made by the women who were coun-selled during the NATO bombings, one can clearly conclude that the life of every woman changed; that emotional states changed many times in the course of a single day; and that the most dominant emotions were des-peration and anxiety, as were the attempts to survive as best as possible and adapt to the limited conditions of life:

> "I am in a horrible fear" . . . "I fear the night" . . . "I am afraid to go
> out further than the grocery shop" . . . "I don't go out" . . . "I sleep in
> the house of my friend" . . . "I cannot concentrate" . . . "I am sensitive
> to all the sounds" . . . "I am frightened that my brother will be mobi-
> lized" . . . "When sirens start, I feel nauseous" . . . "I have lost four

kilos, I broke down psychologically" . . . "Every night I go to the shelter, I feel bad" . . . "When I see soldiers on the street I shudder" . . . "I feel I have dropped from the tracks, everything changed in my life" . . . "I am worried for my future" . . . "I am constantly on sleeping pills" . . . "I sleep in my clothes" . . . "Children in the shelter are very disturbed" . . . "At my workplace men have started to drink intensively" . . . "I am nervous" . . . "I am not afraid of death, but I am afraid of sudden sounds" . . . "It is killing me that I cannot work at anything any more" . . . "My emotional state is changing every hour" . . . "I threw out the TV set, I cannot listen to that language anymore" . . . "Neighbours are spreading apocalyptic rumours all the time" . . . "I am nervous, I go from the shelter to the flat three times in one night" . . . "I feel like leaving this country forever, it is so sickening" . . . "New fears are coming."

Documenting Statements about Mechanisms of Survival

One of the active roles of the Fear Counselling Team of the Women's Centre was to support women's strategies of survival and their positive experiences. Supporting healthy dimensions of behaviour, feelings, and thoughts was the main form of active support of the women we spoke to:

"I am feeling good, I have gone through one war already, I know the rules" . . . "I am focused and rational. I have enough information" . . . "I feel good, I am supporting other women" . . . "I am cleaning the house all day" . . . "I am walking back and forth through town all day" . . . "I spend hours on e-mail" . . . "I have planted many plants" . . . "I am taking my children to the hills" . . . "We are hugging all day" . . . "I am taking sleeping pills, and it works for me."

Documenting Statements of Women of Albanian Nationality in Kosovo

In the first two weeks after the onset of the NATO bombings, the Fear Counselling Team called women and activists in Priština and elsewhere in Kosovo. Women of Serbian nationality expressed their fears of the bombings; women of Albanian nationality feared the bombings, but even more so, the Serbian officials, the army, and the police "of green, blue and masked men." After the first two weeks, many women of Albanian nationality were forced to leave their homes at gunpoint in front of armed Serbian-speaking soldiers. With their families, they were obliged to go to the buses or trains that took them close to the Macedonian border. From Macedonia, some of them called us to tell us that they were alive and well, and some told us of the humiliating and terrifying experiences they had to go through:

"I am terrorized" . . . "a strange silence is horrifying me" . . . "We are sitting in the dark every night, I cannot sleep or eat, but I have coffee and cigarettes" . . . "I don't know what to tell you, nor what to think . . . I am still alive."

Workshops about Feelings

In the first month of the NATO bombings, the Women's Centre organized four workshops entitled "How do we feel?" The exchange of negative and positive experiences was of paramount importance for participants – to help them feel they were not alone in their fears as well as to be supported for their positive feelings.

The Autonomous Women's Centre continues the active telephone support of women and will continue to issue reports and analysis of data obtained.

The Fear Counselling Team of the Autonomous Women's Centre against Sexual Violence (Belgrade) Biljana Maletin, Bobana Macanović, Bosiljka Janjušević, Lepa Mladjenović, and Sandra Tvitić

* * *

These examples of feminist political resistance to the inner processes of fascistization of the political life and minds of people demonstrate to what extent the "normality" of excluding and eliminating the "other" has become the dominant pattern, even in everyday public and private life in Serbia. During the seventy-seven days of NATO bombings in Serbia, we witnessed and went through an unprecedented experience – a new "state of war" – that aimed to make each of us internalize a fear of state violence and paralyze us in every cell of our bodies. It was an experience of organized oppression in which violence and fear became strongly intertwined in so many directions, fragmenting and affecting every level of our realities. This was an atmosphere in which terror threatened to compel us towards one very precise goal: an auto-fixation on solely "our" victimization by NATO bombing. Martial law in Serbia had as its primary aims the paralysis of political resistance; the fascistization of "ordinary" people (including some self-proclaimed "democrats") and the cleansing of Albanians from Kosovo.

The two and a half months of the state of war in Serbia in the spring of 1999 can therefore be defined more accurately as a state of fascism. Fascism is a very active process, a co-operation that is constantly invoked for the normalization of its codes, enacting abstract but powerful demands for each and every individual, and for each and every political subject, to share its norms. It is based on a consensual silence concerning the annihilation of the "other" and a "forcefully voluntary" (*forcement volontaire*) collaboration. It remains to be seen whether race/ethnicity/ nationality in more recent times in the Federal Republic of Yugoslavia and in the other regions of the former Yugoslavia will continue to be used as a political category to define the "other" as someone with whom it is no longer possible to share life. The Women in Black (Belgrade) continues to meet weekly in Republic Square in Belgrade and the Autonomous Women's Centre Against Sexual Violence persists in its work with women across all nationalities and identities. Their struggles are among the building blocks being used to create an anti-fascist future in the region of the former Yugoslavia.

Acknowledgement

This chapter was first drafted in Belgrade, between 20 May and 5 August 1999.

Notes

1 The stages in the long process of fascistization of the symbolic and material social world in Milošević's Serbia can be defined as series of multiple structural mutations: from state socialism to state nationalism, to mafia corporatism, to oriental despotism, to fascistic tyranny.

2 These processes were heavily situated in four levels of identity, which were under extreme and violent turmoil: (1) self-identity; (2) civic/urban identity; (3) gender identity; and (4) identity of the "other."

Neloufer de Mel

Chapter 5

Agent or Victim? The Sri Lankan Woman Militant in the Interregnum

"Appointment with Rajiv Gandhi" is a short story by Sri Lankan author Charles Sarvan, which constructs for us the thoughts of Dhanu, the female suicide bomber of the Liberation Tigers of Tamil Eelam (LTTE), as she spends a restless night before she assassinates Rajiv Gandhi.[1]

The woman in Sarvan's story is unnamed, but from news reports we know her to be Dhanu. In Sarvan's fictional story of the assassination, in which Dhanu eventually ignites the plastic explosives tied to her waist to kill Gandhi at the Madras Sriperumbudur Stadium in May 1991, she looks upon this moment as a wedding, a transformative marriage in which she embraces death as she garlands her bridegroom. Like other brides in her hometown of Jaffna, the Tamil heartland of northern Sri Lanka, she too will be dressed as a bride with care, but this time not by older women relatives and friends, but by men who will wire her up for death.

Dhanu's act of terror is an empowering one. Through it she will break with an oppressive tradition. Unlike the usual arranged marriages, *she* will choose her bridegroom; unlike the traditional virgin bride, she will be touched by men before her "wedding"; unlike the modest woman who shuns publicity, her photograph will be flashed in the world press. And within the ambit of Sarvan's story, in his juxtaposition of Dhanu's childhood reminiscences with the ruthlessness of the present, the "cold-blooded terrorist" is given her individuality.

But even as the woman militant transcends the bounds of traditional female identity, is there a price, other than death of course, to be paid for such "freedom"? I hope to show that there is a price – a loss located in significant ways within the domain of gender constructs and, in particular, the forms of female sexuality and reproduction that are valued within it. This, in turn, reflects the wider issue of a militant's loss of individuality – whether male or female. For the militant's individuality can only be creatively fictionalized as in Sarvan's treatment of Dhanu's story, glimpsed in the discursive contradictions of her/his martial poetry or caught in a moment of hesitancy in conversation. The politics of self-representation otherwise denies the militant a personality and emotional expression of her/his own, and the reality of her/his driving impulses lies in the complete obedience to the will of the militant leadership on whose behalf she/ he struggles. These losses, in turn, mark the paradigms and cornerstones of the anticipated state or social order that militant groups like the Liberation Tigers of Tamil Eelam (LTTE) and the Janatha Vimukthi Peramuna (JVP) struggle for.[2]

From these losses, other important questions arise that have significant implications for feminist struggles within militant nationalism or revolutionary movements. Do women who participate in militant armed struggle enjoy full agency? Does their recruitment to the struggle spell autonomous, individual choice? If so, why and how has there been, historically, an instrumentality with which nationalist/militant patriarchies have enlisted women? How radically have women militants been able to transform their societies to ensure greater social justice and gender equality? And even if, as a result of patriarchal containment within their chosen militant groups, they enjoy only agentive *moments* in an interregnum where normalcy is suspended and there is license to transform taboo and social convention, why shouldn't these women be held accountable for loss of life and the destruction of livelihoods? They have condoned the undemocratic practices of groups like the LTTE and JVP, which resort to summary killings, prevent the return to civilian rule,[3] and sustain themselves through the ideology of militarism.

If, on the one hand, violence draws on the most noble of human qualities such as sacrifice for a collective good, it "expropriates agency" on the other, as it acts to silence both individuals and a majority of people who stand opposed to violence and who want to speak on their own behalf.[4] How should the woman combatant who participates in such an expropriation of agency, even as she transforms her own life through agentive moments *in* violence, be looked at? This is the challenge for feminists in Sri Lanka as well as in South Asia, where militarism is fast becoming an organizing principle in many of its countries, increasingly buttressing authoritarian states and non-state actors, and supporting various cross-border, cross-ethnic conflicts, and where women's participation in violence has taken a significant turn.[5]

Shifting Sites

Women Fighters of Liberation Tigers is a book by Adele Ann, the Australian wife of LTTE theoretician Anton Balasingham.[6] She was a regular spokesperson for the women's wing of the LTTE, which began as an autonomous unit on 1 July 1987, although women combatants had fought side by side with the men since 1986.[7] At first, her function as spokesperson was not disconnected from her foreign nationality, which gave the LTTE a certain credibility, particularly in the eyes of the Western media. As in Sarvan's short story, it is the breaking of new ground for the women of Jaffna that is stressed in Adele Ann's book, and it is particularly in the projection of the LTTE women cadres as being equal with those of its men that this is constructed. In a chapter that describes the military training undertaken by the women, the rigorousness of the training is emphasized and the endurance of the women is admired.[8] The woman combatant is presented as no different than the male in terms of the combat situations for which she is chosen. The ideology and attainment of martyrdom that sanctifies an LTTE combatant's death is within her reach, just as it is for the man. In fact, given the woman's symbolic role as nurturer of society, her participation in violence signals the ultimate moral sanction that can be accorded it.

In the struggle for the anticipated state of Tamil Eelam, the sociocultural role of the LTTE women has undergone and continues to undergo a radical transformation. From that of a conservative, feminized ideal, the LTTE woman combatant is transformed into a public figure, engaged in "masculine" activities, repudiating patriarchal norms of womanhood. In the historical construction of a Tamil identity peopled by men as male warriors, leaders, poets, and philosophers, the LTTE struggle offers women a chance to take their place with these men. *The Broken Palmyrah* points out the attraction of such change for the women of Jaffna:

> One cannot but be inspired when one sees the women of the LTTE, two by two, in the night with their AKs slung over the shoulder, patrolling the entrances to Jaffna City. One cannot but admire the dedication and toughness of their training, seen in the video films put out by the LTTE. One could see the nationalist fervour and the romantic vision of women in arms defending the nation. This becomes a great draw . . . our social set up, its restrictions on creative expression for women and

the evils of the dowry system are some of the social factors that led to their initial recruitment.[9]

The dedication to change, which, in this phase of the struggle for Eelam, is almost surely a call to death, is borne out in a poem written by Captain Vanathi of the LTTE women's wing who died in 1991 at the age of twenty-seven in the battle at Elephant Pass. The poem is entitled "She, The Woman of Tamililam!"

> Her forehead shall be adorned not with
> *kunkumam* (but) with red blood.
> All that is seen in her eyes is not the sweetness
> of youth (but) firm declarations of those
> who have fallen down.
>
> On her neck will lay no *tali* (but) a
> Cyanide flask!
>
> Her legs are going and searching,
> not for searching a relationship with relatives
> (but) looking towards the liberation of
> the soil of Tamililam.
>
> Her gun will fire shots.
> No failure will cause the enemy to fall!!
> It will break the fetters of Tamililam!!
> Then from our people's lips a national anthem
> will tone up!![10]

While the bridal imagery of traditional poetry remains, there is an eroticizing of the martial, and the parenthetical emphases in the poem make it clear that the LTTE woman has rejected the conventional world of feminized identities to embrace a language of death and militancy where there is no place for squeamishness and coyness. Her sexual energy is directed at ushering in a new state and dispensation, not preserving old familial ties.

It is a shift Adele Ann is eager to stress. She writes:

The very decision by young women to join the armed struggle – in most cases without the consent of parents – represents a vast departure of behaviour for Tamil women. Normally young women remain under the control of the father and brother. Male control follows them throughout their lives. The decision to break-out of this cycle of suffo-cating control is a refreshing expression and articulation of their new aspirations and independence. It could perhaps be one of the biggest decisions of their lives. Such a decision makes a social statement about the characters of the young women. It tells society that they are not satisfied with the social status quo; it means they are young women capable of defying authority; it means they are women with independent thoughts. . . . Such young women fly in the face of tradition, but they are the women who are the catalysts for social change. Entering into the military programme represents an extension of the social challenge that young women have made by making a decision to join the national struggle.[11] The implication of this statement is clear. There can be no emancipation for Tamil women without first attaining a new state and social order. The 1991 manifesto of the Women's Front of the LTTE makes this a priority, explicitly stating it in the first clause: "Secure the right of self-determination of the people of Tamililam and establish an independent democratic state of Tamililam." Following this are the specific demands of women, which include the dismantling of caste and dowry systems, equal opportunities in employment, the dispensation to control their own lives, and legal protection against sexual harassment, rape, and domestic violence.[12]

The state as they know it today, administered by the Sri Lankan government, is inadequate and repressive. It has to be recast and women have the potential to play a central role in that recasting. Prabhakaran, the leader of the LTTE, acknowledged this even as he further elicited the commitment of women to the movement. In a statement issued on 8 March 1992 to mark International Women's Day, he wrote:

> Today, young Tamil women are there, carrying arms to extricate this soil in the battlefield. They have performed an immense sacrifice (*arppanippu*) of a kind that amazes the whole world. With pride I can say that the origin, the development and the rise of the women's military wing of the Liberation Tigers is one of the greatest accomplishments of our movement. This marks a revolutionary turning point in the history of liberation struggle of the women of Tamililam. Women can succeed on the ideal path towards their (own) liberation only through joining forces with a liberation movement. (Women) can change into revolutionary women who have heroism (*viram*), abandonment (of life) (*tiyakam*), courage and self-confidence. Only when women join forces with our revolutionary movement that has formulated (a path) to liberation of our women, shall our struggle reach perfection.[13]

A synergy between women's empowerment and revolutionary struggle is established here, but in the line stating that the "liberation of *our* women" has already been determined by the movement, the agency of Tamil women continues to be suspended. By whom was the path to women's liberation determined? Were there women involved in its formulations? And in the possessive "our women," does patriarchy not rear its head in collective control and protection of Tamil women by the male?

Patriarchy in the JVP

The Janatha Vimukthi Peramuna (JVP), or People's Liberation Front, had its inaugural meeting in May 1965 and came into prominence in the late 1960s with an agenda to establish a socialist state. It has had two phases of militant uprisings to date. The first phase began in April 1971 with attacks on several police stations; this first JVP insurrection was defeated by government forces in June of that year. The second phase was from 1987-89 when the JVP took on the UNP government of Ranasinghe Premadasa in a particularly brutal fashion. It conducted summary killings of government officials who disobeyed its orders and of security forces personnel who hounded it, at times wiping out their entire families. These were tactics of terror through which it successfully called for stoppages of work and a boycott of elections, which nearly brought the government down.[14]

The second phase of the JVP was so brutal, both in its own militancy and in the government's counterterror that caused the deaths and "disappearances" of an estimated forty thousand people, that the period is popularly referred to as "the reign of terror." However, despite these violent campaigns, there are many differences between the JVP (particularly in its first phase) and the LTTE that must be noted at the outset.[15] Such an emphasis helps us guard against flattening out all militant groups into one homogeneous set, while illuminating a line of entry to the self-appraisal and representation of the women cadres within the two groups. For instance, the early JVP never saw itself as a nationalist movement the way the LTTE did. Its rhetoric was that of class struggle, and the ideology of militarism was not central to its organizational structure. A JVP woman member like Juliet (a pseudonym), who joined the movement as a schoolgirl of thirteen, would inevitably see and represent herself differently and far less militantly than Captain Vanathi did.

The JVP never saw itself as an army in its own right, unlike the highly militarized LTTE, which has waged a separatist war since 1983. The 1971 JVP insurrection was fought with less loss of lives and property and quelled more easily than the ongoing separatist war. The JVP leaders and cadres who did survive were easily "rehabilitated" into the mainstream even after prison sentences. Many now hold important positions within the state and in non-government organizations. In 2000, the JVP contested elections, won ten seats in Parliament, and formed a coalition with the People's Alliance government, which lost the general election of December 2001. The LTTE combatant, on the other hand, is often killed in battle or, when captured, bites on a cyanide capsule worn around the neck. There are no survivors who can enter the political process.

The ferocity of the LTTE challenge and its dedication to the ideology of violence, then, cannot be matched to the efforts of the early JVP, although in its later phase the JVP mirrored the LTTE in its nationalistic call and had the south gripped in terror. As well, due to the high visibility and efficient organizational structure of the LTTE (the likes of which never characterized the JVP), its international presence through the Tamil diaspora, as well as international media interest in the 1990s in the issue of women combatants, the LTTE women cadres have had more visibility than the JVP women ever did.[16]

In any case, although there had been a tradition of significant women's participation in militant left-wing anti-colonial campaigns such as the Suriya Mal movement, the 1953 "hartal" and other trade-union protests in Sri Lanka, the JVP failed to foster and enlist large scale female participation for its cause because of its patriarchal bent. During the 1970s, the JVP had only five or six women at the action committee level. There were no women on the district committees or the decision-making politburo.[17] Even when the Samajavadi Kantha Sangamaya (SKS), or the JVP women's wing, was formed in 1976, it was assimilated into the JVP patriarchy. Rohana Wijeweera, leader of the JVP until his death in 1989, himself admitted that it was the weakest wing of the organization. When, in 1982, the SKS organized a large international conference, it was the all-male politburo that was invited to its governing board, and its inaugural song chanted the praises of the martyred *brothers* (*sada samramu sohoyuro*).[18] There aren't any woman militants sitting on the LTTE politburo either, nor have any been appointed as members to the LTTE's negotiating team, which is talking to various Sri Lankan governments about a settlement to the conflict. However, the more sophisticated LTTE movement of the 1980s and 1990s was receptive to the political potential of a women's wing and tapped into international funding available for women's struggles and empowerment.

A full-length feminist study of the JVP movement in Sri Lanka has yet to be written, and the experiences of its women cadres yet to be recorded. But Juliet's voice within the first phase of the JVP struggle is instructive as it resonates with the statements, and silences, of the women in the second phase of the JVP. Juliet's family belongs to the Sinhala-speaking bourgeoisie (although her father, a businessman, was conversant in both

English and Tamil) domiciled in the town of Kegalle, about 77 kilometres from the capital, Colombo. Her involvement with JVP politics and recruitment into the group took place through her brother, Sarath Wijesinghe, who was the JVP district leader for Kegalle. After the JVP's first strike on the Wellawaya police station on 5 April 1971, and the subsequent round-up or killing of its cadres by government forces, Juliet regrouped with other JVP members in the jungles of Wilpattu. She lived in and around these jungles for five years, helping with the JVP reorganization. In fact, for about a year after the April insurrection, lawlessness continued in the North Central Province that encompassed these jungles. Public transport was disrupted, communication lines destroyed, and banks robbed. Many of these disturbances were credited to the JVP. However, there were also other gangs and thugs who took advantage of the situation for their own ends.[19]

In an interview with me about her experiences during those five years, it was the breaking of new ground that Juliet stressed. She enjoyed a new-found freedom through her involvement with the JVP. She had been one of seven women chosen to retreat into the jungles because of her adaptability, and although in one sense she was on the run as a fugitive from the law, in another sense she felt free to enjoy the communal living. "We were a group of young people," she told me, "and everyone helped with the chores, so it was enjoyable."[20]

The relaxed tone of such reminiscences reflects, of course, the differences of the JVP then and the LTTE today. But the lack of ferocity revealed by the early JVP campaign, when compared with the LTTE, should not take away from the significance of how women like Juliet set up forms of resistance. The spurning of middle-class cultural norms Juliet took on when she joined the JVP was path-breaking in its own right; so was her active recruiting for the movement at the University of Peradeniya; retreating to the jungles; having to risk her personal safety; living with men; standing against the establishment; and switching dress codes – wearing trousers where previously she would have, in public at least, worn a frock or skirt and blouse as is usually worn by young Sinhala women.

Empowerment and Containment: Duality in the Interregnum

The taboos and impositions of female identity that these women turned their backs on are those that acquire particular significance at times of national crisis. It is ironic that at a time of upheaval, "when in reality social norms are being broken and old values begin to crumble, a stronger effort is made to visibly and vocally reiterate faith in the old morality."[21] This reflects the resistance by the established order, whether it be the state or class/caste interests, which digs in its heels when challenged and, in doing so, reinforces the most conservative aspects of its cultural and political praxis, including the sexual division of labour. But what is of interest is how, on the terrain of gender, those fighting the establishment also mirror it, conforming to a received conventionality, despite their pronouncements to the contrary, in moves that hardly distinguish them from the order they seek to dislodge.

For in the interregnum, as they engage in armed struggle towards the anticipated state, there is a containment within the LTTE and JVP of women even at the moment of their most innovative empowerment. It is a containment most deeply seen at the sites of female sexuality and reproduction. Motherhood is a key construct within female sexuality, a powerful symbol that sanctions nation-building. Much feminist scholarship has been done on the powerful configuration of the mother figure as a signifier of national and communal identity in South Asia.[22] In its continuity as a recurring motif in nationalist/revolutionary discourse lies the control of women by patriarchy in the name of combatting a larger terror that is called state repression, or, if one is on the side of the state, separatist nationalism or revolutionary anarchy. In this trajectory can be found an internalizing of feminized ideals by women and a resistance to them, and, most important, the complex and *protean* containment of women that reflects the shifting goal posts and resilience of patriarchy itself.

In the interregnum, a period in which there is a suspension of normalcy, traditional gender roles are continually challenged. The LTTE and JVP female militant who is willing to both kill and be killed for her cause participates in the public domain in a way that flies in the face of the traditional patriarchal containment designed for her. It was the exigency of the interregnum to which the LTTE was responsive, when by the late 1980s with the war taking its toll on males, the LTTE actively recruited women into its cadres. The early recruitment campaign took a familiar image from revolutionary groups worldwide, combining the role of mother with that of the warrior woman. The woman guerilla, with a baby in one hand and a gun in the other, has been used in revolutionary recruitment and iconography from Latin America to Asia and Africa.[23] Given the gendering of nationalist discourse with its call on women to mother/nurture and birth a new nation through sacrifice and courage, the collapsing of mother and warrior was an easy elision. The 1983 LTTE publication, "Women and Revolution: The Role of Women in Tamil Eelam National Revolution," carried a prominent photograph of a Palestinian woman holding a gun in one hand and a baby in the other.[24] But the notion of mother-warrior did not displace deep-seated notions of normative female identity, which, through popular culture, the media, educational texts, and family conditioning, continued to instruct the Sri Lankan woman on her symbolic value as a sexually chaste, enlightened, altruistic, and maternal being.

As Cynthia Enloe comments, "[I]nterweaving the images of woman as combatant and mother so tightly suggests that as soon as the immediate threat recedes, as soon as the 'war is over,' the woman in the picture will put down the rifle and keep the baby."[25] It is clear from the case of the LTTE that, instead of waiting until "the war is over," its patriarchy had already put in place strictures on women during the interregnum that contained her even as she was invited to step into the public sphere as a combatant. The most bizarre manifestation of such containment was the "10 commandments for women," listed in a poster that was pasted on the walls of Jaffna in late 1984. The dictates included that all young women should wear traditional dress (sari); that married women should not be seen in public in housecoats (Jaffna housewives often buy fish in the early morning from a vendor on the road and come out to do so in their housecoats); that women should wear their hair long; and that they should not ride bicycles, which have traditionally been the mode of transport in Jaffna (all the more important because during the war situation there has been an embargo on petrol). Women who did not abide by these commandments were threatened with being whipped.

The LTTE denied responsibility for the poster. It was signed by a group that professed interest in Tamil culture (the guise of collective authorship is a strategy whereby the impression of popular support for the dictates is created). Despite the LTTE's denial, these commandments were entirely in keeping with a statement issued by the LTTE in their document *Mukamoodikal Kilihinrana* two years later, which declared:

> It is important for women to take care in their dress, in their *pottu* and make-up. It doesn't mean that we are enslaved if we dress according to tradition. Some married women say that it is expensive to wear saris. This is not acceptable. Women should dress simply, and they should not attract men by their way of dressing. Some women say that it is difficult to maintain long hair. These pretensions are wrong. . . . We are engaged in a struggle for national liberation. But, the changes which have been taking place in our culture will only demean our society.[26]

What is significant about this statement is that it reflects a growing unease on the part of the LTTE to the changes taking place in Tamil society, an ambivalence, even, towards some of the social forces which the

LTTE itself had unleashed. That women contested these imposed identities and fashioned their own resistance to them are important indicators of such a transformation. The "10 commandments" were not taken too seriously, but what these commandments stood for was serious enough for the Jaffna Mothers' Front[27] (modelled on the Mothers' Fronts of Northern Ireland and Plaza de Mayo) to protest against them through a written submission published in the Jaffna daily newspapers.

The concern of the Jaffna Mothers' Front was that if such impositions on female identity were not challenged and nipped in the bud, they would grow to form the basis of a dangerous "fundamentalism," which would be particularly inimical to women.[28] However, if the women who joined the JVP and the LTTE as armed combatants were able to shift the parameters, it was clear that within these groups patriarchy would respond and shift its goalposts, too. The LTTE strategy of combining the roles of mother and warrior through a poster and constructing a kind of superwoman liberation fighter is an illustration of such a shift. The mother-warrior ushered the woman into the public from the private and empowered her in an idea of militancy. But these shifts also incorporated the continuing subordination of women even as they were invested, as political participants and combatants, with an agency that was unavailable to them in conventional society.

The central epithets of female containment within these militant groups have been, and remain, discipline and chastity. A militant guerrilla group, by its nature, physically exists as an isolated entity from the larger community, and stricter disciplinary codes are applied to behaviour within it. Sexuality is seen as a threat to discipline and strictures come into place that "police" both male and female sexual desire. Both the JVP and LTTE inculcated a notion of kith and kin. The leaders were elder brothers – figures of authority in both Sinhala and Tamil cultures – and the comrades were younger brothers and sisters. It was a hierarchy meant to deter sexual relations among the combatants, even as it accorded power to a leadership wishing to sexually exploit younger comrades. A former woman activist for the struggle for Eelam told me that women were seen as a "problem" within the LTTE.[29] Marriage was banned on the orders of both Prabhakaran and Rohana Wijeweera (the former JVP leaders) until they themselves wanted to marry.[30]

The move, then, was to "purify" the group and make it distinct from what happened outside of it. Such control becomes all the more important in a terrain in which the usual social boundaries that keep male and female apart do not apply. Within a guerrilla group, the close proximity of men and women "requires" sexual containment. What we have here is an exact replication of the sexual taboos that exist in the outside world despite the militants' denunciation of those very norms. As the Sang-hatana observed of the Communist Party in the Telangana struggle:

> The metaphor of the family constantly used to describe the Party, rein-forced aspects of a feudal culture that continued to assert itself within the organization and perhaps served to keep women in their roles which were extensions of their roles in the private sphere.[31]

This is borne out in Juliet's story. Hers was also a symbolic role within the JVP as she functioned as a mnemonic of her dead brother, the district leader whose death the group mourned. "I had always to set an example," she said, "as my brother's sister. I understand now that I was nothing more than a symbol of my dead brother. I felt burdened by it, but I also accepted it."[32] When persuaded into a relationship with a man, because only then would he agree to be recruited into the JVP, Juliet said the rela-tionship meant a certain "attachment" – they were seen as "belonging" to each other – but there was no physical contact, not even kissing. "In those days," she said, "we were very naive. The revolution was every-thing. Personal matters could come later."

Juliet's womanhood was desexualized. In the interregnum, she had to subsume whatever sexual desires she may have had into the service of her role within the movement. Operating here is a discourse that transforms the sacrifice paid on the personal terrain into a sense of *duty* towards the cause, and the woman militant accepts this as part and parcel of her struggle. She takes on, by choice, identities of abnegation and sacrifice rather than those of individual desire. This reflects, in part, her ideologi-cal commitment to the struggle, her understanding that life in existing society offers no real freedom for the individual, either. But also at play here is an internalization of existing social codes. Curbing sexual desire within the movement would be an extension of, and no different from, the norms of conduct expected from her within her home and until her marriage.

These norms included a collective silence over women's bodies, even when they had suffered transgressions at the hands of the state. None of the JVP women who suffered sexual abuse while in police custody or prison ever talked about those violations, and the JVP male leaders were at pains to deny the incidents. The silence was in the service of preserving notions of women's sexual chastity and virginity.[33] Yet both the JVP and LTTE engaged in an instrumental use of sexuality when it suited them. Despite their silences over the sexual abuses suffered by living women cadres, both the JVP and LTTE made icons out of dead female colleagues who had been raped. The fate of beauty queen Premawathie Manamperi, who was raped and killed by the army in 1971, continued to dominate JVP discourse in a highly sexualized manner; it was her violated body that was remembered and recovered in JVP songs, posters, and articles that appeared in the JVP newspaper *Niyamuwa*.[34]

Manamperi became a mnemonic by which to recall state terror. The JVP discourse of her rape and death was used to transfer the responsibility for acts of violence solely onto the state and to project the JVP as the victim, not perpetrators, of violence in its own right. When Dhanu killed Rajiv Gandhi, the LTTE put out a message that she had been raped by the Indian Peace Keeping Force (IPKF) and that her act of violence was a fitting revenge for her shame and trauma. It is significant that in both instances, rape was publicized only once the women were dead. As for the living female cadre, the sexual abuses they suffered remained silenced, censored. This silence may have allowed the JVP women to re-enter the social mainstream, but it did nothing to redress the wrongs committed by the security forces or to inaugurate a public discussion on women's bodies as sites of war.

The LTTE of today, however, does initiate such a public discourse by warning its women cadres that if captured they will be raped and tortured. To avoid this violence, it insists they commit suicide by biting on a cyanide pill following capture. In this case, the public discourse of women as booties of war may be articulated, but the woman whose chastity is defiled by enemy rape has to be eliminated altogether, even if the justification for the suicide is preservation of one's bodily integrity and the collective good. And when women members have left the LTTE due to ideological differences, it resorted to the rhetoric of sexual shaming to degrade them. Both Rajani Thiranagama and her sister Nirmala Nityanandan, who were once part of the LTTE, were attacked as "loose women" after they distanced themselves from its authoritarianism and violence. Their Christian family background, education in co-ed schools, and freer interaction with men were constructed as grounds for sexual promiscuity.[35]

Vestiges of feudalism also remain in the highly centralized leadership of today's LTTE as it was for the JVP of the past.[36] At the matrix of the LTTE is a personality cult of Prabhakaran that produces, in turn, a pervasive male discourse. Large cut-outs of the LTTE leader dominated Jaffna until Operation Rivirasa, in which the government forces gained control of the town in December 1995. A 14-metre cut-out of Prabhakaran, along with two huge maps displaying what he has achieved and what he hopes to achieve on the road to Eelam, dominate Mallavi in the Vanni.[37]

In the volume of inspirational Tamil Eelam songs entitled *Songs from the Red Blossomed Garden*, released by the LTTE and repeatedly played in public places so that they take the place of the once-popular Hindi cinema music, Prabhakaran is invested with the aura of a deity.[38] However, Prabhakaran is not inventing history. Many guerrilla movements have been dependent for their success on highly centralized organizational structures and leadership cults. That women cadres have to negotiate this reality is implicit in the tension we confront in Adele Ann's *Women Fighters of the Liberation Tigers*. On the one hand, its avowed intent is to present the importance of women within the LTTE. But, on the other, there is an explicit (and political) need to valorize Prabhakaran. Thus, this book on the women LTTE cadres begins with a full page photograph of Prabhakaran with the caption "Mr. Veluppilai Piribakaran, leader of the LTTE who founded the Women's Military Unit of the Liberation Tigers." Homage is paid to him throughout in terms like these:

> He was confident that women had the potential for military training and combat. Unlike many of his fellow cadres caught up in male chauvinistic conceptions of women and their place in society, Mr. Piribakaran was determined that women should have equal opportunity for participation in all aspects of the armed struggle. Even he admits, however, that women have exceeded his expectations of them.[39]

Here is the male who ushers in and creates a space for women within his organization. He is thus the midwife of their agency. That this in itself reinforces gender-hierarchies that keep women in reliance on men is never problematized in the book. Since Ann's project is directed at revealing how Prabhakaran himself has broken out of the rigidity of patriarchal Tamil society, she endorses the construction of LTTE women as a site on which Prabhakaran's foresight is inscribed. The LTTE women refer to him as the "King of the Tigers."[40] And such is the acceptance of this that when members of the "Birds of Freedom," as the LTTE women's wing is known, were asked about feminist concerns, they confessed that there was much confusion within the movement about this, but they "ultimately ended their argument with an expression of faith in their leader's ability to solve all problems."[41]

Such a reliance on the male leader immediately begs the question as to whether the fourth clause of the LTTE women's manifesto – "Ensure that Tamil women control their own lives" – can ever be fully realized. For even as the manifesto is anticipatory, with promises and aspirations for the future, patriarchy in the interregnum has already put into place strictures that will define/confine women. Meanwhile, the woman militant internalizes her containment, be it within the terrain of sexuality, rank, or division of labour. It is not surprising that, accordingly, Juliet the JVP veteran is now firmly rooted within the ambit of traditional family values – married and a mother of three children.[42]

Nor is it surprising that the LTTE woman combatant has internalized her role as martyr in the struggle for Eelam. Heroic death and martyrdom remain important tropes in the rhetoric of recruitment. The University Teachers for Human Rights (Jaffna) report several incidents of young girls forcibly picked up by LTTE recruiters, piled into a van against their will, and taken to LTTE camps for training and "lessons" in the LTTE way of life. Students sitting for the G.C.E. "O" level examination have been told, "One day you will have to die. If you die fighting, it will be a hero's death but if you die a natural death, it will be a coward's death. Your parents may today discourage you from joining. But later they would be ashamed of you."[43]

What does this grammar of recruitment and ideology of martyrdom spell for the suicide bomber who, in being chosen for the task, is accorded the highest honour within the movement? Men and women vie for the honour of being admitted to the Black Tiger squad, from which the suicide bomber awaits her/his call up. This can be viewed as a moment of agency in the militant's life, the pinnacle in a career of dedication. However, because the cult of martyrdom is so ingrained and the concept of sacrifice already gendered, the moment appears to be within the normative, prescribed role for women. The female suicide bomber's choice is already culturally predetermined. More recently, another development has taken place that points to a foreclosing of such moments of agency altogether. Following the failure of some recent suicide bomb attacks, the LTTE has started to wire the suicide bomber's jacket so that it detonates either by remote control or as a time bomb.[44] The human being is no longer in control over the choice of her/his death.

It must be borne in mind, however, that even if recruitment is at times coercive and even as the LTTE tightens its grip on the Tamil population, there are women who resist its culture of violence. There have been LTTE women combatants who have left the movement with the blessings of the LTTE leadership, although it is difficult to ascertain how independent they really are of the LTTE. There are reports that some women members who have been allowed to leave the armed struggle have had to continue to support the movement from the outside, by providing refuge to comrades, sharing intelligence information, or securing funds for the LTTE. They have had the freedom to end their role as a militant, but not their ideological and practical support for the LTTE cause.[45] At least their lives have been spared. Other women have not been as lucky. Two women poets who challenged the LTTE's authoritarianism and its cult of violence immediately come to mind. They are Thiyagarajah Selvanity (known as Selvy), an internationally acclaimed poet, and Sivaramani, a young woman who was born and grew up in Jaffna.

Selvy was taken into LTTE custody on 30 August 1991 and is believed to have been killed.[46] Sivaramani, at the age of twenty-four, got hold of as many of her poems as she could and burned them one night; she then set her room on fire and committed suicide.[47] As Sitralega Maunaguru commented, Sivaramani's tragedy went largely unnoticed – because she did not die by biting on a cyanide capsule in the honoured tradition of the LTTE, she was not praised as a martyr.[48] The ultimate tragedy, then, is of a society trapped in its own epistemic ideology of militarism and violence. Rajani Thiranagama writes:

> If in a society like this, the dominant ideology under which the struggle is organised is itself an even more narrow, revivalistic and romantic one, well sprinkled with images of male heroes and male valour, and if nationalism is a type of aggressive patriotism, then a concept of women's liberation would be working against the inner core of such a struggle.[49]

The grip of a patriarchal LTTE leadership is such that in making this statement, Rajani, too, signed her death warrant: She was shot dead on 21 September 1989 as she cycled home in Jaffna.

Notes

1 Rajiv Gandhi was India's prime minister from 1984 to 1989. He brokered the Indo-Lanka Accord of 1987, which brought the Indian Peace Keeping Forces (IPKF) to Sri Lanka. The IPKF fought the Liberation Tigers of Tamil Eelam (LTTE) from 1987-89 without success. The assassination of Gandhi by the LTTE in 1991 was widely seen as retaliation for these events.

2 The Liberation Tigers of Tamil Eelam (LTTE) has waged a war since the late 1970s for a separate Tamil State, while the Janatha Vimukthi Peramuna (JVP) has had two periods of insurrection – the first in 1971, and the second from 1987-89.

3 In 1998, after sixteen years, municipal council elections were held in Jaffna. Sarojini Yogeswaran of the Tamil United Liberation Front (TULF) was elected mayor, but survived only a month in office. She was allegedly shot and killed by members of the LTTE as was her successor P. Sivapalan. Also killed was Pon Mathimugarajah, general secretary of the Jaffna TULF, who was tipped to succeed Sivapalan as mayor. Through such killings, the LTTE has sent deadly signals that there can be no return to any form of civilian rule that does not have its blessing.

4 Michael Ignatieff, "Nationalism and Self-Determination: Is There an Alternative to Violence?" (Neelan Tiruchelvam Memorial Lecture, Colombo, March 2000).

5 The JVP and LTTE have mobilized women combatants in Sri Lanka; in India women members of the RSS (Rashtriya Swayamsevak Sangh) and Durga Vahini propound Hindutva ideology and participate in violence against the Muslim minority and those deemed "anti-Hindu"; and in Kashmir the Dukhataran-i-millat is a women's wing affiliated to the All Party Hurriyat Conference fighting for Khalistan as a separate Kashmiri state.

6 Adele Ann, *Women Fighters of Liberation Tigers* (Jaffna: LTTE, 1993), pp.8-9.

7 Peter Schalk, "Resistance and Martyrdom in the Process of State Formation of Tamililiam," in Joyce Pettigrew, ed., *Martyrdom and Political Resistance: Essays from Asia and Europe*, Special Issue, *Comparative Asian Studies* 18 (1997), p.71.

8 This has its parallel in the south. A team of journalists who reported on the women cadres of the Sri Lanka Airforce repeatedly stressed the "arduous" and "gruelling" training they undergo in Diyatalawa, which they accomplish with "dedication" and "stamina." See *The Sunday Leader*, 5 March 1995, pp.18-19.

9 Rajan Hoole, Daya Somasundaram, K.Sritharan, and Rajani Thiranagama, *The Broken Palmyrah: The Tamil Crisis in Sri Lanka – An Inside Account* (Claremont: The Sri Lanka Studies Institute, 1992), p.325.

10 Captain Vanathi as quoted in Peter Schalk, "Birds of Independence: On the Participation of Tamil Women in Armed Struggle," *Studies in Lankan Culture* 7 (December 1992), pp.92-6.

11 Ann, *Women Fighters of Liberation Tigers*, pp.8-9.

12 Peter Schalk, "Woman Fighters of the Liberation Tigers in Tamililam: The Martial Feminism of Atel Palacinkam," *South Asia Research* 14 (Autumn 1994), pp.163-83.

13 Schalk, "Resistance and Martyrdom in the Process of State Formation of Tamililiam," p.69.

14 For studies of the JVP movement in Sri Lanka, see A.C. Alles, *Insurgency 1971* (Colombo: Apothecaries' Co. Ltd); C.A.Chandraprema, *The Years of Terror: The JVP Insurrection 1987-89* (Colombo: Lake House,1991); Rohan Gunaratne, *Sri Lanka: A Lost Revolution? The Inside Story of the JVP* (Kandy: Institute of Fundamental Studies, 1990); Kelly Senanayake, "Women, Revolution and the JVP," *Aya* 2 (March-April 1996), pp. 18-20; Manisha Gunasekera, "Gender in Counter-State Political Practice of the JVP 1978-1989" (M.A. thesis, University of Colombo, 1994).

15 Chandraprema draws attention to the divisions within the JVP itself over the issue of armed militancy in *The Years of Terror*, pp.31-2, 34-5. However, the second phase of JVP militancy had much in common with the LTTE and was indeed influenced by the latter. Like the LTTE, its rhetoric was nationalist and class struggle was the duty of the patriot. The cult of martyrdom was adopted by the JVP in the 1987-90 period and the ideology of violence became one of its central tenets. See Jani De Silva, "Praxis, Language and Silences: The July 1987 Uprising of the JVP in Sri Lanka," in Michael Roberts, ed., *Sri Lanka: Collective Identities Revisited* (Colombo: Marga, 1997).

16 This is mirrored in the relative lack of material on JVP women when compared with that available – whether propagandist or not – on the LTTE women

cadres. Moreover, there is a reluctance on the part of JVP women who have now joined the socio-cultural mainstream and have families of their own to talk about their agency in violence. Juliet, for instance, insisted that her name not be divulged.

17 Senanayake, "Women, Revolution and the JVP," pp.18-19.

18 Gunasekera, "Gender in Counter-State Political Practice of the JVP 1978-1989," chap. 4.

19 Alles, *Insurgency 1971*, p.131.

20 Juliet's testimony contradicts Alles's implication that "when the JVP set off on its strike of Balapattuwa, the seven girls [*sic*] in the party went along merely to cook" (Alles, *Insurgency 197,* p.124). As the Stree Shakti Sanghatana noted while recording the experiences of the women in the Telangana People's Struggle, this type of "contributory" historiography, in which the participation of women in militant groups is "analysed and judged not according to their value or importance for women, but according to their 'use' for the movement in question," devalues the complex issues surrounding the woman militant. Stree Shakti Sanghatana, *We Were Making History . . . Life Stories of Women in the Telangana People's Struggle* (New Delhi: Kali for Women, 1989), p.263.

21 Sanghatana, *We Were Making History,* p.263.

22 C.S. Lakshmi, "Mother, Mother-Community and Mother Politics in Tamil Nadu," *Economic and Political Weekly* 20,9 (October 1990), pp.72-83; Sara S. Mitter, *Dharma's Daughters: Contemporary Indian Women and Hindu Culture* (New Delhi: Penguin, 1992), chap. 6.

23 Cynthia Enloe, *Does Khaki Become You? The Militarization of Women's Lives* (Boston: South End Press, 1983), p.166.

24 Sitralega Maunaguru, "Gendering Tamil Nationalism: The Construction of the Woman in Projects of Protest and Control," in Pradeep Jeganathan and Qadri Ismail, eds., *Unmaking the Nation* (Colombo: Social Scientists' Association, 1995), p.164.

25 Enloe, *Does Khaki Become You?* p.166.

26 Maunaguru, "Gendering Tamil Nationalism," p.169.

27 The Jaffna Mothers' Front was formed in July 1984 after an incident in which the Sri Lankan army rounded up between seven and eight hundred males, ranging from twelve to thirty years of age, and forcibly transported them to the Palaly and Boosa camps. In July 1984, the army had begun a new tactic of surrounding a village with armoured tanks and guns in order to comb it for LTTE militants. A plea was issued by the army to the mothers of Jaffna to bring their children with their identity cards for voluntary checking. The mothers did so, and were rewarded at the end of the day with the detention of their male children and their removal to army camps. Frustrated at the acquiescence of their husbands, male relatives, and friends to the government, the women took it upon themselves to organize and formed the Jaffna Mothers' Front. A very successful rally was held with ten to fifteen thousand people attending, which ended in a march to the Government Agent's Office demanding the release of their sons. Sarvam Kailasapathy, personal communication, Colombo, 18 March 1995.

28 Kailasapathy, personal communication.

29 Lakshmi (pseudonym), personal communication, London, April 2000.

30 The JVP leadership had in fact ordered that no JVPer should marry or have romantic links with anyone until the revolution was won (Senanayake, "Women, Revolution and the JVP," pp.19-20).

31 Sanghatana, *We Were Making History*, p.269.

32 Juliet's second brother, Justin Wijesinghe, was also killed in JVP activity.

33 Senanayake "Women, Revolution and the JVP," p.20.

34 Gunasekera "Gender in Counter-State Political Practice of the JVP 1978-1989," chap. 2.

35 Lakshmi, personal communication.

36 This was so when Rohana Wijeweera was the leader of the JVP, although he was never able to control or decimate the many factions within the party as successfully as Prabakharan has done for the LTTE. Wijeweera was killed when captured by government forces in 1989.

37 The University Teachers for Human Rights (Jaffna, Sri Lanka,) *Information Bulletin* 23, *The Island* (2000), p.12.

38 *Counterpoint* 1,8 (November 1993), p.11.

39 Ann, *Women Fighters of Liberation Tigers*, p.7.

40 Schalk "Resistance and Martyrdom in the Process of State Formation of Tamililiam," p.70.

41 Hoole et al., *The Broken Palmyrah*, p.328.

42 Many of the women of the 1987-89 JVP are also married, have children, and are reluctant to talk about their JVP connections partly because, having entered the socio-cultural mainstream of Sri Lankan life, they wish to distance themselves from its violence. They may also fear possible future government reprisals (Manisha Gunasekera, personal communication, Sri Lanka, 1995).

43 University Teachers for Human Rights, *Information Bulletin*, p.23.

44 These jackets, wired to detonate one hour into the operation, were used in the commando-style attack mounted by the LTTE in Rajagiriya, a suburb of Colombo, and en route to Parliament in March 2000. Although the suicide bombers did have to press the switch that activated the timer, the fact that there was no possibility of retraction once the device was switched on meant that they could not subsequently change their minds. This was the first time such a device was used. *Tamil Times*, 15 March 2000.

45 The difficulty at present in accessing information on the LTTE and analyzing its role, particularly for scholars in the south, makes for a reliance on personal communications which are often disparate accounts of the LTTE's policies and activities. Just as there are reports of ex-LTTE women being obliged to continue working for the struggle, there are other accounts that contest this, insisting that within the LTTE there is complete freedom of movement to and from the group.

46 Selvy was awarded the "Freedom to Write" award by International PEN in 1992. The award honours poets who suffer imprisonment or other infringements of their human rights on account of their beliefs and writings.

47 About twenty-three of Sivaramani's poems were with friends at the time of her death and so survive.

48 Sitralega Maunaguru, "Introduction to 'Two Poems of Sivaramani,'" *South Asia Bulletin* 9 (1991), p.147.

49 Hoole et al., *The Broken Palmyrah*, p.327.

Djurdja Knežević

Chapter 6

Gender and Nationalism in the Croatian Media War

Times of intense social change pose both threats and opportunities. When traditional structures of domination are shaken, as they are in critical periods of nation-state formation, the entire population may be mobilized. In these hazardous spaces, women are often "invited" to participate actively in public life. Changes to existing social norms can potentially enable women to overcome the traditional boundaries of their place within society. Thus, a period of crisis may appear as a new opportunity for women.

In this chapter, I consider the behaviour and attitudes of nationalist women and women's groups in Croatia during the period of the war between 1991 and 1995. These women openly advocated a nationalist ideology and approach, giving full support to national state projects. When I refer to a nationalist project, I am referring to a range of collective strategies oriented towards the perceived needs of a nation, with nationalism being the fundamental strategy.[1] My particular interest in this topic relates to the way in which women who are oriented towards nationalism perceive themselves, and what happens to that perception as they forge an identification with the nation.

In examining this particular case, I argue that if the opportunity for women to participate in public life represents solely a bridge to the collective nationalist "solution," then the involvement of women will be neither authentic nor sustainable. This argument is based on two premises. First, women are welcomed into the nationalist state as mother-symbols, or as icons of a community to which an individual is said to owe her/his existence and birth. Mothers appear as an ideal symbol for an authoritar-

75

ian community in which the duties of the individual towards the community prevail over her/his individual rights.

Second, the ruling power in a nationalist community is vested in men. The roles women can play in the nationalist public space are limited to the display of suffering as the basis for condemnation of the "enemy" (every nationalist community legitimizes itself through images of its own victimization), and to acting as caretakers. Women may be allowed to fulfil these roles as long as they never take an active part in the political leadership of the nation. Paradoxically, this "recognition" is an irresistible temptation for some feminist groups. The dividing line between the real and symbolic victimization of women as "Women-Mothers of the Nation" is thin enough to bring together conservative and nationalist women's groups and even some radical feminist groups.

My analysis is based on the statements made by various women's groups and organizations which appeared in the Croatian print media during the period 1992-95. I consider these statements paradigmatic in demonstrating some of the ways in which women who are located in militarized conflict situations become involved in ethnic and national processes. These declarations were made in the early period of political transition after the first democratic elections, the fall of the socialist regime, and during the war in Croatia, which was a time of great social disturbance and change. Nationalism – one of the most important causes and results of the collapse of Yugoslavia – played a fundamental role in societal transformation.

In the following section, I examine the gendered limitations that were placed on the nationalist invitation to Croatian women to participate politically. These limitations were characteristic of the patriarchal framework within which women had to contain their political/public activity, thus restricting any political claims they may have wished to make.

Croatian Patriarchal Frameworks

As long as women's empowerment in a patriarchal state supports the (re)establishment of male domination in society, women, as a social group, will receive political recognition and a certain access to the public space. In the case of Croatia, the turmoil that was a primary consequence of the war launched or accelerated various processes in social development, including changes to the form and dynamics of gender relations. Newly independent Croatia, submerged in the process of building a state structure while still at war, desperately needed the support of women, who represented a large proportion of the population. However, the scope and form of women's political appearance and activity had to be defined and controlled by national male power and limited to a mere supporting role. The ways in which women became involved in ethnic and national processes has been well documented.[2]

There is a wide range of support that women and women's groups can give to nationalists – for example through massive voting for parties that pursue nationalist projects; increasing activism oriented towards organizing social and humanitarian help for "our cause" and "our boys"; and exerting political pressure by encouraging the establishment of programs based on patriarchal values in combination with strong emotional and often religious sentiments. These activities are useful only until the state structure is stabilized. Once women and women's groups are no longer needed for the development of a nationalist project, their public/political work may be terminated, or their activism may take on a different form, or they may lie dormant until they can be (mis)used again at the next political opportunity.

These developments can clearly be seen in Croatia between 1992 and 1998. In the first three years of this period (1992-95), there was massive political support for nationalist women from the government. Women's groups and initiatives with programs based on a nationalist ideology garnered significant and wide-ranging media attention. Reports about their actions appeared on the front pages of print media and in most of the mainstream TV and radio programs. Politicians were almost always present at their events and demonstrations. Delegations of these women's groups enjoyed numerous visits and meetings with the highest officials of the state (Franjo Tudjman, the president of Croatia, was often among them). These groups organized speaking tours outside of Croatia with full financial and political support of the government, as well as with all logistics arranged by politicians belonging to the ruling party. In the section that follows, I examine nationalist Croatian women's experiences on two of these tours outside Croatia.

Croatian Women's Nationalism beyond the Borders of the Nation

The attitude of the state towards the different politics of women's groups is illustrated by two speaking tours made by Croatian women's groups, both organized in the United States. The first tour took place in April 1993, and the second in October of the same year. The first was organized by an American NGO called MADRE, and the tour itself was called "Mother Courage." Women who were invited by MADRE on this tour represented anti-nationalist women's groups from Croatia and Serbia. Even before the tour started, however, the project was heavily attacked by nationalist Croatian and Bosnian groups (working in Croatia). The accusation by these nationalists groups was that the Mother Courage women who were selected to speak for Croatian women did not fairly represent all Croatian women. Their message began, "As representatives of Bosnian and Croatian women's groups . . . we write you to express our concern about the national tour," then continued, "selected women are manipulating and silencing victims of genocidal rape through the simplistic or incomplete line, 'all men rape.'"

Two women who took part in the tour as representatives of anti-nationalist groups were verbally attacked by Americans of Croatian and Serbian origin. In an e-mail message that circulated around the world during the tour – the collective product of five Croatian and Bosnian nationalistic groups, and written under the auspices of Catharine MacKinnon – one woman was called a "pornographer," while another was labelled a "notorious communist." The Croatian media hardly mentioned the tour, although a few scathing commentaries in the newspapers appeared, condemning the whole event without bothering to give much information about it. Moreover, one MP attacked the tour in her speech in the Croatian Parliament, warning her male colleagues not to underestimate the women on the speaking tour, as they were "dangerous."

In October of 1993, the Croatian government organized a speaking tour in the United States in which some of the groups that were signatories of the previously mentioned e-mail message took part. Groups from Bosnia were excluded from the tour because the war had begun between Croatia and Bosnia by the time this second tour began. Under the sponsorship of the Croatian government, some politicians were directly involved in the tour's organization and travelled with the group. In fact, the person who was the main organizer of the tour and who travelled with representatives of these women's groups was the same person who had attacked anti-nationalist groups in Parliament.[3] Croatian state representatives (the Croatian ambassador to the United States and the envoy to the UN) organized most of the tour. Croatian print and electronic media reported the tour on a daily basis, using such titles as "The Congressmen Were Impressed," "Mothers Got Hope," "There is Still Too Little Knowledge about Suffering of Croatia," and "Kindness and Ignorance."[4]

These nationalistically oriented groups in the second tour argued that the only perpetrators of rape were Serbs and that only Croatian and Bosnian women were raped. The number that was repeatedly mentioned was two hundred and fifty thousand rapes by Serbs, although by this time it was already clear that this was an exaggeration. Nevertheless, this figure was repeatedly misused for nationalist purposes. Even Bosnia, a country that suffered the highest incidence of rape, reported approximately fifty thousand cases, which was close to the estimates of the International Red Cross and other organizations.

Turning now to Croatian women's nationalism within their own state-information, I explore this phenomenon through an analysis of selected Croatian print media.

Croatian Women's Nationalism within State Boundaries

Although women's support was welcomed by the new Croatian government, women received public recognition and assistance only as long as they were needed for political reasons. After the stabilization of the national state, in the post-1995 period, government support of nationalist women's groups dwindled; the interest of the state-controlled media diminished; and politicians' visits to these groups, and vice versa, became less and less frequent. One indication of decreasing state support has been that, in more recent times, when delegations of women's groups recognized by the state regime visited government institutions, it was invariably a woman politician of the ruling Hrvatska Demokratska Zajednica Party (HDZ) who was responsible for these groups. In Croatia, appointing a woman to be in charge does not necessarily translate into gender sensitivity; rather, it creates a general sense that finally "the woman's affair" has been put in its proper place, as something marginal and of no importance.

One of the important limitations on women's political/public participation is the content of their political claims. Here we should keep in mind the structure within which women as a social group act – the national state. The conflict and maintenance of boundaries between ethnic-national groups is the most fertile soil for establishing ethnic-national cohesiveness. However, social stratification accompanied by social and economic inequality persists within each ethnic-national group. Even when ethnic-national mobilization towards national cohesiveness is high on the state's agenda, there is usually a dominant group(s) directing and controlling the collective project. Political recognition of women, and their public acceptance by the dominant group(s), can be realized only when women break through the existing patriarchal framework while simultaneously positing their political claims for equality.

For many women in Croatia who are struggling for public acceptance, this has meant acting in a way that is congruent with the common stereotypes of women and their role in society. In male-dominated societies, women can play a subordinate role as supporters, but not an equal role as agents. According to their own understanding of this subordinate role, the nationalist Croatian women's group, "We – For Our Guard," wrote:

> Dear Croatian soldiers in the battle fields, in hospitals, wherever you are . . . we are giving you our tribute and thankfulness for your non-selfish love for "Our Beautiful"[5] and for your heroism in the Patriotic (Homeland) War. We are a miniature part of the Croatian nation that loves you and respects all that you gave up and sacrificed in defending Croatia, our beloved homeland.[6]

Citizenship has historically formed the link between "nation" and "state" for nationalistically oriented women and women's groups. For many women, even a limited and subordinated form of participation in the nationalist project appears to be the easiest and shortest route towards the realization of citizenship, and they may, in fact, perceive it as the only route. What this also illustrates is that nationalist concepts of the state do not recognize the human being as an individual (see also de Mel in chapter 5); this recognition comes through service to the nation.

The domains reserved for Croatian women in the nationalist struggle are spiritualism, emotionalism, religious sentimentality, and motherhood. Among the hundreds of photographs taken at demonstrations in front of the headquarters of international organizations such as the United Nations Protection Force (UNPROFOR), there is only one image to be seen: women dressed in black, with candles and flowers and small children around them. This focus on the religious and irrational creation of the image of "Madre Dolorosa" is based on real premises. Let us not forget that these women are real victims; they are real widows; and the children are real orphans. It is quite a sensitive task to analyze the contradictory use of human tragedy for political purposes.

There are usually two levels of meaning for such photographic images in the print media. On the one level, there are understandable and legitimate claims for the women's dead or disappeared husbands or relatives. On the other, there are overt or discrete messages that advocate support for nationalist state politics. Consider the statement made by "We – For Our Guard":

> This horrible war took thousands of young people's lives, physically and mentally wounded countless people, but it did not kill goodness and our will to defend our homeland.[7]

And as they wrote in another newspaper article:

> They went to the front-line, many of them in jeans and sneakers, but with a heart for Croatia. . . . For thirty-four young, Croatian fighters

the war was their last duty in their lives. Bodies become ashes, the goal
they died for is achieved. Croatia is free.[8]

In Croatian print and broadcast media, images of supporting politicians are discretely placed in the background, while abstract religious
images are used to mobilize emotions. Instead of actual information
being given about an event, an emotive image is used repeatedly. Zdenka
Farkas, one of the organizers of the nationalist demonstration of mothers
in front of UNPROFOR headquarters in Zagreb in 1993, mixes traditional
and modern symbols in her pronouncement that, when confronting the
enemy, the women "will persecute them with the power of spirit and
mind, with the power of love, until they accept us and say 'Long Live
Croatia.'"[9]

Her statement echoes the "flower-power" discourse of the late 1960s
peace movement, which was not a salute to any nationalist project. But
this kind of language, combined in the same sentence with the tribute
"Long Live Croatia," is powerful. The same pattern is repeated often, as
in the following citation made by a member of the Croatian Background
Front in the newspaper *Vjesnik* in 1994: "We started to help our boys
who went to the front in blue jeans and sneakers. We said, 'Let the state
look after the weapons, we, the women, will look after the underwear,
pants, socks, gloves.'"[10] Blue jeans and sneakers are, no doubt, symbols
of modernity. Yet the frequent appearance of these two images – "went
to the front in blue jeans and sneakers" – takes on an ominous synergy.

This discourse draws a clear distinction between the roles of Croatian
women and men. The women should help "our boys," who are defined
as part of a modern, progressive world. However, this role concomitantly
places women in the position of a lesser "background" people. The state,
represented by a strong, dominating male figure, takes responsibility for
supplying "our boys" with weapons that are of fundamental importance
to, and highly symbolic of, the nationalist cause. Women should take care
of those tasks that are ephemeral, less essential. At the same time, the
above excerpts express a female tenderness that is in harmonious balance
with male toughness, and the complexity and ambiguity of male-female
relations at the symbolic level. Here we have the state playing the symbolic role of the tough father; women, the tender, caring mothers of "our
boys"; while "our boys" are in an ambiguously defined position.

As fighters, "boys" have a greater responsibility and therefore a higher
position in the social hierarchy than women. Women, however, being
mothers, treat "the boys" as young, effeminate sons, who need care and
protection. A tragic light is shed on young men when they are defined by
both mothers and fathers as sacrificial candidates *pro patria* (for the

fatherland). The position of "boys" is accompanied by a modestly pathetic heroism. Some "male" characteristics of toughness and lower-scale heroism are evident in this statement by Dunja Vatovac, founder of the Croatian Background Front: "When aggression towards Croatia started, I wanted to transform tears into spitefulness and courage, and my feeling of helplessness into useful work."[11]

* * *

Some women in Croatia were attracted by and took an active part in the nationalist project. These women embraced nationalism as their ideological basis and as the most articulate expression of an irrational sense of belonging to a community. Nationalism offered women a sense of inclusion, giving them an opportunity to enter politics and the public sphere. Thus, they could be recognized as active participants in social life – but only in a bounded way, limited in both social and political respects. For many Croatian women, this limited acceptance created a political and psychological balance with women's own self-understanding of subordination, low self-esteem, and an orientation towards spiritual, emotional, and supporting roles.

In the Croatian women's statements discussed here, we can detect a combination of two discourses: peacefulness and aggressiveness, with an inclination towards the peaceful. It is not that women are biologically more peaceful, but that throughout history, women have been excluded from public and social affairs and, above all, from military structures. Women are less prepared than men to pursue nationalist goals by force, but they are no less nationalist than men.

Notes

1 Sylvia Walby, "Woman and Nation," *Journal of Comparative Sociology* 33 (1992), pp. 81-100.

2 Nira Yuval-Davies and Floya Anthias, *Woman-Nation-State* (London: Macmillan, 1989), pp.1-15.

3 See "There's Too Little Knowledge about the Suffering of Croatia," *Vjesnik*, 26 October 1993; "The Congressmen Were Impressed," *Večernji list*, 25 October 1993; "Mothers Got Hope," *Večernji list*, 24 October 1993; "Kindness and Ignorance," *Večernji list*, 20 October 1993.

4 See the main Croatian papers, especially *Vjesnik* and *Večernji list*, October 1994.

5 The words "Our Beautiful," or "Lijepa naša," are the title and the first words of the Croatian national anthem, and are used as a synonym when expressing tender feelings for the homeland.

6 We – For Our Guard, "Let People Enjoy Peace and Freedom," *Vjesnik*, 1 April 1994.

7 Ibid.
8 We – For Our Guard, "Mothers, Thanks a Lot," *Vjesnik*, 24 November 1993.
9 *Večernji list*, 1 October 1993.
10 *Vjesnik,* 22 February 1994.
11 Ibid.

Part 2

Gendered Violence in Times of Conflict

Malathi de Alwis

Introduction

The chapters in this section address the ways in which communalism or ethnic nationalism, operating within patriarchal structures of power, often involves the advocacy and perpetration of violence, most often sexual violence, against women.[1] In such contexts, it seems that the primary premise of the act of violence is to inflict pain and suffering on the person through the declaration of power over her/him, at the most intimate level. However, as many feminists have argued and as these chapters point out, the sexual violation of woman in times of conflict also seeks to shame subject her family/community/nation, for it is a woman's modesty that signifies the masculinity of her community and nation.

Patriarchal discourses on the modesty of women, as feminists and theorists have noted, are actually about policing their sexuality. Michel Foucault has aptly described sexuality as a "dense transfer point for relations of power . . . one of those endowed with the greatest instrumentality,"[2] whereas Gayle Rubin has defined it as a "vector of oppression," while asserting that much of the oppression of women is "borne by, mediated through, and constricted within sexuality."[3] Ironically, the sexual and moral codes imposed on women are regulated and disseminated through hegemonic patriarchal institutions and instruments, such as the state, law and religious tenets, and their interpreters, the school, the family, and so on. These codes share marked similarities despite their being categorized as Christian or Muslim, Buddhist or Hindu, Bosnian or Croatian, Sinhala or Tamil.

Therefore, it is important to note that all women living within patriarchal structures of power are vulnerable to sexual and psychological oppression and violation – during periods of so-called normalcy as well as during war – though the contexts and forms of violence may differ drastically. The chapters in this section, while specifically focusing on sexualized violence during times of conflict, nevertheless illuminate a surfeit of ways in which violence circumscribes women's lives. While Radhika Coomaraswamy attempts to document and categorize the different forms of sexualized violence against women that she has encountered in her capacity as the UN Special Rapporteur on Violence Against Women, Duska Andrić-Ružičić discusses how the world media reinscribed this violence upon Bosnian women's bodies through intrusive TV coverage and sensationalized reporting.

Selvy Thiruchandran's chapter considers the day-to-day trials of women who are heads of households in Eastern Sri Lanka, many of whom may not have been sexually violated but who constantly live under the sign of its possibility because of their single status – interpreted as "they have no man to protect them" and thus must need one; their insecure lodging situation and desperate economic circumstances; or their inferior class position. Ananda Galappatti, while also marking this constant possibility of daily sexual harassment and violation faced by Sinhala and Tamil survivors of violence (sexualized or otherwise), suggests that Maria Root's notion of "insidious trauma" to describe a woman's acute self awareness that "one's safety is very tentative" – due to the very fact that she is a woman, to begin with – could be used here. Galappatti's argument thus enables us to link socio-cultural, political, and economic hardships that have to be overcome by women war survivors, as described by Thiruchandran, with psychological ones.

These chapters strive to move beyond the simplistic representation of "woman as victim" while simultaneously acknowledging the fact that women continue to suffer indefinitely and in myriad ways after the actual event of violence. Galappatti's thoughtful critique of the medicalization of suffering through psychological labels such as Post-Traumatic Stress Disorder (PTSD) articulates very well the limitations of such a concept, which is perceived as an "affliction of the powerless" and "originates in the White male experience of time-limited events."[4] Similarly, while Coomaraswamy (as well as the other writers and especially Thiruchandran) briefly calls our attention to women perpetrators of violence, she also documents the various ways in which women have coped and sometimes triumphed over their adversities and traumas. But many such victories have come at a cost; the resonances between Coomaraswamy's and Andrić-Ružičić's chapters, in this regard, are particularly thought-provoking.

Both Coomaraswamy and Andrić-Ružičić highlight the crucial role that was played by networks of feminist and human rights organizations around the world to have rape and other sexualized forms of militarized violence recognized as a war crime and a crime against humanity, and to ensure that such interpretations apply to both internal and external wars. In addition, concepts such as mass rape, sexual slavery, and forced pregnancies have complicated the hitherto gender-insensitive discourses of humanitarian law. Yet Andrić-Ružičić sensitively captures the contradictions within our social system, which in order to function is dependent on the sensationalized reporting to engender public outrage and sympathy, the playing of a crude numbers game, the repeated and painful extraction of testimonies, and the withstanding of public censure and humiliation.

What happens to the survivor of violence in the midst of all this? Here is where there is much resonance between Andrić-Ružičić's and Galappatti's work. Women's NGOs were the only institutions that gave priority to the care of the survivor, notes Andrić-Ružičić, who herself works at Medica Zenica, one such institution which does not require that a survivor of violence earn the "right" to receive help: "We leave the job of finding proof of the events to investigators," she writes. Conversely, Galappatti rues the fact that Sri Lanka lacks such sensitive organizations that could enable the "self-actualization" of survivors, while noting the propensity of most counsellors is to view their clients as "candidates for charity and pity" and enthusiastically encourage and reinforce conservative cultural values among them.

In such a context, one wonders whether the relative obscurity of Sri Lanka, in the world's eye, as opposed to the former Yugoslavia – though Sri Lanka has not witnessed rapes of such magnitude as in Bosnia-Herzegovina, for example – has led to the provision of inadequate and reactionary mental health services. Such a conundrum highlights, once again, the inherent contradictions in a social system that requires media sensationalism to inspire remedial measures at the cost of further psychological scarring of these violated women. In conclusion, I wish to reiterate a crucial question, succinctly articulated by Andrić-Ružičić, that must be addressed in such an exchange as this: "Did this really have to happen in Europe for it to be noticed and talked about?"

Notes

1 And I would add men, to a lesser extent, particularly if they identify themselves as or are identified by others as being gay, bisexual, or transgender.
2 Michel Foucault, *History of Sexuality*, Vol. I, trans. Robert Hurley (London: Penguin, 1981), p.103.

3 Gayle Rubin, "Thinking Sex: Notes for a Radical Theory of the Politics of Sexuality," in Carole S. Vance, ed., *Pleasure and Danger: Exploring Female Sexuality* (London: Routledge and Kegan Paul, 1984), pp.300-301.
4 Judith Lewis Herman, *Trauma and Recovery* (New York: Basic Books, 1992).

Radhika Coomaraswamy

Chapter 7

A Question of Honour: Women, Ethnicity, and Armed Conflict

> Most men and women we spoke to were agreed that honour, for losing
> and preserving, is located in the body of women.
> — Rita Menon and Kamla Bhasin, *Borders and Boundaries*

In October 1997, for the first time in the history of the world, a
woman took the stand to testify before the International Criminal Tribunal for Rwanda to describe her experience as a victim of sexual violence during wartime. She charged that what had happened to her was a
violation of international humanitarian law. The Tribunal listened to her
and a year later passed judgment that the violence that had been done to
her was indeed a war crime, a crime against humanity, and an element of
genocide.[1]

In this chapter, I discuss several broad issues pertaining to women,
ethnicity, and armed conflict. After providing a general analysis of rape
during armed conflict, I discuss the relationship between ethnicity,
nationalism, and sexual violence. I then portray a typology of roles that
women inhabit as a result of wars and, finally, reflect on some conceptual
issues that have troubled me during my fact-finding missions as the Special Rapporteur on Violence Against Women to the United Nations
Human Rights Commission.

Rape during Armed Conflict

Rape and sexual violence during war are as old a practice as war itself. Yet rape and sexual violence have been invisible issues in the discussion of international humanitarian law, especially in the last two centuries. They were often dismissed as private acts, the ignoble conduct of perverts, and the regrettable excesses of the occasional soldier; they did not enter the mainstream analysis of war crimes and crimes against humanity.

Recent analysis, however, has focused attention on the fact that far from being an isolated act, rape and sexual violence have often been used as a strategic weapon of war. Though this varies from conflict to conflict (i.e., in certain contexts, sexual violence and rape are more prominent than in others), it is necessary to isolate the factors that make this so. My analysis focuses on case studies of the more extreme variety, but many of the themes are present in most wars of an ethnic nature.

The recent wars in Bosnia-Herzegovina, Rwanda, and Kosovo point to the fact that sexual violence can be a central instrument of terror especially in campaigns that involve ethnic fratricide or nationalist wars. According to testimonies received from most of the conflict areas, rape and sexual violence are used to punish populations for acts that are seen as supportive of the other side. In addition, rape and sexual violence have been used to assert dominance over one's enemy. Since women's sexuality is seen as being under the protection of the men of the community, its defilement is an act of domination over the males of the community or group that is under attack. Susan Brownmiller chronicles in detail the use of rape as an act of domination since prehistoric times – not only domination against women but also against men who are expected to protect them.[2]

Besides their strategic use during wartime, rape and sexual violence are very often employed as a form of torture during interrogation. Rape and sexual violence are also used in ethnic wars to "pollute" and "defile" the other side. Forced pregnancy is a new aspect that has been recorded in modern wars where racial and ethnic purity are valued. Women are kept incarcerated and raped repeatedly until they become pregnant. They are then released, as in Bosnia and Herzegovina, to give birth to "Serb babies." There is also an element of sexual gratification that fuels sexual violence during conflict, leading not only to some perverted sexual acts but also to forced prostitution and sexual slavery.

Recently, stories of sexual violence have lead to greater mobilization of the community against the other side. Such stories have also received greater international attention through the media and galvanized both local and international human rights groups into action. As a result, despite the invisibility of a great deal of sexual violence, figures are also inflated or exaggerated for international consumption. It is now important to corroborate victims' stories to ensure that they are correct. This manipulation of women's trauma is a unique and new manifestation of sexual violence during modern wartime (see Duska Andrić-Ružičić in chapter 8).

Ethnicity and Nationalism

This chapter is entitled "A Question of Honour." In many countries sexual violence is seen as a crime of honour, as an act against the community and not against the physical integrity of the individual victim. This is the civil law as well as the tradition in many Mediterranean and Middle Eastern societies. This aspect is at the core of being able to understand violence against women during armed conflict that involves ethnic, religious, or linguistic differences among groups.

Feminist scholars have focused on the mobilization of the "Moral Mother" during wartime. She not only embodies the nation-state (as in the motherland) but reciprocity for her care and nurture also requires a certain heroism (if they are male) and sacrifice (if they are female) from her citizens/sons and daughters.[3] When the BBC interviewed the mother of Captain Muller, a hero of the Liberation Tigers of Tamil Eelam, she expressed unreserved joy that her son had died for the cause. Stories of mothers asking messengers whether their sons were killed by a bullet in the front or the back before they begin mourning is another archetypal legend produced in wartime.

The mother of the warrior plays an important role in war propoganda. Legends about mothers who urge their sons into battle are present in most societies. In Sri Lanka, among the Sinhalese, the warrior king Duttugemunu, who felt that his mission was to drive the Tamils out of Sri Lanka, had a mother who sacrificed a great deal for her son and who supported him in his crusade.[4] The support of the mother, the person who gave life to the warrior, is an essential ploy in marking discourses of legitimacy during times of war.

But mothers can also speak for peace.[5] Mothers of the disappeared from Argentina to Sri Lanka have taken this mother imagery and turned it on its head. Mothers have argued that they are givers of life and therefore opposed to war. But in other discourses such as Hinduism, goddesses like Durga are seen as fierce warriors. The portrayal of mothers during armed conflict as fearless supporters of war or courageous campaigners for peace is an indication of the power of mother imagery and its resonance in ethnic and nationalist culture.

Typologies of Women's Roles

As I noted above, sexual violence and rape were often seen as an aberrational aspect of warfare. However, this has begun to change. Anthropologists in large numbers are now studying violence and trying to understand its role in society and within communities. In addition, human rights groups are attempting to perfect the strategy of fact-finding missions. As a UN Special Rapporteur, I see the importance of these missions even though they are of brief duration and do not have the weight of academic rigour. These missions have produced a plethora of information on human rights violations during armed conflict, including information on sexual violence and rape. As I review these materials and reflect on my own fact-finding missions, I begin to see a typology of roles that are imposed on women as a result of the violence they experience.

During war, women experience violence at the hands of the men of the "enemy" community as well as soldiers of the "enemy" community. They are most often gang raped in front of family members; their sexual organs are mutilated, tattooed or destroyed; they are sometimes stripped and paraded naked; they are often made to dance naked in front of enemy soldiers; they are sometimes enslaved and made to cook and clean for the men and soldiers of the other communities; and sometimes, as in Rwanda, intimate family members are asked to rape them in public. Finally, after such an ordeal, the majority are killed or left to deal with these traumatic memories for the rest of their lives.

However, the question of honour raises another dimension. Not only "the other" men but also the men of their own communities – often their fathers and brothers – commit violence against them to protect them from their fate or force them to commit suicide. As Ritu Menon and Kamla Bhasin have documented, women who lived during the violence of Partition in 1947 India carried around poison packets, jumped into wells, or set fire to themselves in order to safeguard their "honour."[6] In Rwanda, a psychiatrist told us that one of the major problems he faced was survivors' guilt. The women who did not commit suicide felt that the community's conclusion was that they gave in to sexual violence in order to save their lives, that they no longer had a sense of honour. Many of these women ended up taking their lives after the war was over. In India, children of the next generation recited with pride how their womenfolk took their lives rather than allowing themselves to be violated, thus preserving the honour of the family and the community.

One horrific type of violence that has recently emerged both in Bosnia and Rwanda is forced pregnancy. In Catholic and Muslim countries, abortion remains a difficult proposition, so many of these women had to give birth to children of hate. In East Timor, one mother brought her child born after a rape by an Indonesian soldier to meet us. She told us how she hated and neglected this child until a counsellor and a nun taught her how not to pass on her outrage and anger to an innocent child. The body language of mother and child was plain for the world to see. While other women cuddled the child and played with her, the mother did not touch the child even once, and when she spoke to the child it was always in harsh undertones.

Women not only suffer from armed conflict as direct victims but also make up a large percentage of the world's refugees. They are vulnerable to rape and sexual violence when fleeing battles or on their way to refugee camps, but once they are in the camps, they are also at the receiving end of sexual harassment and violence from camp officials as well as other refugees (see Selvy Thiruchandran in chapter 10). Often, sex is exchanged for favours. If they are in camps as a family unit, observers point to an increase in domestic violence. They are also denied adequate medical care, especially gynecological services. Aid agencies have frequently portrayed women as powerless, helpless, and needy and coupled them with children.

But there is another narrative. Though many women are traumatized by these events, some women are empowered by them. The breakdown of traditional patriarchal norms creates spaces in which women can take control of their lives. This is especially possible when they live in refugee camps close to towns where they can find employment. Once they become economically independent, they begin to make decisions and are not the needy helpless women of the newsreel clips; they regain their dignity and insist on making decisions for themselves. Agencies like UNHCR have responded to this reality by involving women in decision-making with regard to the running of camps. Women's groups are encouraged and women are often urged to fully participate in all activities. Not all UNHCR camps have these practices, but this is the model as spelled out in their guidelines. However, the new-found independence of some refugee women is not always seen as a positive aspect. Malathi de Alwis chronicles how women who go out to work are constructed as being "loose" and immoral as they are no longer under the surveillance and control of their men who remain in the camps.[7]

Women also suffer from the excesses of armed conflict by being thrust into the often stigmatized role of widows. Since most wars are fought between men, it is inevitable that women can become widows overnight. In Rwanda, female-headed households rose sharply after the genocide. This phenomenon has been noted in many other countries as well and has become a serious problem in post-war reconstruction (see Thiruchandran in chapter 10). Menon and Bhasin write that the scale and incidence of widowhood in post-Partition India was so immense that the Indian government set up what was to be its first major welfare activity as an independent state – the rehabilitation of what it called "unattached women."[8] Widows suffer enormous economic hardships as well as trauma, for many have witnessed the deaths of their husbands. Many confess that what keeps them going is the concern for their children. Unskilled, often sexually harassed, and carrying a terrible psychological burden, these women deserve special attention in the work of rehabilitation and reconstruction after war.

Finally, not all women are victims in armed conflict; they can also be perpetrators. When I was in London before my field visit to Rwanda, I read a story in *The Sunday Times* of a Hutu nun named Bernadette who led the Hutu militia, the Interhamwe, into her church and joined them in brutally massacring hundreds of Tutsis who were seeking refuge there. This was the first time that I had encountered a women perpetrator of a crime against humanity. When I was in Rwanda, I requested permission to visit the prison where those accused of genocide had been kept, and who should lead the prisoners' delegation but Bernadette! She complained about the conditions in the prisons and like Lady Macbeth kept asking us for more soap. My heart was stone cold when talking to her, but in time I realized that human rights also means the perpetrators' right to dignity, regardless of their past deeds.

The complicity of women in the violence of their men, especially during ethnic wars, is a very disturbing phenomenon and goes to the heart of the maternalist feminist statement that women stand for peace. Women perpetrators of violence are now present in many armies as well as in guerrilla groups. Does the Geneva Convention adequately deal with the needs of women prisoners of war? Do changes need to be made? These are questions that are just beginning to be asked. And how do we, as women crusaders for human rights, react to women who have joined the military? As someone who believes in the affinity between women and peace, this development, as well as the stories of women who have emancipated themselves by becoming military fighters, troubles me deeply. These are foundational questions about women and human rights and the moral approach to violence – questions that have not yet been adequately answered by any one of our modern theorists.

Some Reflections

What is the quality of honour that allows people to do such horrible things not only to their own people but to themselves? The stories of intracommunity violence and suicide highlight this question of honour in a very stark manner. Also linked to this issue is shame and the fear of shame – *Lajja-bhaya*.[9] In such a context, to take a woman's life in order to prevent her and her community from experiencing shame and humiliation is an act of saving both her own and the community's honour and giving her martyrdom in the annals of collective memory. Obviously, it is not death that the men fear, for they do not kill their sons. It is sexual violence and the anticipation of sexual violence that terrifies them.

This linkage of sexuality and honour, a linkage preserved even in the language of Article 27 of the Geneva Convention,[10] has killed many women during armed conflict. If we are to move beyond this, we have to think of a tomorrow where fathers and brothers tell their women, "You have been raped and we understand your pain and we can forget the shame. Let us help you rebuild your life." If they make that conceptual leap then the fear of shame will disappear and the use of shame and honour as military or nationalist strategies of sexual violence during wartime will no longer be meaningful.

Linked to questions of shame and honour are the issues of ethnic pollution. The hideous stories of forced pregnancy that have come out of the former Yugoslavia point to the fact that men believe that women can be defiled through abuse of their sexuality, which is seen as a boundary marker of an ethnic group. If women are strictly controlled and are only permitted to express sexuality with men of their own community, then it is apparent that the community lays great emphasis on ethnic purity. During war that purity is deliberately assaulted precisely because it strikes at the core of ethnic identity. In communities where purity is not an issue, sexual violence is not such an earth shattering event and may not cause women to lose their desire to live. Pluralist societies whose boundaries shift and in which there is appreciation of hybridity lessen the edge of sexual violence as a means of community defilement. It is the acceptance of hybridity as an important component of the modern condition that will dispel, or make meaningless, wartime strategy that seeks to defile or pollute the other side.

In researching violence, many scholars have noted the difference between the way men and women tell their stories. Valentine Daniel pointed out that men present coherent narratives of violence while women find it very difficult to speak about sexual violence.[11] I found this to be true in my area of work as well. The classic case was a victim of sexual violence who was brought from East Timor to speak to the United Nations Commission on Human Rights. When she was introduced to me, she spoke a few words, but when asked to tell her story in public, she just could not speak. Her mouth opened and closed a few times, and then her eyes filled with tears. Whatever reality she was facing was obviously a devastating one. This went on for about twenty minutes till I finally called it off. Silence, then, is the first reaction of anyone who has experienced sexual violence. It is only with effective counselling and support that women break that silence. It is therefore not unusual that the victims who have been most articulate about their experience are those who have gone through counselling and who have a strong supportive network of women activists.

We also need an adequate methodology to understand the construction of hate within our societies. The case of Tutsi women in Rwanda is a case in point. Tutsi women were constructed as beautiful, seductive, sexual beings. Hatred towards Tutsi women was actively constructed by publications and by Radio Mille Collines, the Hutu radio station that urged the Hutu militia to kill and plunder. They portrayed Tutsi women as a great evil and their sexuality was seen as the greatest threat to Hutu identity. When "the ten commandments" of the Hutu militia were released, the first two related to Tutsi women. The first called on Hutu men not to be seduced by Tutsi women and the second demanded that Hutu wives prevent their husbands from being seduced by Tutsi women. This extraordinary demand portrayed Tutsi women as seductresses and spies and justified violence against them. Thus, sexual violence against Tutsi women was openly sanctioned by the Hutu militia. This was particularly shocking because it is the only context where women have engaged in sexual violence against other women – cutting off their breasts and pulling out their wombs. The extremity of this brutality seems to lie in the construction of hate.

In armed conflict, religion and religious institutions are important sites of sanctuary for women. However, in armed conflict, desecration of sacred places is also a manifestation of hate. In Rwanda, they have preserved these sites of desecration as a memorial to the dead. I was taken to one of these churches. Thousands of mutilated skeletons lay scattered about. The horror of it was made worse by a statue of the Virgin Mary resting on a large pedestal, looking down upon this carnage with compassion on her face. Several skeletons were exhibited in glass cases. The case I was led to held a skeleton of a victim of sexual violence with a pole up her genitalia. There she was preserved for posterity. Such horror in the most sacred of spaces.

The medical way of dealing with the extremities of war has always been through the field of psychology. In Rwanda, a psychiatrist told us that at least 85 per cent of the population was suffering from some form of disorder resulting from the war. They are depressed, they are psychotic, they are grieving for lost ones, they are guilty that they survived, they have children of hate, or they are perpetrators traumatized by the horrific deeds they committed. One of the most comprehensive psychological profiles of a community trapped and scarred by war, in the north of Sri Lanka, is provided by Daya Somasunderam. In his book entitled *Scarred Minds*, he describes case studies of individuals caught in this war and who suffer great trauma and depression. Chronicling the lives of torture victims, combatants, and ordinary citizens who have come to the Mental Health Clinic in Jaffna, Somasunderam gives us a sense of the enormous psychological effects of war.[12] Any program for rehabilitation and reconstruction of war situations must make psychological issues an important component, otherwise a society will never be able to heal itself.

It has been asked what the international community has done about sexual violence during times of armed conflict. Patricia Sellers in her work on war and war crimes against women argues that the early codes of chivalry were explicit about the prohibition of rape during wartime.[13] However, in the nineteenth and twentieth centuries this seems to have disappeared. The Hague Convention and the Geneva Convention speak about the violation of honour, but the Geneva Convention does not explicitly make sexual violence a grave breach that falls under universal jurisdiction and that holds an individual criminally responsible. Luckily, this gender-insensitive approach towards drafting humanitarian law has now changed. Due to the vigorous campaigning by women's groups, the new Rome statute of the International Criminal Court passed in July 2000[14] makes rape and all forms of sexual violence a war crime and a crime against humanity, and ensures that it applies both to internal and external wars. The Rwanda Tribunal looking into the Rwanda conflict goes further – rape and sexual violence are seen as elements of genocide, something that the Criminal Court does not contain in its provisions. This clarification of the normative standards, and the clear enunciation in the Rome statute that rape and sexual violence are grave breaches in and of themselves, is a fitting culmination of the efforts of the international women's movement and its tireless attempts to combat violence against women.

Though the international normative framework has been set in place, the implementation of the framework is still a major problem. The inability of states to arrest and try the perpetrators of the Bosnian, Croatian, and Serbian atrocities is a case in point. Though mechanisms for international accountability exist, states do not have the political will to implement these norms in an objective, impartial manner. In addition, programs of reconstruction such as the one in Rwanda ignore violence against women as an important fallout of armed conflict. The need to make violence against women a central issue in planning rehabilitation and reconstruction cannot be stressed enough. And yet we see bilateral and multilateral programs ignoring these questions when they actually carry out their mandates. It is important that they are sensitized to the problem so that following war, the society can heal in a manner that empowers its women.

When I reflect on women in armed conflict, I remember some of the most affirming memories that I always carry with me – those of the women from Sierra Leone who forced their leaders to make peace; the women of Belgrade who continued to run women's shelters in the midst of the NATO bombings; the Irish coalition of women sitting in the background during the Belfast peace talks, intervening and assisting the mediator; the Indonesian women from all the islands united in their determination to seek justice; and women from all ethnic groups in Sri Lanka signing petitions and planning a campaign for peace, who were vilified in the newspapers and threatened in public, but still determined to continue. It is at these moments that I have felt a part of a greater movement that must surely triumph in the future – the movement of what Oscar Wilde called the "community of the sensitive" – those who make peace and human rights priorities, those who break the vicious cycle of violence and hatred by replacing it with non-violence, compassion, and a respect for justice.

Notes

1 "The Akeyesu Judgment." Reference ICTR-96-4. *International Criminal Tribunal for Rwanda* <http://www.ictr.org> September 2002.
2 Susan Brownmiller, *Against Our Will: Men, Women and Rape* (New York: Simon Schuster, 1975).
3 Malathi de Alwis, "Moral Mothers and Stalwart Sons: Reading Binaries in a Time of War," in Lois Lorentzen and Jennifer Turpin, eds., *The Women and War Reader* (New York: New York University Press, 1998).
4 See Ananda W. P. Guruge, *Mahavamsa, The Great Chronicle of Sri Lanka* (Colombo: Lake House, 1989), pp.611-29.
5 See Malathi de Alwis, "Motherhood as a Space of Protest: Women's Political Participation in Contemporary Sri Lanka," in Amrita Basu and Patricia Jeffrey, eds., *Appropriating Gender: Women's Activism and the Politicization of Religion in South Asia* (London: Routledge, 1997), and Kumudini Samuel, "Activism, Motherhood, and the State in Sri Lanka's Ethnic Conflict," in chapter 13 of this volume.

6 Ritu Menon and Kamla Bhasin, *Borders and Boundaries* (New Delhi: Kali for Women, 1998).

7 Malathi de Alwis, "The 'Purity' of Displacement and the Re-territorialization of Longing: Muslim Refugees in North-Western Sri Lanka," in Wenona Giles and Jennifer Hyndman, eds., *Sites of Violence: Gender and Conflict Zones* (Berkeley: University of California Press, 2003).

8 Menon and Bhasin, *Borders and Boundaries.*

9 Gananath Obeyesekere, *The Cult of the Goddess Pattini* (Chicago: University of Chicago Press, 1984); Shahrzad Mojab, "No 'Safe Haven' for Women: Violence against Women in Iraqi Kurdistan," in Giles and Hyndman, eds., *Sites of Violence: Gender and Conflict Zones.*

10 Article 27 (2) of The Fourth Geneva Convention (1949), Relative to the Protection of Civilian Persons in Time of War, reads: "Women shall be especially protected against any attack on their honour, in particular against rape, enforced prostitution, or any form of indecent assault."

11 Valentine Daniel, *Charred Lullabies* (Princeton, NJ: Princeton University Press, 1996).

12 Daya Somasunderam, *Scarred Minds: The Psychological Impact of War on Sri Lankan Tamils* (New Delhi: Sage Publications, 1998).

13 Patricia Viseur Sellers, "International Tribunals: Justice by Prosecution" (Neelan Tiruchelvam Memorial Millennium Lecture, International Centre for Ethnic Studies, Colombo, Sri Lanka, October 21, 2000).

14 For a detailed study of the negotiations, see International Service for Human Rights, *The International Criminal Court: Towards a Fair and Effective Human Rights Tribunal* (Geneva: International Service for Human Rights, 1998).

Duska Andrić-Ružičić

Chapter 8

War Rape and the Political Manipulation of Survivors

When I speak about war rape in Bosnia-Herzegovina, I do so with trepidation. There are no adequate words to describe the massiveness of the crime and the scope of suffering that women victims have survived. Whenever I address this theme, I am always afraid that verbalizing and objectifying the crime will trivialize it and make the trauma borne by survivors unimportant. I am afraid that I sound like those very journalists and "historians" I berate for their insensitive way of dealing with this theme.

It is my aim in this chapter to clarify how some of the approaches to the subject of war rape have ended up as political manipulation (see also Radhika Coomaraswamy in chapter 7). I hope I do so in a way that avoids injuring our survivors. I begin by discussing the issue of war rape in general terms as a form of violence against women; I then discuss it specifically in the context of war as a part of war strategy, and as a lightning rod for journalists and analysts of war. In the second half of the chapter, I attempt to give voice to survivors by looking at the type of support provided for psychological healing as well as for counteracting political manipulation, and I describe in more detail the approach taken by Medica Zenica, a women's organization which has worked extensively with survivors.

Rape: A Specific Kind of Violence with a Specific Kind of Trauma

Rape is unique as a violent act, because its seriousness (and even the recognition of rape as an act of violence) is for the most part, or even entirely, determined by the behaviour of the perpetrator and his attitude towards the victim. Rape happens to women in marriages or in relationships, in the family, and at the hands of strangers or acquaintances – and finds its fullest expression in the kind of rape that takes place in war. And although rape as an act can have varying consequences for women, depending on both the perpetrator and on the woman's psychological-physiological construction, the fact remains that the woman has been raped – forced to be a passive victim of a sexual act. In its essential form, rape is male violence against women.[1]

As an act of violence by men against women, rape has several levels of significance:

- Rape is a sexually based act of violence.
- Rape is a consciously hostile, degrading, and brutal act against women with the aim of terrorizing and controlling them, humiliating them, rendering them completely helpless, and destroying them.
- Rape is an assassination of their body and soul, their integrity and dignity.[2]

When rape occurs outside the context of war, or some other conflict or crisis, the attitude towards the survivor traditionally has been that it is "Better to stay silent, this brings shame upon you . . . you must have provoked this somehow." Paradoxically, when she does speak, the first question asked is whether or not she defended herself. It is axiomatic that forms of violence experienced by women are ascribed to the woman herself as a participant in this violent act, as simultaneously guilty and even complicitly responsible for what has happened to her.

In contrast to other forms of trauma, rape carries with it some specific consequences that have a determining influence on the survivor's experience of the violence. First and foremost, the consequences of rape are experienced in terms of bodily integrity in the sexual realm, which is more or less a taboo subject in all societies. This fact alone leads to certain consequences for the survivor herself, as well as for the way she is treated in her social environment:

- The survivor is pressured to ascribe blame and the feeling of guilt to herself for having caused or provoked the rape in some way through the manner of her dress, her behaviour, and so on.
- Because sexuality is in many respects regarded as a taboo subject, society generally fails to provide understanding and support to the rape

survivor in the way it does to other victims of violence. The act is not talked about, it is covered up, or it becomes the target of curiosity and voyeuristic interest.

- The victim is sometimes made to bear further responsibility when those in her community are dissatisfied with the mere fact that she has survived. The survivor is considered permanently marked, degraded, and ostracized. The thought expressed is that, essentially, "it would have been better had she died."

Rape is not classified with other acts of pure violence; rather, it is only the sexual element that is exclusively attributed to it. There is a failure to understand that rape is a violent act stemming from the perpetrator's feeling of superiority, need for domination, and desire to make the victim feel she is worthless. The perpetrator degrades, shames, and hurts her, in order to demonstrate his raw power and contempt for the victim herself. In conditions of war, the degradation of the victim's environment and social group of origin is especially stressed.[3]

Rape as a Part of War Strategy

A statistical characteristic of rape is that the number of reported cases of this form of violence against women never reflects the true number. Reported cases are, as a general rule, only the tip of the iceberg. During the war in Bosnia-Herzegovina, rape was recognized as a part of war strategy, which gave the crime, and the reporting of it, political weight. As a result, the survivors were pressured to report these acts (in order to demonstrate the brutality of the enemy).

As long as war has been recorded in history, the rape of "women of the enemy" has been part of that history. The fact is that some women began to speak about their survival of these experiences only fifty years after the events (Russians, Germans, Koreans, Japanese, for example), in the context of systematic and massive rape. It is also true that massive war rape took place in other less politically attractive parts of the world, especially during the numerous African wars (Rwanda is a recent example). But it was immediately after the war in Bosnia had started that people began to speak about rape as a war strategy, although I doubt this was an invention of the Yugoslavian-Bosnian war.

If there is a distinction vis-à-vis the war in Bosnia, it is the fact that the military and political leadership publicly took a stand regarding the rape of women as violence against the enemy (either supporting it or opposing it). While this has made a crucial difference as far as the political weight of the crime is concerned, what difference has it made for the survivors? What is the difference between being a victim of a crime, which has political weight, and one that is "just a random, individual act," with no political confirmation to the survivor that she was a victim?

The Consequences of Defining War Rape as a Genocidal Crime

The recognition of rape as a war crime and a crime of genocide by the new Rome statute of the International Criminal Court and the Rwanda Tribunal, respectively, were historic steps forward (as discussed in chapter 7). The campaign to achieve this goal was carried out on an international level and was based on the active involvement of networks of women's and other organizations around the world.

However, it has been necessary to coax survivors to testify. Only in this way was our campaign to recognize rape as a war crime "justified." At the moment, testifying on the subject of war crimes constitutes a risk, since the criminals are still walking free, some even holding positions in local governments or in other public institutions. Fear of revenge against the witness, against her family members or friends, is constantly present. This fear is aggravated by the tribunal's protracted deliberations and investigations and its inability to provide full and suitable protection of witnesses.

When it comes to testifying for the crime of war rape, every survivor carries within herself not only fear but also deeply rooted shame. Even if she is aware that there is nothing to be ashamed of, the stigma carried by surviving a sexual crime is never completely erased in the eyes of society, even in cases of war rape. The public treatment of these survivors (never discussed in the media, for it would be condemned) is different from the personal treatment. During the war, people who knew about the rapes and had been given varying numbers (the most often cited being 30,000) would ask me, "Is it true that there were so many raped women?" After the war ended (in November 1995), acquaintances would sometimes ask, "Are *these* raped women still coming to you? Now that the war has ended, there probably aren't anymore?"

Is there any point in discussing with people who ask such a question the problem that is at the essence of that question? The severity of a crime, in the eyes of the public, grows above all in proportion to the number of victims. No one gave a thought to the individual horror each victim survived (if she, in fact, survived). These individual trauma victims were not given the "status" of survivors of crimes unless they were considered to be part of a massive group, supported by statistics. These banal questions illustrate the commonly held view that war rape (like rape in general) is something that "comes and goes" – like an act of sexual violence – and is not a lifelong trauma. These questions, once again, emphasize and reinforce the public attitude towards the criminal act of rape.[4]

Therefore, is it any surprise that survivors are less ready to testify than expected? Moreover, from whom is this expected and who has the right to expect such a thing? By keeping silent about the crime that she has survived, the survivor remains alone with her trauma. By turning to women's support organizations like Medica, she receives support but remains anonymous to the public. By testifying in an open courtroom, she exposes herself to the risks of rejection. In the end, no matter what kind of moral obligations society has, its response to war rape revolves around prejudice.

In exposing herself to the public, the rape survivor must carry the burden of being a "good victim." If prejudice is possible even in professional therapeutic work with rape survivors – from whom we would expect a high degree of understanding – what then can we expect from people we encounter in society everyday? What level of prejudice?

> When a helper creates a therapeutic relationship with a survivor . . . the survivor usually feels desperate, helpless, she needs support in order to regain her life step by step. The efforts of both the survivor and helper slowly begin to show results and the survivor becomes more independent. Once this is reached, sometimes the helper may feel, or express openly, criticism towards the survivor. For example, "the way she dresses is provocative," "she's laughing too loudly," "she already has a boyfriend," etc. . . . .In a word, in the eyes of the helper, the client is no longer a "good victim." How come? Wasn't this part of the helper's investment, to help the survivor reach the goal of regaining her life back?[5]

The Role of Media in the Political Manipulation of the Survivors

Journalists were the first to publicize the news of war crimes in Bosnia-Herzegovina – the camps, the crime, the mass rapes. It was then that the international community began to send aid to Bosnia-Herzegovina. Thousands of articles were published, scores of books were written, awards were given to journalists, doctoral dissertations were completed.

An exceptional analysis of the media was published by the historian, feminist activist, and writer Gabriela Mischkowski in her article "War Rape in Bosnia and Herzegovina in Public Discourse in the Federal Republic of Germany." Among other things, she says,

> The media in this war played a decisive role from the very beginning in spreading the image of the internal enemy in the process of disintegra-

tion of the Yugoslav state, and of the violent drawing of new borders and establishing new territorial states based on ethnic homogenization. Women and their bodies were, in this process, given the classic role they have been playing throughout time in the context of nation-states and war – the role of the bearers of children and the objects of protection, the legitimate victims of war.[6]

I recall that, in 1994, while the war was still going on, one of the Bosnian publishers, which considers itself "the conscience of Bosnjakness," published a list of survivors and perpetrators. Only 20 kilometres of road separated the victims from their tormentors. The source of this information was questioned: Was it from one of the state-level centres for documentation? That same publisher described Medica as an organization that was part of a network of clerics who were covering up data on war crimes committed in Central Bosnia by Croats against Bosnjaks. They cited as proof the "fact" that Medica was financed by Caritas Germany.[7]

While the local press, driven by "moral patriotism" or even clumsy empathy with the victims, published articles that could be harmful to survivors, the foreign media, for their part, rushed to sensationalize the issue. I cannot recall a single contact with any journalist in the last seven years that did not contain a request along the lines of "Could you get me an interview with a woman who was a victim of war rape, who was impregnated and had the child?" Is there no end to this tactlessness and insensitivity? And although there may have been, behind the journalistic interest, a genuine wish that these war crimes not be forgotten – especially with those who show this interest now, some years after the war, in the time of waning media interest in Bosnia and Herzegovina – their cold and calculating professionalism is insulting and insensitive. But at the end of the day, these are the articles that are sold to and that sell the newspapers.

There have been several cases of suicide or attempted suicide by women who survived war rape after articles were published with interviews that had been given by the women completely voluntarily. At the time the interviews were given, it was likely that these women were completely unaware of what they were agreeing to. They were in no condition to predict the impact of retraumatization once they saw their testimonies on paper or themselves in the photographs. Or they simply were not aware of the power of the media – for them the journalist is just one of many people to whom they have confessed their story. Is it not up to the journalist and her/his professional and human morality to make every effort not to inflict harm?

Those in Bosnia-Herzegovina who were there to maintain peace and to offer aid have been just as insensitive as the media. After the fall of Srebrenica in July 1995, the reception of refugees (mainly women and children) was organized in a camp near Tuzla. The public media were forbidden entry, but teams from United Nations television were there, and it was their programs that were then shown on Bosnian television and that stated:

> The columns of refugees enter the camp. A reporter stops some refugees even before they have a chance to find a place to sit, to catch their breath after a long and strenuous flight. A woman with a head scarf, who had obviously spent her life isolated in a small village, speaks frantically about what has happened to herself and her daughter as they were expelled, waving her hand in the direction of the young woman who stands cramped over behind her.[8]

The fate of those expelled from Srebrenica is one of the greatest tragedies of the Bosnian war; but does its severity justify the documenting of this tragedy in a way that goes beyond the boundaries of human dignity? Does the reporter wonder at all whether this woman was aware of who it was she was speaking to? Does a peasant woman from an isolated village know what a camera is, or the power of the media, or how many and which people will hear her story? How, then, can we find ways to document these crimes without doing harm to the survivors? What numbers are necessary for the heinousness of the crime to be "recognized"? And finally, the one other question that still bothers me: Did this really have to happen in Europe for it to be noticed and talked about? The silence of the media – or the mere whisperings along the way – contributed to the invisibility of the crimes of war rape that took place in Uganda, Rwanda, Sierra Leone, Somalia, Sudan, Indonesia, Afghanistan, and the countries of Latin America, to name just a few.

The Origins of Community Support for Survivors

At the end of 1992 and throughout 1993, the Bosnian Muslim community made some attempt to protect the dignity of survivors. For example, the Islamic religious leadership of Bosnia-Herzegovina issued a *fetwa* (*fatwa*), saying that women survivors should not be rejected by their families, friends, or communities, but that they needed to be supported and helped. Children born as a result of rape were to be brought up as Muslims and not distinguished from other children. The position taken by the state helped to soften the time-honoured negative, judgmental view of rape survivors, regardless of the circumstances of the rape. But the state still has not developed adequate mechanisms to help survivors.

In the summer of 1993, during a meeting attended by women from Zenica and other women who had fled to Zenica to escape the killing, we spoke about the possibility of organizing help for the women victims of war rape. One of the participants (then working for the wartime government) suggested that the Centre for Social Work could open a special unit to which women could turn in order to make use of services that would be available within the system. This was her response to Medica's suggestion that there was a need for a network of women's centres (within the NGO sector) that would be open to women who were surviving all kinds of trauma, including this specific one. As a politician by profession, although not lacking empathy for victims, she offered a rather clumsy solution. But this is a political consequence of misunderstanding. How can we give ourselves the right to consider these women as collective victims and, as such, to consider them as "public concerns," in terms of the institutionalization of the problem? How much can this benefit the needs of the survivors? How much do they really want to emerge from anonymity? Thankfully, this kind of institution was not created. A solution was developed via the public health-care system without opening "special units."

Medica Zenica's Therapeutic Principles

Women's NGOs are actually the only institutions whose priority has been to care for survivors and not to count them, publicize their stories, and hunt for war criminals. The effects of sexual abuse are long-term, while the interests of the state in this issue are only short-term, lasting as long as the situation can be used to win political points and gain sympathy from the international community.

Medica's work with traumatized women, including survivors of rape, is based on nine basic principles, which were established during the project's development and which continue to serve as the basis of our work. These principles are outlined here.

1　To relate to the woman as a person, not as a victim of violence, but as one who has survived violence.

2　To nurture solidarity and unconditional trust through psychotherapeutic work with the survivor on a personal, individual basis, without asking for proof of her story. She does not need to earn the "right" to receive our help.

We must keep in mind the mental state of our clients, how much can be said, what must be left unsaid, how much she chooses to reveal about herself. The foundation for ongoing work lies in the initial step of providing a survivor of violence with a sense of security and control so that she may have greater trust in the therapeutic process. Therefore, we leave the job of finding proof of the events to investigators, if a woman were to decide to present her case. As we work with a woman survivor we proceed slowly, one step at a time, through therapeutic work, allowing her to come to terms with her traumatic experience by gradually reconstructing its mosaic, allowing her to be the one to set the tempo of her own recovery.

3 Protecting the woman against sensationalism, political exploitation, or other experiences that do not contribute directly to her recovery.

Of course we cannot forget the important role the media have played in bringing the issue of war rape to the public's attention. The media helped to mobilize the public into action, organize help for the survivors, and contribute to a broader understanding of the problem. But the media have not always used an appropriate approach as I describe above. Even during the war, we attempted to protect survivors from media exploitation for sensationalistic purposes.

One of our efforts has been directed at shifting the term "victim" to the word "survivor," which illuminates a different aspect of this problem and gives dignity to the individual. We generally agree that women who survive rape need neither media attention nor the attention of society if that attention is intended to portray a pitiful victim. On the contrary, survivors need and deserve understanding, compassion, and respect. With such support they will be able to go on living a fulfilling and useful life.

4 Supporting a woman's right to choose.

A woman must have the right to make decisions about all questions related to her personal life. We do not have the right to pressure her or decide for her. We can help her according to her wishes and offer suggestions for help, such as how to decide what to do about a pregnancy, which is one consequence of rape – to accept the child, to choose to give it up for adoption, to choose to prosecute the perpetrator, or to testify in the court for war crimes.

5 Supporting and helping a woman realize her right to choose.

This includes human and professional support, psychological, medical, legal, and other help, which Medica is able to offer. We also co-operate with other institutions, both governmental and non-governmental, in order to fulfill these rights.

6   Offering assistance regardless of nationality.

From the beginning of its work, Medica has been open to women from all nationalities. We established the Centre and began our work during the period of the most violent conflict between nationalities since the Second World War. If we had not been in this situation, we would have taken for granted this kind of approach, but as it is, we value our client's womanhood above all her other social characteristics.

7   Every honest human interaction has its own therapeutic value.

Especially in cases of trauma caused by human beings, there is a need for a human commitment to fight for human rights, which includes an understanding that violence is a violation of human rights and that violence is a basic injustice. The commitment to these principles is critical for the survivor's recovery.

8   There is a necessity to take broader public action within our
     community.

The problem of rape is that not only does it involve a relationship between the victim and the perpetrator but it also has a broader social context. Rape is perpetrated as a consequence of a power imbalance. Because of this power imbalance and its violent consequences, there is no place for an attitude of moral neutrality. Honest commitment to the work itself is a moral struggle, which addresses not only the consequences of violence, but also its causes.[9]

9   The importance of documentation.

It is important to record events so that they enter the historical record and become a part of collective memory. It is important, therefore, to speak of crimes that have taken place so that they are not forgotten and not repeated. The questions that troubles us are, How do we achieve this without hurting the survivor, without threatening her? Do we have the right to ask for testimony? We can strive to provide an environment in which a survivor can make her own decision about testimony without feeling subject to public pressure. We can also strive to provide for her – should she decide to give her testimony – a completely safe context in which to do so.

* * *

Today, Medica-Zenica continues its work with women victims of violence in Bosnia-Herzegovina as this country reconstructs, rebuilds, and repairs the life of the individual members of its multi-ethnic community. We continue to work across the borders and boundaries of ethnic-nationalism.

Notes

1 Women's groups from the region of the former Yugoslavia (and the network of European feminists) have discussed the issue of war rape and again underscored the idea that, in the end, war rape is essentially male violence against women, and that the foundation of that violence is the torturing of women who "bear" the enemy, by being someone's wife, mother, or sister. They have noted that history simply did not record this crime with the same political weight as is now the case (see Coomaraswamy in chapter 7). But the core notion has been the same throughout the centuries. For expressing this opinion, these feminists and activists were accused and condemned according to their place of origin, political affiliation or religion (Chetnik, Ustasha, fascist, communist, clerical, Muslim-haters, pro-West bitches, and so on).

2 Monika Hauser, "The War against Women and How They Are Defending Themselves," *Medica Bulletin* (January 1996).

3 Edita Ostojić, "Silovanje – Specifican vid nasilja, specifićna trauma," Drugi pogled 2, "(Ne) živjeti s nasiljem," *Medica Zenica – Infoteka* (April 1999).

4 Ibid.

5 Edita Ostojić, "Opasnosti koje nam stoje na putu pružanja adekvatne pomoći," iz "Priručnik za pomagače i pomagačice koji rade sa žrtvama i preživjelima nasilja," Edicija Drugi pogled, *Medica Zenica – Infoteka* (November 1999).

6 Gabriela Mischkowski, "Kriegsvergewaltigungen in Bosnien-Herzegowina im öffentlichen Diskurs in der BRD," in Krieg, Geschlecht und Traumatisierung: *Erfahrungen und Reflexionen in der Arbeit mit traumatisierten Frauen in Kriegs- und Krisengebieten* (Dokumentation von Medica mondiale e.V.,IKO-Verlag, Edition Hipparchia, 1999).

7 Caritas Germany is a German non-governmental organization aid organization.

8 This is the author's interpretation of the news reported on 12 July 1995.

9 Edita Ostojić, "Osnovne vrijednosti na kojima počiva naš rad sa traumatiziranim osobama," iz "Priručnik za pomagače i pomagačice koji rade sa žrtvama i preživjelima nasilja," Edicija Drugi pogled, *Medica Zenica – Infoteka* (October 1999).

Ananda Galappatti

Chapter 9

Psychological Suffering, "Trauma," and PTSD: Implications for Women in Sri Lanka's Conflict Zones

In recent years, humanitarian workers in Sri Lanka have become increasingly concerned with the psychological consequences of war. Non-governmental and state institutions at the international and local levels have been propelled into "psychosocial interventions" by the terrible psychological toll that is exacted by war and by the heightened interest in this area of work within the Sri Lankan and international donor community. As in many other conflict zones around the world, the framework that has been hastily adopted to respond to the psychological needs of survivors of violence has been oriented towards the concept of psychological "trauma," in particular, the diagnosis of Post-Traumatic Stress Disorder (PTSD). This chapter raises concerns about how the notion of "trauma" is currently deployed in Sri Lanka, and explores the implications this may have for acknowledging and responding to women's experiences of psychological suffering in the conflict zones of Sri Lanka.[1]

Recent Sri Lankan history has been marked by violence. The North and East of the island have been in the throes of an ugly war that has been waged for over two decades. Whether brutalized by this war or not, other regions of the country have also experienced armed violence associated with the rise and fall of the Janatha Vimukthi Peramuna (JVP), first in 1971 and more recently in the late 1980s. Individuals caught up within this violence, both as civilians and combatants, have experienced terrible events. It is often claimed that tens of thousands, if not millions, are suffering the psychological consequences of conflict-related violence.

115

However the estimates may vary, what is significant is that these people have been "traumatized." A proposal submitted by a local NGO working with survivors of armed conflict argued that

> it is easy to overlook the need for psychological care because it is not a need felt even amongst the traumatized. This can be attributed to the inherent reluctance of the Sri Lankan to see his/her problem as a psychological one. The tendency is to seek medical explanation and allopathic treatment for what is clearly a psychological manifestation. The fact remains, however, that they have been traumatized and this must be addressed.[2]

Women and children, and widows and orphans in particular, are often cited as the most vulnerable groups that "can never be expected to lead normal lives again."[3] This emphasis on women's vulnerability is not peculiar to Sri Lanka. The international literature on Post-Traumatic Stress Disorder, the now ubiquitous construct, elaborated by Euro-American psychiatry, goes as far as to list the condition of "being female" as a "risk factor" for developing this disorder.[4] It is necessary to examine the implications of such assertions. The psychosocial circumstances that cause women to be at risk for PTSD must be analyzed, as well as the theoretical and moral underpinnings of that psychological diagnosis.

"Trauma"

The origins of the notion of a relationship between psychological trauma and a consequent disorder have been traced to Jean-Martin Charcot's work on hysteria among survivors of railway accidents in the 1880s. Subsequent work by Pierre Janet, Joseph Breuer, and Sigmund Freud laid the basis for twentieth-century conceptions of "traumatic memory" that lead to the pathology of the mind.[5] According to Breuer's and Freud's 1893 definition, a trauma was any experience that precipitated distressing affect, whether fright, anxiety, shame, or physical pain. Though their notion of trauma differed somewhat from that which is widely accepted today, their concept was significantly formulated *in terms of the reaction to particular events*. Freud's broad view of potentially illness-causing trauma included the domain of experience that would be categorized within the set of "stressful events."

The distinction made today between traumatic and stressful events is seen as crucial. Within contemporary clinical psychiatry and psychology, a trauma is understood to be an experience that is more extreme, is exceptional, and has "more overwhelming . . . psychological consequences" than a "stressful" event that is less severe. The attempts to define traumas as terrible experiences (for example, witnessing a murder, childhood sexual abuse, involvement in a major road accident) failed, since individual responses to these varied. Therefore, as with the formulations of a century ago, traumatic experience is still necessarily identified and defined by the psychological response to events.[6] Consequently, the dominant description of post-traumatic psychological effects of the last twenty years (i.e., PTSD) is based on both *an aetiological event* as well as *a subjective response to that event* in order to establish that a traumatic event (and a subsequent stress disorder) has occurred.[7]

On PTSD as a Description of Psychological Suffering

Post-Traumatic Stress Disorder has been welcomed by many for its insistence on an external causal factor in defining a psychological condition. Because it is one of the few diagnoses defined within the primary catalogue of psychological disorders (the *Diagnostic Statistical Manual-IV* of the American Psychological Association), some researchers have claimed that PTSD moves "one step away from the individual model of responsibility that pathologises a human response to intensely frightening experiences."[8] Certainly, in late-twentieth-century North America and Western Europe, the popularized notion of a post-traumatic stress reaction provided an important means for acknowledging the harm suffered by women and men who had lived through terrible experiences. It enabled greater understanding of the difficulties of veterans of the Vietnam War and also of the psychological consequences of domestic assault, rape, and other violence faced by women. In the context of contemporary Sri Lanka, it has been argued that the PTSD construct has provided a much needed voice to the suffering of people of North Sri Lanka, upon whom the psychological impact of war has been long ignored by the state's mental health establishment.[9]

However, it is now apparent that there are also many limitations and failings of the current construct of Post-Traumatic Stress Disorder. Criticisms of PTSD have made much of the value judgments implicit in the prescription of what constitutes an abnormal reaction to a traumatic event. The symptoms that characterize this disorder are essentially excessive expressions of what are considered acceptable reactions to a trauma. The validity of emphasizing the persistence of complaints as a crucial diagnostic criterion has been questioned even within the context of Euro-American cultures. It has been argued that to pathologize distress three months after experiencing an extremely stressful situation, whether it be combat, rape, torture, or a death camp, is to delegitimize suffering through its transformation into a medical condition. Arthur Kleinman suggests that this is indicative of a particular cultural orientation, namely, that "suffering in North America is thought of as perhaps no longer normative, or it would seem, normal."[10] Within Sri Lankan cultures, and certainly in the context of repressive political violence, it seems that difficult life situations are often given meaning through prolonged suffering and its expression.[11] However, it is a pathologizing biomedical view of psychological suffering, though sometimes in a humanist guise, that prevails in the humanitarian policies of the local and international non-governmental organizations working in Sri Lanka.

Despite being the most popular viewing frame for psychological suffering caused by extreme events, Post-Traumatic Stress Disorder is by no means the only diagnosis available for this among the biomedical models of mental well-being. The World Health Organization has included definitions in its most recent revision of *The International Statistical Classification of Diseases and Related Health Problems,*[12] in which it acknowledges a greater variation of responses to extreme events than does the *Diagnostic Statistical Manual-IV.* As well, many researchers have drawn attention to other forms of depression and various dissociative disorders associated with experiencing "traumatic" events. Some investigators, like Judith Herman, have stressed the limitations of PTSD in describing the effects of prolonged and repeated suffering in instances such as torture, imprisonment or captivity during war, chronic spouse abuse, extended childhood physical or sexual abuse, and organized sexual exploitation. There is still vigorous debate on the appropriateness of using PTSD to describe the wide range of human responses to extreme events even from within the Euro-American culture, which has formulated that diagnosis.[13]

Nevertheless, despite the potential drawbacks of the current definition of Post-Traumatic Stress Disorder, its global predominance has meant that it is the primary, often the implicit, reference point in discussions concerning violence-related psychological suffering in Sri Lanka. The enthusiasm with which the diagnosis of PTSD has been brought into Sri Lanka may have much to do with its widely perceived progressive nature within the scheme of Euro-American biomedicine. "PTSD is about the only psychiatric diagnosis that people do not object to being given," writes Stephen O'Brien from the UK. He continues,

> It is as if PTSD in particular is an acceptable face of mental illness, more understandable than schizophrenia and easier to associate with. There is an acceptance that it could happen to "anyone, even to a member of my family."[14]

This view might well be valid within cultures that have absorbed the many post-Vietnam War movies and Euro-American media stories in which PTSD is defined as an element of the injustice visited upon war veterans and disaster survivors. However, in Sri Lanka's war zones, post-traumatic distress is viewed as a sign of psychological weakness or pathological morbidity. In America or Europe, a diagnosis of PTSD can bring a sufferer legal compensation and vindication. In Sri Lanka, it will only make the sufferer a candidate for charity and pity.

These attitudes seem to be implicit in the assumptions made by many humanitarian workers, who also associate psychological vulnerability with socially and materially constructed powerlessness of persons in those areas. This is particularly true in relation to humanitarian ideas about women in conflict zones – for example, expectations of "traumatization" would be greater in the case of a woman whose spouse is murdered than in the case of a man in the same position. The sexist underpinnings of the presumption of psychological weakness notwithstanding, it is instructive to examine the possibility of a gendered psychological vulnerability in relation to the issue of power.

Women, PTSD, and Powerlessness

Writing in an era when PTSD is a common diagnosis, Judith Herman describes the psychological consequences of trauma as "an affliction of the powerless":

> At the moment of trauma, the victim is rendered helpless by overwhelming force. When the force is that of nature, we speak of disasters. When the force is that of other human beings, we speak of atrocities. Traumatic events overwhelm the ordinary systems of care that give people a sense of control, connection, and meaning.[15]

The analysis of trauma through the lens of power can speak profoundly to the experiences of women, and offers some explanation of why *being female* increases the risk of suffering the psychological effects of trauma. Although it is not clear whether women are more likely to experience violence during their lifetime than men, "women are often understood to be more vulnerable to the development of posttraumatic states."[16] Data from North America suggest that women have a greater chance of being exposed to events likely to produce PTSD (e.g., rape, childhood sexual abuse, adult physical assault) than are men. This finding has led to the explanation of the significant rates of PTSD (and other post-traumatic states) among women and people of colour in North American culture in terms of the social inequities that increase their risk of victimization. Certainly, within Sri Lanka, violence against women is legitimized and accommodated by social constructions of femaleness and masculinity. There are inadequate data to indicate whether women in Sri Lanka's war zones would be more "at risk" of being diagnosed with PTSD than men. While it has not yet been possible to assess whether women in Sri Lanka are more likely to live through potentially traumatic experiences than men, it is necessary to study how structural powerlessness mediates women's psychological responses to these experiences.

The current diagnosis of PTSD may not reflect the reality of women's lives. Although it was the first diagnosis to recognize the psychological toll exacted of survivors of rape, domestic violence, and sexual abuse and which incorporated much of the 1970s feminist literature on violence against women, it is now essential to examine its relevance for women.[17] The suffering experienced by women is often common, repeated, and current, and may not be represented within the notion of "post"-trauma, which largely "originates in the white male experience of time-limited events, often singular in nature versus the prolonged, everyday effects of rape and sexual and physical assault."[18] The nature of organized violence in Sri Lanka has superimposed upon these atrocities of "civil" society the protracted experiences of torture, living in areas under military control, and, during terror campaigns, disappearances and single or multiple displacement.

In fact, conditions of conflict have increased many women's structural vulnerability, producing new threats to their physical and sexual integrity. Post-Traumatic Stress Disorder, with its construction historically situated within the circumscribed experiences of mostly Western male combat veterans of "Vietnam" and the world wars, does not seem equipped to deal with women's experiences in arenas of conflict in Sri Lanka. Women's suffering within the context of war does not revolve around discrete or even chronic "traumatic" events alone.

Psychological Suffering in Two Conflict Zones, Present and Past

Most parts of Sri Lanka could be loosely mapped as being within a zone of armed conflict, either vulnerable to the organized violence of the "ethnic" war or somehow affected by the violence associated with the Janatha Vimukthi Peramuna insurrections of the 1970s and late 1980s. The following material is derived from research undertaken between 1997 and 1998 within the districts of Vavuniya and Monaragala, both sites of severe armed brutalities – Vavuniya within the context of the "North and East" war, and Monaragala within the context of violence in "the South." The stories shared by women in these two districts seem to say that even though their experiences often were vastly different, they were at times fundamentally similar.

The Monaragala district is generally considered a conflict zone of the past. The violent killings, disappearances, and terror came to an end by 1992, and though jungle-side villages along the district's eastern perimeter are sometimes attacked by the Tigers (the Liberation Tigers of Tamil Eelam), these incidents are given little significance at a national level.[19] Although the atrocities of the past are no longer apparent, for many women in this area the violence is far from being a faded memory. Even seven or ten years later, the violence is still very immediate and often painfully remembered every day.

During this time, still referred to as "the terror," many women were widowed, their husbands taken from their homes by armed men. Other women were themselves the targets of attack for their roles in local politics, their husbands' suspected political affiliations, or for reasons that remain obscure even to them. JVP activists predominantly attacked families with connections to the armed forces or the civil administration, and the families of suspected "subversives" were targeted by the army, police, and shadowy state-sponsored paramilitary groups. However, under the cover of this terror, a great many others died, too. It was a time of false tipoffs that served personal vendettas or business interests, of sack-covered *goni billa* informants at security checkpoints, of ruthless punishment for disobeying JVP-imposed curfews and regulations. Civil administration was paralyzed. There was a large-scale detention of "suspects" by the military, and abduction and torture by all parties. Corpses were left by the roadside, dumped in rivers, or hung from lampposts as warnings. Many people, mostly men, simply disappeared, never to be found again.[20]

Although there has been no record of sexual assault of women on a comparable scale to that within the North-East conflict arenas, there have been a few reports of rape by army personnel, and male ex-detainees have claimed that they were forced to sexually abuse female detainees while in army custody.[21] It is almost certain that the frequency of such rape and assault was far higher than reported, given the tremendous social stigma attached to suffering such abuse. My co-researcher and I also learned of at least one instance of abduction and forced marriage of a woman in Monaragala to a man associated with the JVP.

Many women in Monaragala today live with the legacy of that period. They very frequently refer to the events during "the terror" as having transformed their lives. Widowed mothers speak of having struggled alone to "bring up children well" in one of the most deprived rural areas of Sri Lanka. The unequal and meagre employment opportunities available to them as women often made the job of being a working mother all the more difficult, often the most arduous and self-defining task of their lives.

Their changed status within the strongly patriarchal Sinhala culture of Monaragala has caused many women hardship, even as they have struggled to overcome terrible adversity. Families and neighbours have harshly censured widowed women who attempted to adjust to life as the head of their household (see Selvy Thiruchandran in chapter 10). When they went out to work or to sort out compensation claims for the loss of a spouse, neighbours would accuse these women of carrying on "secret affairs" and neglecting their duties as mothers, allegations that seriously compromised their social status. Remarriage, or even a hint of courtship, was sometimes enough for a woman's in-laws to sever all contact with her, attempt to acquire the property shared with her dead or disappeared husband, denounce her as complicit in her husband's death, or try to take her children away from her. However, choosing to live without male "protection" has often meant living with sexual harassment and the very real threat of rape. While legal or common-law remarriage has brought financial, emotional, and physical security to many women, others have been victimized by their new partners. The mothers, wives, lovers, and sisters of the disappeared continue to live with painful uncertainties: "Is my child still alive?" "When should I stop waiting for him to return?" "Should I keep looking for my brother?"

Women in Monaragala do not necessarily make a strong distinction between their experiences during "the terror" and the trials of life since that time. Some women often consider these to be inextricably linked, with the troubles of the present having their causal origins within the violence of the past. Attempts to demarcate boundaries within the continuum of their experience may make little sense to these women. Their suffering appears to be seamless, implicitly understood as a generalized predicament that merely inhabits different forms as it persists through time. Other women do not explain their current difficulties in terms of hardships suffered during "the terror," although they may experience potentially psychosomatic complaints that could date back to that time.

It is apparent that many women have experienced great distress as a consequence of the difficult and often extreme circumstances they have faced. Some women speak of "not knowing what was happening" for over a year following the murder of their spouses. Others speak of mothers who have become "mentally ill" after the death of their husbands or lovers. Many women have spent years visiting army camps and consulting "light-readers" (local shamans), searching for some news of an abducted husband or son, only giving up when their financial resources were exhausted. When attending health clinics years later, widowed mothers often reported that they and their children would cry "almost every day" at home, when they thought about their situation.

Women have also tried to contain the pain of their situation by taking on religious and cultural practices or investing new confidence in their belief systems. For some women, giving "alms" on behalf of the disappeared sometimes has become an "obsession," taking priority over all other concerns. Others see these terrible circumstances that have befallen them and their families as "karmic" explanations to existential questions. Emotions of anger, residual fear, hopelessness, extreme sorrow, and nearly unbearable grief remain with these women.

In addition, some women complain of an intense and debilitating pain in their head, chest, limbs, and lower back, although doctors insist that there is nothing physically wrong with them. These may be somatic expressions of their psychological state, yet very few of these women (or doctors in the area) seem aware of this possibility. Others are troubled by nightmares and disturbed sleep. They are sometimes "visited in their dreams" by the dead and the disappeared, even by the perpetrators who committed the violence against them. While this can be comforting (in the case of lost family or friend), for many it is an upsetting event. Whatever the origins or nature of their distress, these psychological experiences are very immediate to these women, seriously affecting the way in which they live their lives today.

Attempts to delineate direct causal relationships between psychological hardships and their consequences for women in Vavuniya are as challenging as any such efforts in Monaragala. Over the last twenty years, the Vavuniya district has been occupied by the Liberation Tigers of Tamil Eelam (LTTE), the Indian Peace Keeping Force (IPKF), the Sri Lankan Armed Forces, and other Tamil paramilitary groups. The district has experienced ethnic riots, large-scale population displacement, periods of "low-intensity hostilities," and full-blown war. During the war, the district was divided into "cleared" (i.e., government-controlled) and "uncleared" (i.e., LTTE-controlled) areas, each served by parallel systems of administration. The material in this chapter was gathered within the "cleared" areas, which were easier to visit from "this side," since travel across the "border" was tightly regulated by both the Sri Lankan Ministry of Defence and the LTTE administration.

The "cleared" portions of Vavuniya were a primary buffer zone between the war zone and the more southern parts of Sri Lanka. Hundreds of thousands of persons displaced by military offensives in other districts were been "temporarily" placed in camps in Vavuniya, and many cannot leave for years to come. The camps are overcrowded and lack adequate hygiene and sanitary facilities, and inmates of these "welfare centres" are unable to leave the premises without special permission. During the war, all residents of "cleared" areas were subjected to tight military and police control, their movements regulated through a system of "passes."[22] In addition to the civil and military administrations, there existed a regime of extortion, torture, and intimidation by independent paramilitary groups (i.e., the People's Liberation Organization of Tamil Eelam, the Tamil Eelam Liberation Organization, and the Eelam People's Revolutionary Liberation Front), which were depended upon by the Sri Lankan Armed Forces to control LTTE activity in the district.

Whether living in the camps or outside of them, women in Vavuniya have experienced tremendous hardships and horrors. Tens of thousands have lost family, friends, acquaintances, homes, and material possessions to acts of war and violence. Tamil women have been subjected to sexual assault by Sri Lankan armed personnel, members of the Indian Peace-Keeping Forces, and others;[23] they have been disabled and injured by gunfire, shelling, mines, and torture; and many have been separated from their families, children, and spouses as they fled advancing battlefronts and were placed in "refugee" camps. The material hardships of the camps, along with the withdrawal of personal freedoms and loss of privacy and personal dignity, are unbearable to many. Suicide is becoming increasingly frequent among displaced women who are unable to cope with the conditions they live in[24] (see also chapter 10).

For women living in Vavuniya, who have experienced the uncertainties of war and displacement for many years, the psychological implications are similar to those described by women in Monaragala. Many experience sleeplessness and recurring dreams of shelling and other threatening incidents in their lives. Many report that their lost family members are constantly in their thoughts and stay with them "even if [they] close their eyes." "I hate the nights," said one woman. Some women experience sudden fright and "shivering" at the sound of gunfire or an aircraft; they say it is only death that will end their fears. Grief, loneliness, and sorrow deeply affect the lives of these women, resulting in their "crying all the time." Others report forgetfulness and a numbness of emotion. They speak of giddiness, loss of appetite, and other physical complaints like chest pains that occur when they think about what has happened to them. Some have very strong reactions to reminders of events that have befallen them, collapsing unconscious at the sight of blood, for example. For others, their experiences have caused a crisis of faith and they have abandoned prior beliefs in astrology and stopped visiting places of worship. Others have renewed faith in their god or gods.

The chronic nature of the stress experienced by women in Vavuniya makes it difficult to understand their psychological states in terms of causal events and exacerbating, "maintaining" factors. Indeed, it may not be helpful to force these stress responses, or those of the women in Monaragala, into the popular frameworks of post-traumatic stress reactions. Certainly, concepts like PTSD can be used to describe some of the experiences in these conflict zones. However, it is necessary to find ways of responding to the conditions of fear, somatic complaints, hopelessness, grief, helplessness, and existential doubt in a way that does not compartmentalize and medicalize these various, and arguably reasonable, reactions to life-situations in Sri Lanka.

It would not be wise to posit psychological "distress" purely as a form of protest against the intolerable. Such an approach will likely cause the actual suffering of women – many of whom desperately wish a release from the recurring nightmares, headaches, chest pains, and sleeplessness that plague them – to be misunderstood.

Towards a Wider Framework for Psychological Suffering

In light of the many shortcomings of the medicalized models used for diagnosing the effects of psychological trauma, the newer concept of "insidious trauma" may be useful in considering how living in uncertain and potentially harmful conditions in Sri Lanka affects women. Maria Root's work suggests that the notion of "insidious trauma" could be a valuable tool in describing women's lives in such situations. She locates its effects in women's acute self-awareness that "one's safety is very tentative."[25] This awareness is created by experiences that show that a fundamental, unchangeable aspect of one's identity (i.e., *being female, being of a particular ethnicity*) can increase the risk of personal danger. In Sri Lanka, this is manifested in a fear of being raped, visiting government officials or passing checkpoints alone, of intruders at night, and so on. Just as many women are acutely aware of being female and of the personal risk this status entails, others are aware of their ethnic or social status and know that this status is unsafe. This awareness helps women survive and should be recognized as signalling a form of significant and legitimate psychological hardship.

The concept of "insidious trauma" could also provide an important means to better understanding the experiences and cognitive schemas that determine the subjective experiences that define a traumatic event.[26] Certainly within the particular conditions of areas like Vavuniya and

Monaragala, this notion of "insidious trauma" could be an appropriate means of acknowledging suffering. It could also contribute to a better understanding of how transgenerational processes mediate psychological distress in Sri Lanka and elsewhere.

Responding to Psychological Suffering

A legitimate view of psychological suffering contains a moral imperative to alter the social and material realities that enabled the suffering to be created. Perhaps in the truly desperate situations that women face in Sri Lankan conflict zones, it is appropriate that the dominant "adjustment-based" therapies be abandoned. It may not be possible or proper to expect these women to adjust to "normal" behaviour and emotions when the notion of normality itself is uncertain and when present-day reality is unacceptable.

Adjustment-based approaches to psychological distress can be repressive, particularly for women, as they can support the acceptance of existing social norms, even if this means that women remain in subordinate roles. In Sri Lanka, many of those who "counsel" women reinforce conservative cultural values by emphasizing the importance of women's roles as mothers and wives, absolving men from the responsibility of nurturing and communicating with their children. Likewise, women are often encouraged to support their husbands emotionally, but men are seldom encouraged to support their wives.

Counsellors also tend to discourage clients from maintaining unconventional emotional and sexual relationships in order to minimize social outrage at this behaviour; and they very often act out of personal moral conviction. Some humanitarian social workers even arrange marriages for single women who have been sexually abused, since they perceive this to be the principal solution to the women's problems. A woman's inclinations to protest the inhuman conditions of the war zone or other social injustices would, similarly, be dampened (often for very understandable reasons of her personal safety). Professional humanitarian orientations towards apolitical assistance could discourage the assertion of personal or collective agency in the face of outrageous conditions.

It seems now that some major change is necessary. For women in Sri Lankan conflict zones, reorienting the "therapeutic" approach towards "self-actualization" may prove more appropriate and liberating. From this perspective, the criterion of an "improved psychological state" does not mean an adjustment of expectations but the development of one's desires and potentials and the fulfilment of one's own needs. Self-actualization will mean different things for different women: some will reject the traditional social roles; others will redefine those roles; and still others will use the traditional roles as a framework for achieving self-actualization. Self-actualization may also involve self-definition through reformulating personal ethnic and class identities. All this may mean a greater lack of adjustment to "norms," pain, and confusion in defining and living different roles, and an increased risk of social disapproval and personal harm.[27] It may also mean greater personal involvement in efforts for social transformation.

It is possible that developing an "internal locus of control" might help women to transcend their suffering.[28] Of course, implementation of such an approach to "therapy" will present numerous ethical dilemmas for anyone supporting women's self-actualization. From a mental health professional standpoint, a support person's personal agenda is all the more pertinent in a violent context where individuals are often structurally powerless.

Although it may appear ethically precarious to initiate potentially inflammatory "therapy" within areas where a process of self-actualization may lead to a woman being in greater personal danger, it could be argued that to do otherwise is to deny the nature of suffering being experienced in conflict areas of Sri Lanka. To describe being female as a "risk factor" for PTSD or other distressed psychosocial responses to extreme events seems an offensively passive understanding of women's suffering; it issues no moral imperative for change, nor does it legitimate women's pain and difficulties.

Notes

1 The considerations raised in this chapter arose out of research and conversations with Dr. Gameela Samarasinghe. The material pertaining to women's experiences in Vavuniya and Monaragala was received from a survey we carried out under the auspices of the International War-Trauma and Humanitarian Intervention Trust and the Social Scientists' Association, Colombo. The research was supported by NOVIB, The Netherlands. In addition, I am very grateful to Professor Daya Somasundaram for some keen observations and comments on an earlier draft.

2 "The Peace Program" (Colombo: Family Rehabilitation Centre, 1996), unpublished proposal.

3 Editorial, "Caring for the Mentally-Ill," *Daily News*, Oct. 5, 1998.

4 M.J. Friedman and A.J. Marsella, "Posttraumatic Stress Disorder: An Overview of the Concept," in A.J. Marsella, M.J. Friedman, E.T. Gerrity, and R.M. Scurfield, eds., *Ethnocultural Aspects of Posttraumatic Stress Disorder* (Washington, DC: American Psychological Association ,1996), p.23.

5 Allan Young, *The Harmony of Illusions: Inventing Post-Traumatic Stress Disorder* (Princeton, NJ: Princeton University Press, 1995), pp.32-8.

6 J. Busfield, *Men, Women and Madness: Understanding Gender and Mental Disorder* (London: Macmillan Press, 1996), pp.210-11.

7 "Criterion A" for Post-Traumatic Stress Disorder, as described in the *Diagnostic Statistical Manual-IV* is as follows: "The person has been exposed to a traumatic event in which both of the following were present: (1) The person experienced, witnessed, or was confronted with an event or events that involved actual or threatened death or serious injury, or a threat to the physical integrity of self or others. (2) The person's response involved intense fear, helplessness, or horror. Note: In children, this may be expressed instead by disorganized or agitated behavior."

8 Maria P. Root, "Women of Color and Traumatic Stress in 'Domestic Captivity': Gender and Race as Disempowering Statuses," in Marsella et al., eds., *Ethnocultural Aspects of Posttraumatic Stress Disorder*, p.374.

9 Daya Somasundaram, Professor of Psychiatry, personal communication, Jaffna University, Colombo, 1999.

10 Arthur Kleinman, *Writing at the Margin: Discourse between Anthropology and Medicine* (Berkeley: University of California Press, 1995), p.181.

11 Patricia Lawrence, "Grief on the Body: The Work of Oracles in Eastern Sri Lanka," in Michael Roberts, *Sri Lanka: Collective Identities Revisited*, Volume II (Colombo: Marga Institute,1998), pp.271-94.

12 International Classification of Diseases-10, 1992.

13 Judith Lewis Herman, *Trauma and Recovery* (New York: Basic Books, 1992); Robert W. Robin, Barbara Chester, and David Goldman, "Cumulative Trauma and PTSD in American Indian Communities," in Marsella et al., eds., *Ethnocultural Aspects of Posttraumatic Stress Disorder*, pp.239-54.

14 Stephen O'Brien, *Traumatic Events and Mental Health* (Cambridge: Cambridge University Press, 1998), pp.2-3.

15 Herman, *Trauma and Recovery*, p.33.

16 John Briere, *Psychological Assessment of Adult Post-Traumatic States* (Washington, DC: American Psychological Association, 1997), p.18.

17 Friedman and Marsella, "Posttraumatic Stress Disorder"; Herman, *Trauma and Recovery*, pp.9, 118-22.

18 Root, "Women of Color and Traumatic Stress in 'Domestic Captivity,'" p.373.

19 These sporadic attacks, however, are all too meaningful for the few residents of that lonely area, who stay alert to danger night and day, defenceless but for the few shotguns issued to them by the Sri Lanka government.

20 The figures of people who disappeared or died during this time are contested. Conservative estimates put the numbers killed at around forty thousand. The UN Working Group on Enforced and Involuntary Disappearances reported processing over three thousand cases of disappearances for the period between 1988 and 1990 in the Southern and Central provinces alone. Another seven thousand cases for that period were unprocessed at the end of the Group's first visit in October 1991. Following its second visit in 1992, the Group reported receiving an additional five thousand cases to be processed in late 1992. Sasanka Perera, "Beyond the Margins of a Failed Insurrection: The Experiences of Women in Post-Terror Southern Sri Lanka" (paper presented at the University of Edinburgh, 31 October 1997).

21 Perera, "Beyond the Margins of a Failed Insurrection."

22 During the war, internally displaced persons and visitors received passes for limited periods of time (one day, five days, two weeks, or one month). Residents applied for a three-month pass. Travel south of Vavuniya District was only possible for those with a special category of "open" passes. The bureaucratic procedures for obtaining and renewing passes were often tedious, sometimes humiliating, and were reportedly corrupt, despite occasional attempts by the police administration to clean up malpractices that undermined the security agenda. Failure to have a valid pass in Vavuniya resulted in arrest.

23 Rajan Hoole, Daya Somasunderam, K. Sritharan, and Rajani Thiranagama, *The Broken Palmyra: The Tamil Crisis in Sri Lanka – An Inside Account* (Claremont: The Sri Lanka Studies Institute, 1992), pp.201-203, 305-21; and personal communication with internally displaced persons, health personnel, and community workers, Vavuniya, Sri Lanka, 1998.

24 Personal communication with internally displaced persons, health personnel and community workers, Vavuniya, Sri Lanka, 1998.

25 Root, "Women of Color and Traumatic Stress in 'Domestic Captivity,'" pp.374-5.

26 Ibid.

27 Dorothy Smith and Sara J. David, *Women Look at Psychiatry* (Vancouver: Press Gang Publishers, 1975).

28 Stephen Joseph, Ruth Williams, and William Yule, *Understanding Post-traumatic Stress: A Psychosocial Perspective on PTSD and Treatment* (New York: J. Wiley and Sons Ltd., 1997).

Selvy Thiruchandran

Chapter 10

The Other Victims of Terror: Households in Chaos

The phenomenon of large numbers of female-headed households is a post-war development in Sri Lanka. This chapter analyzes the situation within these households by focusing on the psychological, socio-cultural, and economic challenges faced by these women. In 1997, I carried out in-depth research in two districts in the Eastern Province of Sri Lanka – Trincomalee and Amparai – interviewing two hundred primarily lower-class, displaced women from all three communities: Tamil, Muslim, and Sinhala.[1] The sample included women living in refugee camps (ironically called welfare centres), as well as those who had been relocated to newly constructed villages. The research concentrated on capturing the qualitative aspects of these women's lives – their feelings, emotions, and daily routines.

The political causes of the war in the north and east of Sri Lanka are well documented, though each version carries its own biases. The centre of the conflict was first Jaffna and then Batticaloa, but Trincomalee, a particularly sensitive region because of its important natural harbour, was also drawn into the conflict, especially during the final decade of the twentieth century. In Trincomalee, people often referred to 1990 as a year of a major event, and it was, in many ways, equal to 1983, the year of the major communal riots directed against the minority Tamils by the state in the south. In 1990, there was a huge massacre of civilians in Trincomalee by the army. The LTTE attacked the police station in Pothuvil in the Eastern Province, killing many police officers. The army retaliated with force in Trincomalee, creating shock waves and paralyzing the people for several months.

Households in these two regions can be described as units, which are structured around domestic and subsistence activities. Their members live under one roof, pool their resources and labour, and cook and eat together. A household can be made up of one nuclear family or an extended family, several families or a group of unrelated persons. These households are not homogenous, undifferentiated units. They operate within class and caste structures and create differential patterns of expectations and norms. As well, they are constantly subjected to changes, either due to circumstantial, environmental, political, or socio-economic upheavals. When a woman becomes the head of a household, the relationships within the household, as well as between the household and the rest of society, can be disturbed radically.

Relationships within Households in Trincomalee and Amparai

When women assume the role of a head of household in wartime, they are often doing so after having witnessed the brutal death of their spouses (and possibly other family members) or having been left with uncertainty and fear as to why and how the spouse was "disappeared." In addition, they have been displaced many times, are very poor, and are uncertain of what the future holds for them both politically and economically. The women interviewed in the two districts are so severely traumatized that eighty-one of the two hundred women we interviewed had contemplated suicide at some point. They said that the only reason they had resisted this form of escape was the fear that their children would be reduced to orphans and end up roaming the streets as beggars.

It is in the midst of such suffering that these women have to rear their children, which includes trying to help them overcome their own traumas and anxieties. Thus, it is not surprising that many women said they felt that they had become inadequate mothers. One woman remembers trying to change her behaviour after overhearing her ten-year-old daughter complaining to her friends, "My mother is not like others. She does not dress well. She is always worried and unhappy. She gets angry too often or for nothing."

Many women also find it difficult to discuss what they are going through with their children. Some confess that they have hidden the fact of their husband's death from their children and continue to pretend that he has gone abroad temporarily. Some children are too small to comprehend what has happened to their fathers, but others who are either told or find out how their fathers have died have difficulty coping with their grief and anger. They can become a great source of worry to their mothers who do not know how to respond to either their emotional outbursts or sullen silences.

The relationships these women have with their teenage sons are the most troubling to them. At the time of our interviews, several teenage boys had dropped out of school on the pretext of finding jobs or avenging their fathers' killers. They are now unemployed and idle and take out their frustration and bitterness on their mothers, blaming them for all that has befallen the household and resenting their mothers' attempts to discipline them. One boy said, "You should have died, too. Our father will not beat us and scold us. You are ordering us, you tell us don't go there and here, come home before dark. We don't want you. We want our father."

Another boy said, "If *appah* (father) was alive he would give us rice. You are starving us. You have no job, no money. We have no education. What kind of a mother are you? We have no shoes to wear to school. When we come home, we have no food." Some even beat their mothers, but it was the verbal attacks that hurt the women the most, and they sobbed uncontrollably when repeating them to us.

Yet there are also many children who are described as being very helpful to their mothers and who seek to comfort them by contributing to the family's finances, doing odd jobs, helping around the house, and counselling their mothers. Their words and actions frequently remind the mothers of how quickly the war has aged them: "Don't worry, we will look after you. We will get a job soon. We have to be strong and face the future." It is the presence of these children, the women note, which is the only redeeming factor in their lives. As one mother told us,

> They need my love. For their sake I have to live, I have to laugh. If not
> for them, I would have gone mad. I would have committed suicide. I
> forget my worries when I look at the children. I depend on my chil-
> dren for my mental peace. They make me function.

The women said that their suffering as well as their difficult relationships with their children would not have deteriorated as much if they were not so poor. Though some children blamed their mothers for their poverty, these households have always been poor, even before their breadwinners died. The difference now is that they have become completely dependent on what was originally a supplementary income provided by the women, and so they have become the poorest of the poor. The continuation of the war has also made their lives worse by reducing mobility, raising the cost of essential items, and introducing scarcities. These women barely eat one meal a day, and they find it especially difficult to watch their children suffering hunger pangs.

However, this does not mean that the women sit around helplessly waiting for handouts. They try to manage as best as they can by turning their household into a site of production. Some women weave mats and *cadjans* from dried coconut leaves (when sewn together into clusters, *cadjans* can be used to build fences along one's property and as roofing materials), sew clothes, pound paddy, or prepare foods like hoppers and stringhoppers. Others rear poultry, goats, or cattle in their backyards, or convert their front verandas into small shops. As household head, breadwinner, and family caretaker, these women barely have time for relaxation or even sleep. They wake at 4 a.m. and go to bed late at night. Many of their children lead similarly arduous lives, often going from house to house to sell items produced by their mothers before they set off for school and return home to go to bed hungry.

Relationships between Households and the Community

These households are not these women's dominion, a shield against market forces, or havens of expressive love, care, and religiosity. The women I interviewed described their households as places where they carry out most of the labour and have experienced much violence, sacrifice, and suffering. These woman-headed households, though no longer dominated by a patriarchal authority, are not completely free of patriarchal influence in the form of gossip, sexual harassment, and other forms of exploitation and oppressive intrusions from the public domain. At the same time, because of their now socially stigmatized position as widows, as well as their extreme poverty due to the loss of their breadwinners, these women find themselves isolated and alienated from their former friends, associates, relatives, and the community as a whole.

While the women who work outside their home as agricultural labourers or weavers have to worry about how they will be perceived and treated by their employers and co-workers, most of the other women's day-to-day interactions with society are restricted to friends, relatives, and people in their neighbourhoods, and to institutions such as schools, the state, and NGOs.

The Schools

All the mothers say that it is very important to educate their children. However, one of the biggest problems that they have to contend with is how their children are treated at school and their resultant unhappiness and reluctance to go to school. In the same derogatory way that the Tamil and Muslim mothers are referred to as widows, and as "those who have eaten their husbands," their children are also made the butt of hurtful comments from their neighbourhood peers. They are told that they have "eaten their fathers" (*tahapanei tintani*), and sometimes they are ridiculed as "refugees" and "strangers," as those who do not belong to the village. These children are frequently isolated by their peers and not accepted into games and other extracurricular activities.

The absence of a father becomes a stigma when it is translated into the notion that he has deserted the mother and the children. A common comment is "You are the son/daughter of a father who was a terrorist and who ran away." The stigmatization of fatherless households is particularly strong among Muslims. The social status of these households is devalued and they stand condemned in the public eye. What could be sympathy is transformed into derision: "You have no father, how do you manage? What do you eat?" ask the neighbours.

Kaimpenn Valarta kalusarai, kavali, or "the rowdy, the lowly son brought up by a widow," is a term commonly used to describe children who have no fathers. It is not uncommon to hear the child's peer group at the school and in the neighbourhood say, "*Vaapakku etiraha irunta soru tinnavilli* (You don't sit with the father and eat your meals)." This Muslim expression is also an indication of how the status of the child is related to the presence (or not) of a father. Muslim women recognize their own relative powerlessness and tell their children:

> You have no father. Therefore you should not get into unnecessary
> arguments with your friends. No one will stand up for you in the event
> of quarrels and fights. Their fathers will come out and side with them
> and protect them. I can't do that.

Sometimes the children are also humiliated by their teachers, who scold them for not having brought their school fees on time, thus providing additional fodder for derision by the other students. Fortunately, such insensitivity on the part of teachers is an exception rather than the rule, and many of the women are especially thankful for the kindness and caring extended to their children and themselves by school teachers and principals. The mothers told us that sometimes the teachers, who were mostly men, tried to be surrogate fathers to their children. They testified to innumerable instances when the teachers and principals bend rules to waive or reduce the facility fees for the children, buy them pencils and exercise books, and send notes to the mothers requesting special meetings if they notice that the children are psychologically troubled or neglecting their studies.

The State

The women's primary interaction with the state is in the context of procuring financial compensation for the death of their spouses and for the rehabilitation of homes damaged or destroyed by the war. Some women also receive food stamps and charity allowances as widows (these amounts vary according to the number of children they have), while others have been included in state schemes like the Janasaviya program, which provides loans to the poorest of the poor.

However, the financial aid they receive for the repair/construction of their houses is used instead to feed their children and themselves. Much of the monies given as compensation for the death of their spouses is handed out to others who exploit and take advantage of the women because of their gender, their single status, their ignorance of state bureaucracies, as well as their low class and low status in society. Relatives, neighbours, and bureaucrats come forward to help these women to fill out forms, then take them to the officer concerned to expedite the process. When finally the money (on average Rs 50,000) reaches these women's hands, these "helpers" are often the first to lay claim to the money. Only a few women have managed to invest part of this money in small businesses (shops, boutiques) or other income-generating activities such as poultry rearing.

Non-governmental Organizations

The non-governmental agencies (NGOs) have provided assistance to these households in various ways and at various times. They have donated household items in kind as well as given money to the women to purchase items such as books and clothes for their children; they have funded house repairs; they have given repayable, interest-free loans to buy sewing machines and kitchen utensils and to help start goat and poultry rearing. However, much of this support has been in the form of emergency aid rather than in the form of long-term income-generating assistance. Even the few income-generating activities that have been supported by the NGOs have been discontinued because of inability to sustain the activities. When we asked about the demise of these projects, we were told that the women have been unable to pay back the loans. This is sometimes blamed on the NGOs for providing skills training or assistance for self-employed activities. However, the temporary alleviation of poverty through projects the women have started have helped them to pay school fees, hospital charges, or buy medicines. But the assistance of the NGOs and the state to alleviate the extreme situations of poverty in which these women live has been negligible.

Households in Refugee Camps

What I have described so far have been the travails that displaced women encounter whether they are in relocated settings or in refugee camps. However, it is important to document some of the conditions that are unique to refugee camps, which have also made the lives of female heads of household especially difficult. Some of the refugee camps are located at Love Lane, in the Technical College in Anandapuri at Puliyankulam in Trincomalee. A number of these camps are occupied exclusively by Sinhalese. Adjacent to the Sinhalese refugee camps are those occupied by Tamils.

Unlike the resettled villages where women can live in their own homes, the refugee women control only a few metres of ground in large warehouses, which are packed with people. The partitions, which mark each family off from the other, are rarely even made of cardboard; more often they are made with saris and sheets donated by others. The women eat, sleep, and change clothes with little privacy. They often ask other woman or girls to stand watch when they change clothes so that "peeping Toms" can be chased away. It is the same scenario when using the toilets and when bathing. Both men and women have to bathe from the same containers, in which the water is collected from the lorries on a daily basis. Unused to bathing in public under the stares of men and within earshot of their comments, these women find this to be an extremely uncomfortable experience. Yet if they wait until the area is clear of men, there is no water left for them.

In such a context, mothers are especially fearful for their young daughters who are frequently sexually harassed, just as they are, and so the mothers are constantly guarding their daughters. The women note sadly that refugee men protect "their" women – their daughters, wives, and mothers – but look upon other single women as sexual objects. The single woman becomes sexually vulnerable because she is not "owned" and therefore not protected. However, they describe a certain solidarity among the women, so that if a mother leaves the camp to run errands, other women will watch over her daughters.

The refugee camp is seen as a very dangerous place for young children of both sexes. Since their mothers are busy at work inside or outside their makeshift homes all day, the children tend to socialize with the neighbouring adults who play cards, drink, gossip, or indulge in "vulgar sexual jokes." The women complain that these children have not only learned to enjoy this life of idleness but have also been privy to intimate acts between adults. Nor are there many private moments between mothers and their children because the children prefer the "interesting" company of the adult males in the camp. Completing school is also a difficulty. Most school dropouts in our sample are from refugee camps, and this is not surprising since the atmosphere in these camps is not conducive to serious studies. Dim lights, noisy people, and radios and TVs at full volume are the norm.

The Sinhalese women in the camps subscribe to very similar cultural patterns of behaviour as the Muslim and Tamil women. All are concerned about their children's education. As well, they all suffer from a suicide syndrome and experience loneliness and feelings of alienation, including the indifference of relatives. In these respects, their membership in a politically hegemonic ethnic bloc does not necessarily confer any special privileges. Stories similar to those that we heard from the Tamil women are repeated by the Sinhalese women, sometimes using the very same words and phrases.

However there is a difference vis-à-vis widowhood. The rigid patterns of seclusion, and the cultural and social marginalization to which the Tamil women are subjected, are absent among the Sinhala people. There are no rules and conventions imposed on them culturally. Like the other groups interviewed, they too, do not want to marry. But this is not because they are culturally conditioned to the idea of "one man in my life," but because they fear that the children will not be accepted and treated well by a new husband. Unless absolutely necessary, Sinhalese women do not leave the camps, even for neighbourhood socio-cultural events. They express both the fear of leaving their children alone in the camp and personal financial constraints as reasons for avoiding these events.

The Sinhala women whose husbands have been killed by the LTTE did not tend to express anti-Tamil feelings. Their experiences with their Tamil neighbours have helped them to formulate more tolerant attitudes. One Sinhalese woman said that when the LTTE killed her husband, the Tamil neighbours hid the rest of the family in their house. Another woman said,

> We are very friendly with all the neighbours. We do not think of ethnic belonging, whether Sinhalese, Tamil, or Muslim. We mix with all of them freely. We take part in their festivals. When I burned myself, Tamils looked after me and my children. They are generally very helpful.

However, the same kind of feelings are not always expressed by the Tamil women, particularly those from Trincomalee who have not had the opportunity to interact with Sinhala civil society or to enjoy their Sinhala neighbours' company or hospitality. Proximity to the "other" is a major factor in the process of reconstructing either friendship or hostility across ethnic boundaries. The mass killings and disappearances caused by the state apparatus and the attendant brutality have led Tamil women to refer to the state as the "Sinhala State." State terrorism, inter-ethnic tensions and rivalry have constructed a series of antagonistic feelings among all ethnic groups. A Tamil woman said,

> The Sinhalese community in uniform shoots, mutilates, tortures, arrests, and kills the Tamil and Muslims.

A Sinhalese woman said,

> The Tamils want to have a bigger share of the cake, they are selfish and destructive like the LTTE.

Another Tamil woman said,

> The Muslims want to drive away the Tamils from the Eastern province and want to enjoy all the benefits. Not only the Sinhalese, but the Muslims are also against us.

While they are always not anti-Sinhalese in the way they conduct themselves on an everyday basis, two of the Tamil women have sons who have vowed to avenge their fathers' killers. However, their mothers oppose them and say there is no point in harbouring feelings of hatred towards anyone, just to become killers and, in the process, destroy themselves.

The general pattern of consciousness among the women interviewed was that they hated violence and war and longed to have peace and tranquility. There were many women in all three ethnic groups who wanted the state and the LTTE to put an immediate stop to the war brutality. The women in the refugee camps were more articulate than the displaced women living outside refugee camps in their expressions of this view.

Both in the village and in the school, refugee children from all ethnic groups are treated as outcast vagabonds. Among the communities that are affected by war, poverty, and insecurity, there is a refugee hierarchy that defines "refugees" versus "those who belong to the land, to their own habitat." Refugee children, like their parents, are cast in an idiom of other-ness and referred to in a derogatory way as *ahatipillaikal,* which is translated as someone who is socially and economically marginalized. This construction is not a caste or class variation of a hierarchy; it is based on a concept of non-belonging to the very habitat and land of one's birth.

* * *

In most households in Sri Lanka, labour is usually gendered. Food, dress, and emotional needs are taken care of by women, while men concentrate on the finances and the discipline and education of the children. Sometimes, if women are well-educated professionals, they may take on some of the male tasks in the household, but rarely is this reversed. In the lower-class, poverty-stricken, female-headed households that we studied, we found that women are struggling to accomplish both the female and male tasks within their households. Their sons resent them when they try to discipline them, while also accusing them of letting them go hungry and unclothed. So, in trying to be both father and mother to these children, these women sometimes feel that they cannot adequately be either.

The women believe that they are constantly judged and exploited by others in the community, and as a consequence, frequently feel helpless and vulnerable. They express a loss of self-worth, which they say exacerbates the difficulties they confront as heads of their households. Isolated and alienated, it is not surprising that these women cling to their children for support and affirmation and at the same time act as their caretakers and protectors. Yet, despite all these hardships and traumas, the most heartening message is that they continue to struggle and survive. They are sometimes passive and forbearing and frequently restrain their sexuality in order to adhere to rigid patriarchal and societal norms, but they are never silent. They complain, weep, wail, curse, and argue. Though controlled, their protests are loud. They experience patriarchal domination, which manifests itself variously through sexual harassment and in other ways, and they are against the war, against the killings, and against the ethnic/communal violence perpetuated by all sides.

These women are still hoping for a future of peace and tranquility. A return to normalcy is their first desire in terms of their priorities. Often this is expressed through sentiments regarding their children, the children's future, their education, their jobs, and their daughters' marriages. Their children are their nearest kith and often the only hope in their lives. These are some of their statements:

> "I must live for the children." "I must work so that my children can have at least one meal a day." "My aspiration is to educate the children." "My daughter(s) should be married . . . married to good husbands." "The fatherless children should be shown the right path. They must grow up to be good."

They are aware of the patriarchal context in which they live and yet they speak out forcefully against the war, the killings, and ethnic/communal chauvinism. As one woman put it:

> The nation as a whole is under siege – a siege of hatred, suspicion, and "mutual murders." Our children are affected. What do we hope for them . . . insecurity, worries, tension poverty, and starvation? The war must stop!

Notes

1 See Selvy Thiruchandran, *The Other Victims of War: Emergence of Female-Headed Households in Eastern Sri Lanka*, Volume I (New Delhi: Vikas Publishing House Pvt. Ltd., 1999).

Part 3

Politics and Cultures of Resistance

Edith Klein

Introduction

The chapters in this section offer a rich perspective on women's organizing and resistance in the countries which are the subject of this volume. They illustrate the difficult issues that women and men must confront in coming to terms with the political violence of inter-ethnic war and in defining their roles in reconfigured political spaces. A central concern for all the authors is the effectiveness of women's strategies in organizing as women. Here we are shown opposite outcomes from the strategy of affirmative essentialism – where, in Sri Lanka, this strategy has in some cases resulted in the marginalization of women's groups, while in Bosnia it has met with some success in such areas as resettlement and refugee return. Elissa Helms describes in chapter 14 the way in which women's traditional roles in Bosnian patriarchal culture were used to achieve certain political goals; and, indeed, makes the case that those goals might have been unattainable in any other way. Still, in neither of these cases has the resistance of women to the politics of war and nationalism fundamentally challenged the shape of the political terrain, nor has it yet widened the democratic space.

Nowhere is this dilemma seen so clearly as in the way that women's groups organizing against political violence invoke the symbol of motherhood – both as an appeal to a set of universal values and as a strategic weapon. The strategic advantage lies in the unassailable credibility of the maternal ideal within the cultural mainstream, but it can also be exploited and manipulated within the hegemonic nationalist discourse, often to a grotesque degree. The maternal ideal can be a helpful way to mobilize women around an anti-war cause, but, as Kumudini Samuel demonstrates in chapter 13, the Sri Lankan experience shows how entirely possible it is for women to be undermined by more powerful nationalist forces that want to play the same maternal card for nationalist purposes. The Bosnian women of Zenica, for their part, appeared to show sufficient awareness of this danger and responded by keeping their goals narrowly defined and by distancing themselves as much as possible from the much discredited male world of politics. The mutual lessons here may lie in the necessity of women reorganizing against political violence to be clear about separating their mission from that of other political forces – even those with whom they may be in temporary alignment.

It is also worth noting that the strength of the Bosnian women's groups described in this section may be found in the way they absorbed the predominant cultural values into their strategies of resistance rather than overtly challenging them. If expansion of the democratic space to include women was not one of the immediate outcomes, this does not mean one should discredit the strategy. The Bosnian women acknowledged their cultural context in realistic terms – an overwhelmingly patriarchal social order (crypto-matriarchy notwithstanding), highly averse to "feminism," and with idealized and well-defined ideas of male and female roles. They understood that going outside the cultural norms would be strategically counterproductive.

The dominance of the prevailing cultural discourse in Sri Lanka is described by Neluka Silva in chapter 11. She examines the intersection of gender with ethnicity as part of the social fabric in Sri Lanka through the lens of cultural production. The author has studied in a detailed way the language, text, plot development, and visual imagery of several Sri Lankan teledramas that have dealt with the subject of intermarriage. Silva demonstrates that, at least in mainstream cultural production, even "progressive" messages are overwhelmed by the overarching structure of the dominant gender and ethnic discourse. The dramatic depiction of intermarriage appears to be a device that is designed to illustrate for the media-consuming public the dangers and ultimate failure of such relations, but in a gendered language that conflates the feminine, the victim, and the minority individual who is destined for assimilation and loss of her own identity.

Different sorts of questions are raised with regard to the unity and diversity of feminists in Serbia who, while not directly confronted with political violence in the same way as their sisters in other regions of the former Yugoslavia, nevertheless were faced with the challenge of interpreting the violence and atrocities committed by their co-nationals beyond Serbia proper against members of other ethnic groups. They were also challenged by the effort to situate themselves within the larger dilemmas posed by inter-ethnic war – questioning their own sense of national belonging, their understanding of violence, and their roles as mothers, sisters, wives, women. In chapter 12, Lepa Mladjenović concludes that diversity of opinion and mutual tolerance are keys to opening up the democratic space that ought to be, in the view of many of the authors in this volume, an important goal for feminists no matter where they may be.

Confronted with protracted nationalistic violence, Sri Lankan, Bosnian, and Yugoslav feminists and activists have responded, as these authors demonstrate, from a variety of positions that bring diverse interpretations of symbolic ideas and approaches to strategic resistance. From these experiences, several instructive points can be taken. First, sensitivity to cultural conditions needs to be weighed against the costs of violating them, an accounting that can bring different results, depending on the setting. The example of the dramatic fictional treatment of the issue of intermarriage in Sri Lanka on the one hand, demonstrates that even more liberal interpretations of cultural norms can be co-opted by the dominant patriarchal structure. In that same setting, those women's resistant movements that organized around a single issue and adhered closely to cultural norms found themselves eventually dominated by nationalist forces. On the other hand, the careful use of traditional values and confinement to the associated norms can yield important gains, if they are linked, as they appear to have been in the Bosnian case, to specific, highly focused goals. When there are external actors involved – for example, if international non-governmental organizations provide aid during the conflict – the balance can also be affected.

A second point is the connection between politics and resistance. Women's linkages with the mainly male-dominated political arena may be an important factor in ultimately expanding the democratic space to include women in decision-making and to establish women's issues on the political agenda. In the fragile and much contested political space that is at the core of inter-ethnocultural conflict, the windows of opportunity for the fostering of women's issues are rare indeed; yet it is often the case that it is the women in these conflicts who are best positioned to take up the responsibility for inter-ethnic dialogue and reconciliation.

The third point is that the intersection of gender and nationalism in Sri Lanka, Bosnia, and Yugoslavia yields further confirmation that women are "othered" in many possible configurations, whether as rape victims, partners in mixed marriages, family members of deserters or pacifists and, most certainly, as feminists. What is most alarming is how easily that "othering" becomes part of the cultural fabric. It can also survive a conflict long after the cessation of violence.

Neluka Silva

Chapter 11

The Politics of Intermarriage in Sri Lanka in an Era of Conflict

I n 1998, a brigadier of the Sri Lankan army commented that the solution to the ethnic conflict in Sri Lanka lay in Sinhala soldiers marrying Tamil girls. This comment cannot be read as either facetious or idealistic. Rather, it falls within a discourse that has recently been promoted in public and that has gained recognition on a variety of fronts. In 1998, popular television, through the state-owned Rupavahini Corporation, telecast as well as produced several Sinhala teledramas whose focal points were the issue of mixed relationships/marriages in the arena of conflict. The positive codification of these relationships sharply contrasts with previous representations of the traditional antipathy associated with ethno-racial intermixing.

Just as established institutions, socio-political certitudes, and ideologies are thrown into crisis by conflict, so does the issue of intermarriage undergo shifts and mutations. In this chapter, I locate the politics of intermarriage within a discursive framework that has experienced certain historical shifts. I begin by foregrounding the debate on intermarriage in the public discourses during the colonial era, particularly during the movement for Independence. In this discussion, I examine the popular sentiments reflected in the works of ideologues like Anagarika Dharmapala, and the ways in which these sentiments were reinforced in the media of their time. I also demonstrate how the dominant Sinhala Buddhist discourse on intermarriage is transformed and appropriated by other ethnic groups to institute their ethnic superiority.

In dealing with the contemporary scene, post-1983, my discussion begins with the Sinhala teledrama *Sura Asura*. This series marks a water-

147

shed in teledrama history because it charts the relationship between a Sinhala man who is married to a Tamil woman and maps the politics of conflict and how it impinges on their marriage. In the final section, I analyze
the shift in attitude that has occurred since the screening of *Sura Asura*,
vis-à-vis recent representations of the ethnic conflict and the negotiation
of mixed relationships, by examining the three teledramas *Yugavillakuwa*,
Parameshwari, and *Ira Handa Yata*.

The Rise of Sinhala Buddhist Consciousness and Intermarriages

Although Ceylon did not experience a protracted and violent anti-colonial struggle as did some other British colonies, the escalating political
tensions of the late nineteenth and early twentieth centuries were
nonetheless a transformative moment in which competing ethnic identities defined and informed political and personal relationships. The rise of
ethnic-centred nationalisms was a defining characteristic of Ceylon even
in the early years of anti-colonial resistance. Christianity, Westernization,
and British rule were placed along one continuum, and it was felt that all
three had to be rejected:

> It was in the form of a revival of Buddhism and a rejection of the
> efforts of missionary organizations to convert people to Christianity
> that the resistance movement manifested itself as its first and, in retro-
> spect, most profoundly effective expression.[1]

Anagarika Dharmapala's denigration of the colonial project and the
valorization of a "glorious" Sinhala past are recognizable strategies in the
formulation of nationalist thought and sentiment. Part of his nationalist
agenda included designing specific "rules" for the Sinhala Buddhist
layperson, which incorporated a distinct set of prescribed standards of
conduct for women. His brand of Sinhala Buddhist consciousness was
embraced and propagated in cultural production, notably in the novels of
the time and on the stage.

Scholars such as Jayawardena, Obeyesekere, and Roberts, Raheem,
and Colin-Thome[2] have charted the trajectories of identity formation in
the anti-colonial struggle vis-à-vis Westernization. The agenda of the
nationalist ideologues was not simply to construct and maintain a distinct, and what they felt was a pure, ethnic identity but also to police the
boundaries of their groups. Thus, disavowing mixed marriages ensured
the purity of the Sinhalese. Piyadasa Sirisena, a disciple of Dharmapala,
published several Sinhala novels, which, according to E.R. Sarachchandra
were instrumental in the "re-awakening of the national consciousness."[3]

Mutual hostility between ethnic groups is reflected in writings and media representation in this period. Inevitably, negative presuppositions about ethnic groups are most prominently unveiled during moments of familial or socio-political crises, and most perniciously enforced in social rituals such as marriage.

The form of identity politics, which marked the period of decolonization, has re-emerged in post-colonial Sri Lanka with significant differences. Apart from the changes in the socio-political structures, escalating tensions between the Sinhalese and Tamils, which led to racial riots and to the beginning of the current armed conflict in 1983, have reconstituted the terms of reference in the construction of the ethnic "other." In the contemporary culture, the Tamil character is stereotyped and portrayed in racist terms, evident in popular plays like *Uthure Rahula Himi* (Monk Rahula of the North), and teledramas like *Yashorawaya* and *Sura Asura*. Burghers[4] and foreigners are still maligned in a narrowly nationalistic and xenophobic idiom.[5] Such stereotyping of ethnic minorities has created mutually exclusive identity categories, which impinge upon inter-ethnic relations. The rupture of relations is perceived to occur most prominently in the case of mixed marriage.

Sura Asura

Sura Asura, written by Sumithra Rahubadda and directed by Bermin Lylie Fernando, was first screened on the state television channel Rupavahini in 1992-93. The series begins with the courtship of a Sinhalese man, Suranimala, and a Tamil woman, Lakshmi. From the outset it is evident that vehement parental opposition hampers their relationship. When it comes to marriage, both sets of parents are appalled that their children intend to marry outside their ethnic group and religion. Their arguments against the marriage are attendant upon an ethno-racial, cultural, and religious exclusivity that I have described above. It is felt that in transgressing these boundaries, they are betraying community identity. Lakshmi's father demands of her, "Have you forgotten your race?" Her mother follows with, "We can't watch you destroy your life." Her mother also invokes memories of the anti-Tamil racial riots of 1958, which forced them to flee Colombo and find refuge in Jaffna, when she recalls the racial riots of 1977. Underpinning the ethnic antipathy of Lakshmi's parents is an anxiety over how the reverberations of a mixed marriage will affect the rest of her family; one possibility is that it will mar the marriage prospects of the younger sisters. Thus ethnic identity, and the maintenance of it, provides security along with a sense of respectability for the entire family.

In this teledrama, Sinhala chauvinism also forges its identity markers in similarly narrow parameters. Significantly, Suranimala's father, representing the voice of patriarchy, invokes ethno-sexist stereotypes in his objection to his son's marriage. He says to his son that when "a Tamil woman hangs around your neck," it is a sign of her "cunning," and concludes that "even a street woman [prostitute], if she is Sinhalese, is acceptable to us, rather than a Tamil," thus imputing a higher value to Sinhalaness despite the negative gender stereotyping. Similar patriarchal overtones resonate throughout the series, and Suranimala is frequently guilty of wielding his dominance over his wife. For example, when Lakshmi voices her desire to go to Jaffna with her children, he reacts by saying, "In this house, I make the decisions" – an assertion of the intrinsic power relations within the familial domain. His children are brought up as Sinhalese, and there is no indication that any attempt is made to teach them their "mother tongue." Rather, all the interactions take place in Sinhala, even between the mother and children. Lakshmi's language, therefore, is not provided a space in what Suranimala perceives as a "Sinhala" household.

The ethnic riots and subsequent events shore up the rupture in their relationship. Lakshmi's mental and physical trauma are effectively captured as she is placed at the mercy of her husband and his parents. After losing their home (which is looted and burned), her parents-in-law use the excuse of the children's safety to take them away from their mother. I use the term "excuse" here because it becomes an expedient device by which the grandparents can ensure that the Sinhala religious and cultural norms are systematically transmitted to the children, portrayed, for instance, in the Buddhist Jataka stories related to them by their grandfather. Every effort is made to inculcate Sinhala values in the children, and this is manifest during the family's visit to Lakshmi's parents home in Jaffna. The children are unable to interact with their grandparents and aunts in Tamil, a testimony to the influence of majority politics in personal relationships. Nira Yuval-Davis and Floya Anthias have emphasized the significance of consciously teaching and transferring the cultural and ideological norms of ethnic and national groups.[6]

After the riots, Suranimala's underlying racial prejudices are made visible in the seemingly facetious comments he makes about Tamils to his Tamil colleague Sathya. "Two Tamils make an association," he sneers and constantly remarks on their perceived "stinginess." These prejudices also have an insidious effect on his marriage. Suranimala's suspicion of Lakshmi's friendship with a Tamil doctor is based on the assumption that their Tamilness is a point of attraction and commonality. His jealousy, and subsequent maltreatment of Lakshmi, is vindicated by such essentialist statements as "two people of different races cannot live together." While Suranimala makes racist comments about the ethnic conflict, Lakshmi's opinion is negated on the grounds that "you have no right to talk about the Sinhalese." Suranimala's attitude of ethnic superiority is bolstered by patriarchal notions, which assume that when a woman gets married, part of the assimilation process requires that she abandon her premarital identity.

The culmination of *Sura Asura* is the "rescue" of Lakshmi and the children from the militants by Suranimala who goes to Jaffna to find them. Although the estranged couple is reconciled, the overwhelming impression created throughout the series is that a mixed marriage has negative consequences. A lukewarm ending, encoding an optimistic tone, does not rehabilitate the series from the overwhelming negativity engendered by the overlay of religio-cultural differences portrayed in Suranimala and Lakshmi's relationship. The stereotypes that the series sought to perpetuate were an attempt to prove that unions between two ethnic groups are impossible.

It is perhaps this ideological climate that determined the reluctance on the part of the Censor Board to air the series on the state television station. Some members of the Censor Board insisted on getting clearance from the Ministry of Defence, and clearance was only granted after much editing. The director pointed out that audience reactions were fairly negative: "One person told me that after watching six episodes he had forbidden his family members from watching this show."[7] It is perhaps the ambivalent ending, which does not portray the mixed relationship as unproblematic, that accounted for the negative reception at the time *Sura Asura* was screened in 1992.

A simplistic depiction of intermarriages, which does not confront or problematize the overarching gender or ethnic hegemonies, is blatantly promoted as the replacement for the *Sura Asura* paradigm in an abundance of recent teledramas. This shift in the ideological stance can be situated within the present socio-political matrix. The People's Alliance was voted into power in 1994 on a mandate to solve the ethnic conflict, though it is now committed to a military solution. Public discourses, via conduits such as the media, sought a range of approaches to grapple with the conflict such as the state-funded Sudu Nelum (White Lotus) campaign, which attempted to promote understanding among Sinhala, Tamil, and Muslim communities.

Recent Teledramas

In the past, the war itself or, more precisely, armed combat and its conse-quences, has not entered the public arena except in news reports on televi-sion or in the newspapers. Recently, however, large segments of combat footage have been interwoven into some of the new teledramas. In *Yugav-illakuwa* and *Parameshwari*, these scenes reach a point of overkill. At least one or two scenes in each of the twenty-odd episodes of *Yugavillakuwa* concentrate on combat scenes. Inevitably, this becomes tedious. However, these scenes are a point of departure from earlier representations of the conflict, and what is of particular interest is the way in which mixed rela-tionships are a point of focus within the framework of armed combat.

In the above two series, as well as in *Ira Handa Yata*, there is little variation from the *Sura Asura* intermarriage theme: a male Sinhala sol-dier falls in love with a Tamil girl, but unlike the earlier instances, parental opposition is lukewarm. Although the stereotypical arguments are invoked, there are other characters who enthusiastically support the rela-tionship. Inevitably, the family comes to terms with their son's choice of a marriage partner. The only virulent opposition is from militant Tamil men, who see the soldier as diluting their separatist cause by falling in love with one of "their own" women.

In *Parameshwari* and *Ira Handa Yata*, the Tamil girls are clearly posi-tioned in the role of victims. Each one lives with a family that has lost one or several members to the conflict. Their near-refugee status is dis-rupted by the intervention of a Sinhala soldier. In *Parameshwari*, he is injured by the militants and nursed by Parameshwari and her family, and the soldier in turn rescues her from death when the militants discover her liaison with the enemy. In *Ira Handa Yata*, the soldier helps the Tamil girl's family when they flee to a refugee camp and, as in *Sura Asura*, pro-tects her from death. The soldier in each case rejects a Sinhala fiancée (who is approved by his family), for the sake of the Tamil girl.

Such scenes are underscored by a confluence of socio-political, gender, and cultural dynamics. War, especially nationalist conflict, is a "male drama," as Elleke Boehmer has noted.[8] Conflict harnesses the myth of masculine stoicism, the ability to endure any physical or emotional hard-ship, and such images are aligned with the heroic. In her exploration of the Gulf War, Malathi de Alwis illustrates how war and heroism are gen-dered within public discourses where first, war is perceived as "man's work," and second, military training requires a discourse on humiliation that relies on using feminized terms such as "girl," so that "a recruit becomes conditioned to prove himself in opposition to these identities."[9] These images are exploited in the teledramas where the physical prowess of the soldier is heightened through shots of him in combat. Even when he is injured (as in *Parameshwari*), and although it appears that the pain is excruciating, his manner suggests masculine stoicism. He is almost always portrayed in army fatigues, so the viewer is rarely allowed to forget that he is first and foremost a soldier.

By placing the woman at the mercy of the Sinhala soldier, the notion of victimhood is crucial, not only to deny her any possibility of agency but also to secure the soldier's masculinity by conferring a degree of heroism upon him. The departure here from the norm is that, on a figurative level, he is defending his "motherland." On a literal level, the woman he physically defends is one of the enemy. This position is denigrated because he, like the non-hero, the revolutionary, the pacifist, and the soldier who is emotionally incapacitated by armed conflict, falls outside the parameters of dominant discourse. As the commanding officer in *Parameshwari* reminds him, "It is a shame to go after the enemy." Interestingly, though, the teledrama ensures that whoever he protects does not destabilize his masculinity. He maintains his masculinity by warding off the Tamil (male) militants who attempt to kill his fiancée.

Such definitions of masculinity bolster the representational efficacy of nationalist conflict, and are used to counterpose certain idealized feminized images of woman-as-nation.[10] While the image of mother has very striking resonance in iconographies of conflict, in terms of the teledramas I am examining, the female roles correspond to a romanticized notion of the "daughter" who is dutiful and chaste and assigned value as a "future" mother. However, the solidity of this position is fractured by the protagonists' transgression of the ethnic boundaries through intermarriages. Since circumstances make them traitors to their ethnic group, the threat has to be dispelled by its self-appointed sentinels, the male militants. The women become the malefactors in the equation, providing validation for the Sinhala soldiers to protect them from their own kind.

Despite the initial, overt antagonism and traditional arguments that are espoused, these mixed relationships are eventually endorsed by the (Sinhala) families and their social networks. The terms of approbation reach a level where, for instance, in *Ira Handa Yata*, after having discarded their son for marrying a Tamil woman, it is the daughter-in-law who finally provides the greatest support to the family during her father-in-law's illness, leading to the parents' acknowledgement that "it is only you that we can turn to." In *Parameshwari*, although the commanding officer initially condemns the relationship, he then sanctions it on the grounds that "we must have mixed marriages, and a mix of cultures, because if not, those who win will be the terrorists or the nationalists."

In *Yugavillakuwa* the relationship between the Sinhala army doctor, Charitha, and the Tamil doctor, Revathi, is represented as ill-fated from the start. Despite their attraction to each other, the couple resists emotional involvement until the very end, when Revathi flees to Charitha's army camp in Jaffna. What is striking here, in contrast to previous attempts at presenting interracial relationships, is the rationale for avoiding such a liaison. Revathi's reluctance to become involved with a Sinhala man is not based on the obvious reasons of ethnic, religious, or linguistic differences, but rather on her commitment to the civilians of Jaffna. Other characters in the series also recognize and accept their attraction to each other. The final moments of the series could thus be read as a visual enactment of larger societal approval. They meet their deaths while attempting to rescue a child who seems to be abandoned in the middle of the road (it is a ploy by the militants). Besides the pathos, the final image of the interracial "family" gestures towards a different future, perhaps of the kind alluded to by the commanding officer in *Parameshwari*. Increasingly, the image of the future evoked here is of a male child, once again securing the future of the Sinhalese race. Assimilating into another ethnic group seems to imply that a son will carry on the father's name and race.

Similar articulations occur in *Parameshwari* and *Ira Handa Yata*. However, the configuration of the interracial relationship promoted in the media and the public discourses seems to adhere to a paradigm that is problematic. In the teledramas explored, the woman belongs to the Tamil minority, while the man is drawn from the Sinhalese majority (the converse situation has thus far not merited representation in the public arena). In marrying a Sinhala man, the politics of assimilation come into play. It can be assumed that these women will relinquish their Tamil surnames and accept their husbands' Sinhala names, omitting a vital component of their identities. Although in *Sura Asura* Lakshmi continues to wear the *pottu* (a mark of her ethnicity), in *Ira Handa Yata* the protagonist discontinues wearing this, a further effacement of her Tamilness.

Language is also a crucial determinant of these relationships' parameters. In every case, the woman communicates with her husband/lover in Sinhala, while the man does not endeavour to learn or converse in Tamil. When it comes to the question of mixed marriage, it is perhaps presupposed that the minority has to succumb to the linguistic hegemony of the majority. The children from such a union are also forced to embrace Sinhala, thereby perpetuating the dominant power structures. Language in these media representations is problematic. Escalating ethnic and nationalist conflicts reinvest power in the national language because it signifies cultural integrity and transmits a sense of homogeneity. Jingoistic nation-

alist sentiments, transmitted through and defined by linguistic constructions, become the cutting edge for racism.

Concomitant with implausible story lines, these inbuilt hegemonies
prompt a simplistic resolution to an immensely complex conflict, making
it easy to dismiss these teledramas on the grounds of ethnic chauvinism.
While it is important to foreground these limitations, it is also necessary
to recognize their progressive content. Thus, I am loath to read these representations as a conscious state-instituted strategy to bolster Sinhala
nationalism. Rather, I read them as a problematic attempt at assimilation,
and an extremely naive one at that. Judging from the reality and preva-
lence of intermarriages and intermixing throughout Sri Lanka's history, it
may be possible to see these teledramas as striving towards negotiating a
fundamental reality that has hitherto been suppressed, thus counterbal-
ancing the erasure of a phenomenon that takes on threatening overtones
in an era of conflict. At the same time, the gendered nature of these kinds
of hegemonies within a "liberal" project is completely lost. Even if there
is no conscious effort to overtly promote the dominant ideologies, it is
evident at a subtextual level.

* * *

Culture, especially that which appears on state-controlled television, is
inevitably tied up with the requirements of the nation. The very real economic and political forces threatening its sovereignty and legitimacy determine the regulation of cultural production. As Lila Abu-Lughod argues:

> A close examination of the strategies writers and others pursue to con-
> struct national identities through constructing cultural essences reveals
> that because their efforts are tied so closely to contemporary national
> debates and dilemmas, they are likely to be undermined by conflicting
> ideologies and the actual social experiences of the people to whom they
> are directed.[11]

The urgency of promoting mixed relationships in recent teledramas is
related to the controls imposed by the state and the attempt to strengthen
the fabric of a nation, which has been threatened by ethnic conflict.
While playwrights and filmmakers who can perform or show their works
in relatively secure places, shielded from the exigencies of the state, offer a
more challenging range of ethnic possibilities, those who aspire to reach
wider audiences still have to engage with the constraints imposed by the
Ministry of Defence as alluded to by the director of *Sura Asura*. This disjuncture between theory and practice reveals the anxieties of a nation in
crisis. When atypical circumstances force a breakdown of "traditional"
social and gender values, it is also the moment that hegemonic institu-

tions most vehemently reinforce ethno-racial and sexist chauvinism in socio-political praxis.[12]

Notes

1 K.M. de Silva, *A History of Sri Lanka* (London: C. Hurst, 1981), p.339.

2 Kumari Jayawardena, *Feminism and Nationalism in the Third World* (London: Zed Books, 1986); Kumari Jayawardena, "Some Aspects of Religious and Cultural Identity and the Construction of Sinhala Buddhist Womanhood," in Douglas Allen, ed., *Religion and Political Conflict in South Asia* (New Delhi: Oxford University Press, 1993); Gananath Obeyesekere, "The Vicissitudes of the Sinhala-Buddhist Identity through Time and Change," in M. Roberts, ed., *Collective Identities, Nationalisms and Protest in Modern Sri Lanka* (Colombo: Marga Institute, 1979), pp.279-313; M. Roberts, I. Raheem, and P. Colin-Thome, *People in Between: The Burghers and Middle Class in the Transformations within Sri Lanka 1790's-1960's* (Ratmalana: Sarvodaya Press, 1989).

3 Quoted in Roberts, Raheem, and Colin-Thome, *People in Between*, p.10.

4 Burghers are the descendants of the Europeans. As a situation unknown in some erstwhile colonies, Sri Lanka's long history of colonialism led to the formation of an ethnic minority that was distinct from the English-speaking Sinhalese or Tamils. These were descendants of the Portuguese and Dutch, mostly Christian and whose first language was neither Sinhala nor Tamil.

5 Neluka Silva, "Representation as 'Othering the Other': Non-Sri Lankan in Sinhala Theatre," in *Pravada* 1,9 (1992), p.32. The two teledramas *Yashorawaya* and *Sapphire and Silk* position the Burgher woman and the foreign woman within a narrowly xenophobic discourse. These two characters are portrayed as promiscuous, Westernized, and responsible for the disruption of the traditional family unit.

6 Nira Yuval-Davis and Floya Anthias, "Women and the Nation-State," in John Hutchinson and A. D. Smith, eds., *Nationalism* (Oxford: Oxford University Press, [1989] 1994), p.314.

7 Bermin Lylie Fernando, "The Story Behind Sura Asura," *The Sunday Times*, June 21, 1992, p.13.

8 Elleke Boehmer, "Motherlands, Mothers and Nationalist Sons: Representations of Nationalism and Women in African Literature," in Anna Rutherford, ed., *From Commonwealth to Post-colonial* (Aarhus: Dangaroo Press), p.223.

9 Malathi de Alwis, "The Manliness of War and the Abstractions of Death: A Feminist Critique of the Gulf War," *Pravada* 1, 2 (1992), p.26.

10 Neluka Silva, "The Representation of Nation and Gender in Selected Contemporary Writing from India, Sri Lanka and Pakistan" (Ph.D. diss., University of Leeds, 1997), p.10.

11 Lila Abu-Lughod, "Asserting the Local as National in the Face of the Global: The Ambivalence of Authenticity in Egyptian Soap Opera," in Ali Mirsepassi, Amrita Basu, and Frederick Weaver, eds. *Localizing Knowledge in a Globalizing World: Recasting the Area-Studies Debate* (Syracuse: Syracuse University Press, in press), p.22.

12 Silva, "The Representation of Nation and Gender . . . ," p.23.

Lepa Mladjenović

Chapter 12

Feminist Politics in the Anti-war Movement in Belgrade:
To Shoot or Not To Shoot?

"**G**ood girls go to heaven, bad girls to Ljubljana" was the title of the Fourth Yugoslav Feminist Meeting held in May 1991 in Ljubljana, Slovenia. The organizers of that conference could not have known at the time the depth of meaning that "heaven and hell" would have in the context of the pain that was to devastate many women across the homeland in the years of war and fascism that followed.

Women's groups in the former Yugoslavia were just beginning to organize actively in the early 1990s. Feminist activists from Ljubljana (Slovenia), Zagreb (Croatia), and Belgrade (the former Yugoslavia) were planning a meeting of the SOS Hotlines (the three initial feminist services for women survivors of violence) to discuss issues of male violence for the first time. New initiatives were being organized to support women in policy-making: a forum entitled "Women's Parliaments" was held in Belgrade and Zagreb; a Women's Party was established in Belgrade; and a Women's Lobby was set up in Belgrade, Zagreb, and Ljubljana. Feminists across the former Yugoslavia were collaborating, learning from each other, and enthusiastically enjoying the beginnings of feminism together. New issues and ideas were being raised, such as changes to the legal system; support for women in political parties; the launching of women's studies courses and programs; new theoretical work on the "woman question"; and the consolidation of feminist lesbian initiatives in Croatia and Slovenia. Feminists were forging links across the regions and the continents, and all this activism was occurring when women's groups still lacked space and money.

In 1991, in the state bordering the Adriatic Sea, which is now called the former Yugoslavia, there were twenty-two million inhabitants, twenty-one languages, twenty-five ethnic groups, and six republics. Thirty-nine per cent of those employed were women. Neither nationalism nor abortion was yet an issue among feminists; abortion had been legalized in 1976 and was provided free through the national health system. The state position on nationalism was "brotherhood and unity." On average, more than 70 per cent of urban families had washing machines. Kindergartens were free, although there were not enough of them. Education and medical care were paid for by the state. While trade unions did little for workers' rights, at least they made certain that workers and their families had holidays. "Communism before 1991," we used to say, "was a paradise for children."

On 27 June 1991, the lesbian and gay group ARKADIA was having its first public discussion in Belgrade on the "Right to be Different," when the 7:30 p.m. state-TV news announced that the first Slovenian soldier had been killed by a Yugoslav soldier in Slovenia. It was a sunny and warm day in Belgrade, and people were enjoying the beaches on the local river. While I was not aware at the time that this was the first day of the wars to come, and that just three months later I would be one of the founders of the Women in Black group, the feminist in me wondered how men could walk off the beach, pick up guns, and kill other men. Belgrade, the city in which I live, became a symbol of the Serbian regime, a place for manufacturing fascist politics and nationalism, a home to killers, war rapists, and war profiteers. The years of war shaped many of us as feminists in Belgrade. During this period there were numerous disagreements among activists on every issue except one: that the dictatorship of the Serbian regime had to go.

Some of the most hurtful issues in wartime come up around the question, *To shoot or not to shoot?* Disagreements and misunderstandings among Belgrade feminists have been frequent, but during the war they were often particularly painful. Many of the issues experienced by women in war zones are also experienced by feminists who work in states that are not at war. However, the nearness of torture and death and the level of fear intensifies differences. Thus, disagreements in wartime do not always remain simply different points of view: some perspectives incorporate the logic of revenge, which result in choosing militaristic options and death. Many of these issues are not talked about, in order to avoid pain. Before I discuss the question of *To shoot or not to shoot?* I will describe three moments of women's lives in war.

Dilemmas of Everyday Life in a War Zone

Everyday life throughout the women's peace movement in Belgrade in 1991 did not involve the same survival issues as those faced by women from Bosnia and Herzegovina, Croatia, and Kosova, where war swept over their bodies. However, the echo of their pain was always present – as a background to the activist work of those of us who were not "on the front line." We heard their voices through letters and stories told during and after the war, and through the workshops that we organized in our peace movement. Their voices held fear and hope, which in wartime are always associated with militarization.

A young activist, who was seventeen years old when the war began in Bosnia, describes her desperation and exhaustion after four years of war, sniper hits, bombings, concentration camps, rapes, and killings:

> Every day I did something in order to survive war, small things, supporting others, finding food, keeping warm . . . and then at nights I wished that someone would hit us with a huge bomb, an atomic nuclear bomb, anything, and kill all of us together so that all this horror would be over for everyone, once and for all.

Another woman from Bosnia wrote to us in the third year of war, in 1994:

> Some of us in Sarajevo have a daytime dream that foreign planes will circulate above the Serbians' hidden places in the hills from where they shoot at us every day, and bomb them, kill them all, and finish with this bloody Bosnian story forever.

An Albanian woman from Kosova describes the fears she felt in 1999:

> When the NATO bombing started in my town, Djakova, there was a fire on the third day. We called in the fire brigade. Serbs who were working there said: "NATO is bombing you from above and us from underneath." We had a fear of bombs, but we knew that there would be an end to Milošević's tyranny after NATO, so that fear was nothing compared with the fear we had of the Serbian police. After ten years of Serbian repression and humiliation, the fear of the Serbian police was enormous. My whole body shakes now even when remembering.

In the last decade of the twentieth century, approximately five million people from the entire territory of the former Yugoslavia had to move from their homes at least once. These people are called refugees, displaced persons, exiles, immigrants, and deserters. The last ethnic cleansing took place in Kosova in 1999, when 750,000 people of Albanian nationality were expelled by the Serb police and the military over the course of seventy-seven days to Albania and Macedonia. After their return to Kosova, more then 220,000 citizens of Serb and Roma nationality were then expelled by the Kosova Liberation Army.

Contradictions among Feminists

To Shoot or Not to Shoot?

> When a soldier comes to your door to shoot at you or your daughter, what should you do? Shoot back or not?

This was one of the first questions that some of us posed to each other in 1991. Feminists at that time had little experience with a culture of ethics that would suggest an easy answer. The former Yugoslavia had suppressed religion and, in any case, Yugoslav feminists derived few ideas if any from religious morality. Marxist politics had argued that we should defend our ideas "even if it came to blood." However, by 1991, Marxism had lost its popularity in the everyday lives of Yugoslavs. And finally, the former-Yugoslav system had annihilated the notion of human rights. Thus, feminist activists found themselves in a political void with limited knowledge of the history of human rights or international peace politics.

Nor had feminism as a theoretical body or a movement developed sufficiently to effect social change or to influence women's consciousness. At that moment in time, those of us living in a non-war zone (i.e., a zone that was not affected by direct military actions) did not know how other feminists would answer the question, *To shoot or not to shoot?* Our first three dilemmas were:

1. If we shoot, then there is no end to shooting, we enter the *circuit of revenge*.
2. If we don't shoot, maybe they/he will shoot me?
3. Is it not motherly to want to shoot the one who wants to shoot my daughter? (See also chapters 13 and 14.)

Feminists who declared that they would *not* shoot felt hurt by those who said *yes,* they would shoot. Those who said *yes* to shooting felt betrayed by those who said *no*; they believed that the pacifists were prepared to let anyone be killed and therefore did not trust them. Feminist pacifists were not sure of the line between shooting to defend and shooting to kill, and therefore did not trust those feminists who said they would shoot. With the outbreak of war, women found themselves divided on the question along the lines of pro- or anti-nationalist feelings and interests. Women whose relatives were in combat were perplexed, especially those who had already made a very clear decision not to shoot.

Pro-nationalists would defend shooting in defence some of the time, but not all of the time. Feminist pacifists asked, How shall we be feminists if we say *yes* to shooting? How shall we be pacifists if we follow the line of the "Big Serbian Intellectuals" who cite "the nation's father" Dobrica Čosić as saying, "Serbs have a historic excuse to shoot first in defence"? And all of us asked:

- Where is the line between shooting first and shooting second?
- Are all feminists supposed to be pacifists?
- Are pacifists always and totally against any shooting?
- Are pacifists cowardly or courageous?
- Do we have examples of history being changed and wars being stopped by *peaceful resistance*?
- Is it easier to say *no* to taking up the gun if you are outside the war zone than if you are being shot at daily?
- In the very moment when your nation is attacked, how is pacifism interpreted: as a betrayal of the national interests or as a no-war option?
- Can we end all wars by means of wars?

There were many different responses to these questions among feminists in Belgrade. It was clear that all of us engaging in these discussions were still sitting in our homes and were not yet threatened by war. The dilemma around to shoot or not to shoot had other dimensions in the early period of the war, which we feminists explored and deconstructed by asking the following questions:

- Are you speaking from the site of a nation that is a "victim" or one that is an "aggressor"? In other words, what was your address when the war started?
- Do you have emotional bonds (relatives, ties to a birthplace, religion, friends, spouses, lovers or memories of lovers) in the region of the "other" (the enemy)?
- Do you have strong national feelings for the region in which you live (relatives, ties to a birthplace, religion, friends, spouses, lovers or memories of lovers)?
- What experiences of violence have you have had in your life (previous wars, male violence, prison, sexual violence)?
- Are you a mother of male children who may be recruited into the military?

These were just some of the political issues that were crucial in making the decision to shoot or not to shoot. However, the way one responded to these questions was not always determined by whether or not one was a feminist – the emotional imprints of life often had a more important role to play in answering this question. We learned that asking if feminists should be pacifists would always be an open-ended question, as would asking if pacifism meant not shooting at all (under any circumstances).

Military Intervention: Yes or No?

If military intervention will stop the war, what would you vote? Yes or no?

This new dilemma developed during the military intervention in Bosnia and Herzegovina in 1995, and in the Federal Republic of Yugoslavia in 1999; and it developed in relation to new historical facts. In 1995, the forty-month siege of Sarajevo ended after seven days of international military intervention by air. The Serbian snipers finally stopped shooting the citizens of Sarajevo after NATO bombed Serb military targets (and the dream of many Sarajevans came true). After many unsuccessful previous efforts, this intervention led to the peace initiative in November 1995.

The 1995 intervention shifted the discussions from *To shoot or not shoot?* to a new dilemma of *Military intervention: yes or no?* Feminists were again split along the lines of pro-nationalist and anti-nationalist sentiments. Those with pro-nationalist feelings did not like the idea of a big power shooting at "their soldiers" and were therefore against military intervention. Feminists who believed that their role was first of all to understand the "other" felt that Bosniacs had been freed after the military involvement and that this fact must be taken into consideration in deciding *yes* or *no* to military intervention. Their pro-intervention standpoint was not usually stated publicly because it was unsafe to do so. Instead, they publicly criticized their own fascist regimes as a way to oppose the war. Feminist pacifist groups like Women in Black, and their leader Staša Zajović, always proclaimed themselves as anti-militarists. For this group, there was no excuse for military action and they argued that all sides should stop military activities immediately.

However, anti-militarist activists were not always pacifists. The founder of the Centre for Anti-War Action in Belgrade, Vesna Pešić, supported international military intervention in Bosnia and Herzegovina even before it actually happened. But when the 1999 NATO bombings began on her territory of Belgrade, she opposed it. Sonja Biserko, the director of the Serbian Helsinki Committee of Human Rights (Belgrade), agreed with the military interventions in Bosnia and Herzegovina as well as in the Federal Republic of Yugoslavia. It was clear that not only feminists but also human rights activists had diverse opinions on military intervention.

In 1999, two military actions occurred simultaneously: the NATO bombings of the FR Yugoslavia, including Serbia, and the Serbian regime's ethnic cleansing of the Albanian citizens of Kosova. This created more divisions in Belgrade, including divisions among pacifists themselves. To understand this political situation, it is important to know that by not signing the Paris and Rambouillet treaties, Slobodan Milošević indirectly "signed" an agreement to allow the NATO bombings. Feminist anti-fascists regarded him as being responsible for the bombings, while feminist pro-nationalists claimed that NATO was responsible. Before the NATO bombings, all foreign monitors and the international community had to leave the FR Yugoslavia and Kosova; this created the perfect condition for Serbian fascists who forced Albanian citizens out of Kosova. The ethnic cleansing plan was carried out during the same seventy-seven days of the bombings. Thus, anti-fascist feminists took the position that Milošević was responsible for both the NATO bombings and the ethnic cleansing. Pro-nationalist feminists opposed military intervention and took the position that NATO was responsible for the bombings; they did not talk about the ethnic cleansing.

After the NATO bombings, the Serbian regime was forced to relinquish its power. The ten years of low-intensity war against the Albanian population in Kosova had ended, as well as the seventy-seven days of ethnic cleansing. With the culmination of these events, *Military intervention: yes or no?* became an issue for feminists from Kosova. Most said *yes*: their immediate experience of military intervention was the elimination of ten years of Serbian fascism in the period immediately following the NATO bombings. A few individual peace activists from Women in Black Against War in Belgrade sided with them. They were disgusted with ten years of constant Serbian fascism and regarded the international military intervention as the only way to stop this. Anti-fascist feminists in Serbia who were not so explicitly against military intervention wanted to reach beyond their personal feelings of fear by trying to understand the feelings and positions of feminists from Kosova. Many other feminists in Serbia who had lived through the bombings and the accompanying terror did not have any doubts that they were against military intervention, now that it had happened over their heads. The vast destruction of the infrastructure and the increase of hatred and fear was enormous, considering it had "just" been seventy-seven days.

During these days of bombings there was a complete political turnover: the *peace option* became an ideology of the Serbian fascist regime expressed through official "peace concerts in the piazza." Republic Square, which was the site of the vigils by the Women in Black against the Serbian regime, was taken over by the regime whose slogan became "For Peace!" In addition to local patriotic militaristic music (from the First and Second World Wars), flags appeared on the streets, together with patriotic badges, hats, and postcards.

Fear had shaped most of the political options during the seventy-seven days of bombings. The Kosova Albanian women testified that they feared the Serbian police and paramilitaries during the NATO strikes far more than the bombings. They saw the Serbian regime as the only source of war; while the Serbians only feared NATO and saw NATO as the only source of war. The regime controlled the media so completely that citizens in Serbia did not receive news of the ethnic cleansing of Albanians. In such a concrete historical situation of two concurrent wars, anti-fascists and pacifists had to be careful. Now the dilemma was whether it was a realistic option or an idealistic option to take a pacifist position against both NATO and Serbian fascist ethnic cleansing. NATO bombings had not only destroyed the military and police headquarters (which pleased some anarchists and anti-fascists) but also the lives of five hundred citizens, and most of the industry and infrastructure. Yet Albanian citizens felt grateful to NATO for ending their pain. Their experience was one of liberation, for which they had waited many years.

Feminist anti-fascist politics in Serbia in 1999, therefore, did not always accompany a non-military intervention option. As well, the many different peace groups had a variety of political analyses of military actions. Peace was not the absolute choice for each peace activist, anti-fascist, leftist, human rights activist, anarchist, or feminist. Some peace activists who chose to agree with the military intervention in 1999 still remained Women in Black peace activists, although Women in Black was against all militarist action, ethnic cleansing, and NATO bombings. In 1999, the terms "feminist" and "peace activist" in relation to the question *To shoot or not to shoot?* became even more complex.

In the meantime, the notion of peace in the international community changed. The so-called European Left parties, which in the 1990s were peace-oriented by definition, voted in their respective parliaments in 1999 *for* NATO intervention because global politics had changed. The function of the United Nations as the anti-war institution changed as well, since it too had voted for NATO intervention. In this highly militaristic international context, feminist peace activists who chose peace as a means of reaching peace became a small, radical, and brave group of women. Despite the fact that during the ten years of war in the region of the former Yugoslavia the peace movement did not change the militaristic course of the war, its persistence was extremely important as a statement of the possible existence of civil society even during fascism.

* * *

The first dilemma that I discussed in this chapter was *To shoot or not to shoot?* The second dilemma was *Military intervention: yes or no?* which emerged during the NATO military intervention. The increasing complexity of these two dilemmas during the ten years of war in the region of the former Yugoslavia can be summarized as follows:

- The lack of military intervention in July 1995 in Srebrenica, Bosnia and Herzegovina, led to the disappearance and massacre by the Serbian military of eight thousand Bosniac men in a period of two weeks. After this, the decision was made to prepare military intervention against the Serbian military and paramilitary around Sarajevo, which was carried out two months later.
- The politics of peaceful resistance led by the Kosova political leader, Ibrahim Rugova, during the low-intensity war against Albanian citizens from 1989-99 was unsuccessful. Ten years of *peaceful resistance* by Kosova leaders had not succeeded in attracting the attention or the help of the international community! Only after the Serbian regime had committed grave violent crimes of mass killings did the international community react in support. One can argue here that only violent acts are noticed and registered, that violence is the reaction to them, and that this is the patriarchal cycle of male violence, which is based on a cycle of vengeance through violence.
- The war in Bosnia and Herzegovina ended after a week of international military intervention by air against Serbian military positions in September 1995, which resulted in the signing of the Dayton Peace Accords in December 1995.
- The Serbian repression of Albanian nationals in Kosova ended after the NATO bombings in the spring of 1999.

These examples from the former Yugoslavia, in which military intervention ultimately put an end to the violence of war, suggests that the orthodox peace position needs to be rethought in order to include many different peaceful dimensions and positions. These examples also demonstrate that the patriarchal military system is part of everyday life (see Elissa Helms in chapter 14). This then leads to a new question, *Who asks for military intervention and for what reasons?* Obviously, some pacifists would say *yes* on some occasions and *no* on others. Peace as a means to peace is not part of the patriarchal operational mechanism; rather, it is and always was a revolutionary path.

In the end, *To shoot or not to shoot?* becomes a multi-layered historical question. Do we have a friend who might have been saved if there had been a military intervention in Srebrenica? in Rwanda? If we imagine that the genocide of half a million people in Rwanda could have been stopped by a military intervention, would we have voted yes? And would we have sent ourselves or our friends to the military squads to bomb Rwanda in order to stop genocidal war? Or would we have done it for Bosnia or Kosova but not for Rwanda? Are the private and political in this instance completely intersecting again?

My experience is that there are two feminist pacifist positions and, at different times, both have moral considerations that bother us:

- The first position: If we choose at all times to be on the pacifist *no shooting* side, and we meet a friend who was saved in Bosnia or Kosova after the military intervention, we are embarrassed when facing her. She tells us that our position is idealistic and that her reality is something else. We still believe that a world without militarism is possible. Our friend can understand us, she can even believe the same politics herself, for having been in war, she hates war. But her reality is different. We look into her eyes and end up with an ethical problem, because our position has not included her reality.

- The second position: If we have a basic pacifist position of *no shooting* at any time, but in certain concrete situations we say *yes* to military intervention, we face our own pacifist politics and feel a moral embarrassment in siding with the military intervention. Our friend was saved and we have thought about her while choosing. But we have betrayed our own peace politics, we have said *yes* to shooting, while we ourselves would never take up arms and shoot.

It pains me that patriarchy as manifested in a military system has placed us in positions in which our free desire has no expression that can be recognized by the patriarchal reality. Patriarchy damages each free choice that we make.

Kumudini Samuel

Chapter 13

Activism, Motherhood, and the State in Sri Lanka's Ethnic Conflict

S ri Lanka's ethnic conflict, widespread state repression and human rights violations, and market-driven changes in macro-economic policy have forced new gender roles on women. Political repression and violence have accounted for a large number of widows and female-headed households.[1] However, Sri Lankan society still values a married woman over a single woman, and a wife over a widow.[2] Furthermore, in times of war and socio-political insecurity, the figure of the mother becomes a central signifier of racial and cultural values, national pride and purity, and is intrinsically connected in this way to the concept of a nation's honour.[3] Conversely, violence against women increases with heightened militarization and with the patriarchal power play that accompanies political violence and war.

Within the parameters of political activism, Sri Lankan women have been able to use their "motherhood" as a political force to bring about significant changes in the political power balance. But they have not been able to sustain this activism or use it as a means of achieving genuine empowerment or political leadership. The use of a socialized construct such as motherhood has also meant that there has been no critical re-examination of the place of women in Sri Lankan society. Instead, women have helped to perpetuate the same stereotypes that marginalize them from both society and the political process, consciously or unconsciously colluding in maintaining their own oppression.[4]

At the grassroots level, both traditional party politicians and the armed movement have appropriated women's activism. They have used women's contributions at critical moments in time, but have never invested them with any power within the political process. Likewise, women's aspirations for peace, and their activism within the peace movement, have not been translated into the determination of either the content or the direction of any peace process by the state or the Liberation Tigers of Tamil Eelam (LTTE).

This chapter explores four key women's coalitions/organizations that emerged in the 1980s in response to Sri Lanka's ethnic conflict. I specifically look at the activism of these groups, their appropriation of motherhood as a form of struggle, and their relationship with the state. This chapter is based on my personal experience within the human rights and women's rights movement since 1980 and draws from the activism of women's groups in Sri Lanka's predominantly Sinhala south and Tamil northeast. I deal specifically with the experience of the Northern and Southern Mothers' Fronts and with two coalitions – the Women's Action Committee and the Mothers and Daughters of Lanka. This chapter is by no means a comprehensive study of all the political activities played out at the national or local levels, but it does draw out some significant strands of women's activism in these regions.

The Northern Mothers' Front

In response to the round-up in Velvettiturai and transportation to the south of over eight hundred Tamil youth in August 1984, Tamil women spontaneously mobilized in Jaffna to demand the release of their children. Thus, the Northern Mothers' Front was formed. At its inception, the Mothers' Front was an autonomous grouping of women who came together to demand the release of their children. Tamil politics during this period was on a collision course with the predominantly Sinhala state and Sinhala majority government of President J.R. Jayawardene. The women of the Front, therefore, had no compunction in displaying a significant degree of militancy in making their demands to the Tamil Government Agent (GA), who was the government's representative in Jaffna. Defying the hostile presence of the military and police in Jaffna, the Front organized a march from the central bus station to the Kachcheri building that housed the GA's office. It was estimated that five thousand women participated in the demonstration, while the press in Jaffna placed the figure at ten thousand.

In a mood of militancy and anger, the women stormed the office of the GA, climbed onto his conference table, and read their demands to him. They wanted him to contact the appropriate officials in Colombo immediately and ask for their assurance that the youth rounded up in Velvettiturai would be returned to their families. The Minister of Defence requested that ten representatives of the Front travel to Colombo in order to negotiate with him, but this was summarily spurned, and the Minister was forced to assure the mothers that their children would be returned within the week. Except for thirty children who were detained in Colombo for further investigation, the rest were returned to Jaffna within a few days.[5]

In a situation where the representation of Tamil parties in Parliament was outlawed and the only articulation of Tamil aspirations was through violent militant struggle, this mobilization of Tamil women in a non-violent, peaceful protest was a significant move in contemporary Tamil political participation. It was also the first attempt at using the notion of motherhood as a way to protect life, in a climate where civil protest was difficult and dangerous to organize. The invocation of motherhood was used as much as a protection against reprisals as a legitimate moral duty and obligation to safeguard life. Thus, the Front was able to make significant gains in its demands from the state. Following the August protests against disappearances, the Front staged a demonstration in Jaffna, calling on the state to "Stop the Rape of Women," saying, "We live amidst fear and in tears." The Women's Action Committee in the south, which lent their support to the women of the north, wrote a letter to President Jayawardene on 19 December in which they adopted the demands of the Mothers' Front.

The Mothers' Front was made up of women who spanned many ideological orientations – from feminists to militants, to women from the traditional left, to women who did not subscribe to any form of women's politics but organized merely as mothers concerned about the security of their children within the context of the ongoing ethnic conflict. The leadership had to define an identity for the Front that was different from the individual identities or politics of its members. Significantly, at its inception, the Front articulated political positions independent of the militant groups in the northeast, especially vis-à-vis the LTTE, which was becoming more and more powerful in the region as it systematically decimated other Tamil militant groups with which it was competing.

However, by 1987, the Indo-Lanka Accord was signed and the LTTE had consolidated its power in the region. At the time, the LTTE moved in to determine the work and the direction of the Front, and the Front's independent leadership moved out, some of them leaving the northern peninsula altogether. The women who stayed to actively run the Front converted its work to projects of a purely charitable nature, such as the production of "Jaipur" feet for the disabled.

Thus, the use of motherhood as a political force could not be sustained as a means of genuinely empowering women. The LTTE obviously considered the Mothers' Front expeditious at the time of its mobilization and allowed it to survive. As the LTTE gained physical control of the northern peninsula, the need for the Front's existence within the dictates of patriarchal nationalist politics evaporated. The women themselves were unable to sustain the organization or even attempt to transform it into a more positive, useful political force, particularly because it was based on a notion of motherhood that did not fundamentally challenge gender roles of power and domination.

The Southern Mothers' Front

In another significant mobilization of motherhood, the Southern Mothers' Front was born in the southern town of Matara in 1990. This formation, according to its conveners, was inspired by the Northern Mothers' Front as well as by the Mothers of the Plaza del Mayo in Argentina. In response to continuing abuses of human rights, especially disappearances in the district, over fifteen hundred women, predominantly mothers, attended an inaugural meeting, and soon the Front spread its activities to almost all the other Sinhala-majority southern districts.[6] The mobilization of the mother figure was manifest in the name of the Front. It was also strongly present in its logo, which used the image of the Sinhala alphabet "M" (*mayanna*), denoting the first letter of the word *mava* (mother), cradling the image of a child in its fetal-shaped curve. The Southern Mothers' Front, however, was organized under the auspices of the main party in opposition, the Sri Lanka Freedom Party (SLFP), and its conveners were two male Members of Parliament.

As the Front grew in strength, it was used as a political weapon against the ruling United National Party. Its first national convention and rally were held in Colombo in February 1991, amid heavy military presence, threats, and malicious diatribes in the state-owned national press. The Front, however, was a powerful presence. Admittedly many of its members were also members of the SLFP, but it had within its ranks women with no party affiliation, mothers and wives of police and military personnel who had been killed, and even a few Tamil women who had lost family members in the ethnic war.

Present at the national convention was a woman who came to symbolize the Front, Dr. Manorani Saravanamuttu, the mother of assassinated journalist Richard de Zoysa. Middle class and Tamil, Saravanamuttu strove to keep the movement non-partisan and to keep its peace-seeking goal in focus. In a speech to the convention's audience, she emphasized, "Make no mistake, our aim is peace, our method is peaceful.

We have wept alone and have come together for comfort. From this has arisen our desire to collectively seek peace in our country." As a way of keeping peace, the Front would act as a peaceful watchdog over whatever government was in power. She also noted the Front's political linkage and said, "The most important facet of this political linkage at the start is that it gives the mothers some measure of protection in the initial stages of their campaign." And she stressed, "As the women learn to fend for themselves, and develop their organization, they will become independent."[7]

Another woman present at the convention was Chandrika Kumaratunge, then on the fringes of the SLFP, and herself the recent widow of an assassinated politician. She would be elected president of the country three years later. Kumaratunge was the hope and the inspiration of the convention, both for the mothers and the onlookers. In a powerful speech, she asked the mothers not to be taken over by politicians or political parties but to "take the struggle into their own hands and make it their struggle."[8] Kumaratunge's exhortation was to no avail – neither she, the SLFP, nor any other independent representation within the Front was able to divorce the mothers' needs from the exigencies of party politics. The SLFP clearly made use of the Front, not to reinstate democracy or to see justice done, but to overthrow the incumbent government and secure political power.

The appropriation of motherhood was to be both positive and negative. The women used their gendered role of motherhood as a positive expression of anger and emotional outrage in a situation where traditional male forms of struggle were either ineffective or impossible due to political violence and terror. The methods of struggle adopted by the Front were clearly innovative and accessible to the women. Marches and demonstrations were interspersed with ritual invocations to the gods, in the form of *Kannalauwas*,[9] for the return of their children and, more powerfully, to wreak vengeance on those guilty of taking them. While the issue of democracy and human rights, disappearances, extrajudicial executions, and accountability became the political slogans in the campaign to overthrow the United National Party (UNP), the mothers' invocations to the gods became the psychological weapon that disturbed the incumbent president the most. At the same time, the use of *Kannalauwas* kept the women's activism in the realm of the irrational, and reinforced both for them and for society at large that recourse to the irrational was the preserve of women. It did not give the women any independent or sustainable political strength.

The presence of the Southern Mothers' Front was without doubt a powerful catalyst in shifting the balance of political power. The political issues rooted in questions of democracy and peace were epitomized by the presence of the Front. Many politicians, both women and men, were to take on the issues of peace and democracy in their political campaigning. A number of women politicians of the SLFP, in particular, espoused the peace-seeking cause of the mothers. Chandrika Kumaratunge made the resolution of the ethnic conflict, the reinstitution of democracy, and the protection of human rights the main planks of her election platform.

However, the Southern Mothers' Front disintegrated with the electoral victory of the People's Alliance (PA) Party. Women party activists put their faith in the newly elected president for the delivery of justice. Not having been politically independent from the SLFP but dependent on it for leadership, the Front could not convert itself to the watchdog body envisaged by Manorani Saravanamuttu. As with the Northern Mothers' Front, its mobilization was based on women's role as mothers and on their duty and moral obligation to protect their children, so it could never challenge the disempowerment or limitations of gendered roles. Although it was an important catalyst in pushing the process of democratization forward, the Front could not translate that gain into the political empowerment of its members. Although they influenced the political process, they would never acquire positions of power that allowed them to participate in decision-making.

The Women's Action Committee (WAC)

Since the early 1980s, a number of women's groups in Sri Lanka have increasingly challenged issues of human rights, ethnic politics, and the armed conflict, and in particular their impact on women. The first significant coalition of these progressive women's groups was within the Women's Action Committee, which was established in 1982. The Committee was conceived of by a group of women, most of whom were at one time part of, or influenced by, the radical politics of new Left groups and the socialist feminist and women's movements of the 1970s, particularly in England and the Netherlands. It was formed out of a critique of the Left and sought to incorporate a democratic, non-partisan, decentralized structure. Based predominantly in the Sinhala south, the groups within the Committee were autonomous and organized among urban, middle-class women, working-class and peasant women, writers, poets, students, and so on. The WAC also had contact with Tamil women's groups in the northern city of Jaffna and among Tamil women from the plantation sector in the central hill country.

The work of the Committee included documentation and dissemination of information, consciousness-raising, networking, campaigning, lobbying, and advocacy. Its public activities at the national level were centred on International Women's Day, International Human Rights Day, and International Labour Day. WAC sought to discuss the basis of women's oppression from a feminist perspective, locating it within patriarchal power structures both in the private and the public spheres. It discussed ethnic and class oppression within this framework as well, and sought to link women's rights with human rights to establish a democratic culture that respected diversity and pluralism. In the context of the ethnic conflict, the Committee consistently and systematically called for political negotiation as opposed to military confrontation as a means of resolution.

Although I only discuss the work of the Women's Action Committee in relation to the ethnic conflict, it organized and campaigned as much on gender- and class-based issues as it did on ethnic issues. At the micro level, WAC concentrated on raising awareness. At the national level, the ethnic conflict was discussed at its national conventions, and issues in relation to the conflict were taken up in public campaigns that took the form of demonstrations, marches, public appeals, and pickets.

Throughout the 1980s, WAC joined other women's groups to speak about the consequences of war; the right to the self-determination of the Tamil people; the need for the redress of Tamil grievances; and, in particular, highlighted human rights violations perpetrated against the Tamil people and the institution of non-democratic structures and the abuse of state power. It also linked the ethnic conflict and the politics of violence to the deterioration of democracy and its consequences for all ethnic communities.

One of WAC's first public actions was to call for the repeal of the *Prevention of Terrorism Act* in 1983. It also campaigned for the release of Nirmala Nithiyananthan, then the only woman political prisoner held at the Welikada Prison in Colombo.[10] Both of these demands were immensely unpopular in an increasingly Draconian state. In solidarity with the newly formed Mothers' Front in Jaffna, WAC took up the demand of the women from the north to "Stop the Rape of Women." In an open letter to President Jayawardene in December 1984, which was later distributed as a leaflet, the Committee made the link between rapes, militarization, and the continued pursuit of a military solution instead of political negotiations to resolve the ethnic conflict. It also warned that more and more men from the south would be pawns in the war machine, and expressed its condemnation at the resultant destruction of life. WAC called upon all parties in the conflict to resume talks with the commitment of bringing about a just solution to the conflict. This' appeal was made in the aftermath of the All Party Conference, which ended in a shambles and gave free reign to warmongering and chauvinism. Women were the first citizens to again broach the subject of peace through dialogue.

Following the signing of the Indo-Lanka Accord in 1987, this climate of fear and insecurity was to take a new and more dangerous turn. Strong opposition to the Accord and any attempts to devolve power to the minorities emerged in the south, spearheaded by the Janatha Vimukthi Peramuna (JVP) and its affiliate organizations, such as the Maubima Surakime Viyaparaya (the Movement to Safeguard the Motherland). This opposition was soon to take on a militaristic aspect, which resulted in hundreds of politically motivated assassinations of those seen to support any political solution to the ethnic conflict. Progressive groups such as WAC, which had consistently campaigned for a political solution within a plural and democratic framework, were targeted by the JVP as being anti-patriotic and pro-Tamil. A number of individual women and women's organizations within WAC had to work underground; WAC itself found it too dangerous to work in public and, by 1989, most of its constituent members decided to create a new organization, which they called the Mothers and Daughters of Lanka (MDL).

Significantly, the Women's Action Committee was involved in one last action, which was very different in form and content from its previous work. It produced a leaflet to mark International Women's Day on 8 March 1990. The leaflet attempted to depict the trauma of disappearances in a creative form, picturing the Jathaka of Kisa Gothami adapted to the Sri Lankan political context.[11] The motif was powerful in its message. It used a central illustration of a mother with the corpse of a child in her arms. Surrounding the "mother" were a series of medallions akin to the picture compartments making up a traditional *Vesak pandal*.[12] Within these medallions were depicted images of the sorry experience of mothers going in vain from pillar to post to find help in the search for their children – mothers at police stations, detention camps, prisons, the homes of neighbours or politicians, and the offices of the media and the NGOs. Significantly, WAC militancy also resorted to using the mother in her accepted role as giving life to, nurturing, and protecting her young, invoking the moral duty of mothers to safeguard the sanctity of life.

Mothers and Daughters of Lanka (MDL)

In response to state- and JVP-led terror and armed conflict, the reformulated WAC, under the new name of Mothers and Daughters of Lanka (MDL), once again mobilized women and went public with an appeal calling for a "Stop to All the Killings." The appeal was accompanied by this poem:[13]

Tell me, my children
how can I,
your mother,
remain silent any longer?

Carrion consumes the flesh
that I nurtured, with sleepless nights,
amidst hunger and deprivation;
the flesh
that is all that remains
of my son,
my daughter,
of the child who looked up at me
with love in its eyes
after a childhood quarrel.

The blood that flows
over village and town,
on the roadside and in the rivers,
is the blood that once flowed in my veins
as I suckled you, my child.

No matter what arms you bear,
No matter what power you have
Who is it who gave you those arms,
Who is it who gave you the power
to destroy a life
that a mother brought forth?

Wait.
Heed your mother's cry.
Call a halt to this cycle
of violence and hatred.
Stop this killing
and seek solutions.
Stop killing.
Stop killing NOW.

As in the north, women's political activism in the south shifted in response to the immediate human rights violations of disappearances and summary executions. But the response came from women who identified as mothers and who located the mother as the central figure initiating protest by virtue of her motherhood as the poem above aptly illustrates. In a statement following the poem, MDL laid claim to a universal motherhood:

> We have come forward as MOTHERS of LANKA to demand justice and
> fair play for all human beings, who are like sons and daughters to us
> . . . no matter what divisions and differences there may be between us,
> the love we bear our children is the same.

Invoking their biological functions, MDL noted,

> We nursed a thousand hopes in our hearts from the day a child was
> conceived in our womb to the moment when we heard its first cry;
> surely all this was not to see the lives of our children destroyed at any-
> one's hand.

Taking on a note of censure and advice, MDL next addressed the "children" they perceived as being among the killers (a clear appeal to the
JVP), saying,

> You who are our children. . . . Your mothers cry out to you that mur-
> der cannot bring about the cessation of murder. You must above all
> learn to respect human life.

Finally, striking a militant note, the statement ends with an appeal to all
women

> to come forward to defend our right to life, to demand an end to this
> wanton destruction of life and to organize and build a movement dedi-
> cated to the seeking of solutions to problems we face today.

The statement ends with the demands to call a halt to the practice of
politics at gunpoint; to create a society free of divisions of race, creed,
and caste; to build an atmosphere in which one can live without fear;
and, in bold print, to "REFUTE BARBARISM!" "END THE WAR!" and paradoxically, "BRING DOWN PRICES!" MDL, however, maintained their autonomy and political ideology in relation to both the ethnic conflict and
women's issues, resorting to the use of the mother image purely as a tac-
tical means of survival.

By 1990, the JVP uprising was crushed by the state, and its leader,
Rohana Wijeweera, was executed. The JVP itself gradually moved into
representative politics in the mid-1990s. By the end of 1990, MDL's work
and statements gradually revoked the use of mother imagery, although it
did not change its name. The original debates a year earlier, which critiqued the invocation of motherhood and included space for daughters in
a name that was seen to be exclusively addressing mothers, had died
down. The politics of the coalition reverted to the politics reminiscent of
the Women's Action Committee. A fundamental concern of the coalition
remained the ethnic conflict, although increasingly the connection

between violence against women and the violent politics of state and extra-parliamentary groups was made.

* * *

In times of severe political crisis, particularly when there is an extreme loss of life, why do women resort to the "safe" construct of motherhood? The experiences of the Northern and Southern Mothers' Fronts and the Women's Action Committee, which later transformed into the Mothers and Daughters of Lanka, indicate that accepted notions of motherhood can and have been used as a tactic at particular moments in time. This approach may help to deal with severe crises in the short term and facilitate longer-term survival, but the construct of motherhood by itself, with no critique of its meaning or of its repercussions, has not been a sustainable source of power for women.

Motherhood was used as a shield behind which women and political entities in opposition to the state sought to mobilize in moments of political crisis, particularly when traditionally male forms of organizing were not possible. In the cases of both the Southern and Northern Mothers' Fronts, this mobilization was strictly controlled within the confines of centralized and patriarchal party power structures, that is, by the SLFP and later the LTTE. This ensured that any potentially empowering political ambition was limited strictly to women within their control (that is, women within the party or political organization). The vast majority of women, who were activated in struggle, could as easily be deactivated to suit particular political expedience. The Fronts' relationship with the state and their struggles against state power disintegrated the moment they lost the "protection" and authority of the SLFP and the LTTE.

Each of these organizations internalized patriarchal notions of women in their use of the mother figure. As Neloufer de Mel observes in chapter 5 (and Elissa Helms in chapter 14), they continued the practice of vesting in the person of the "mother," the totality of a woman's identity.[14] In so doing they made use of its power as a symbol in their struggles against the state and, in particular, against state and extra-state repression. Motherhood was also a safe and non-challenging construct around which women could be "allowed" to enter the public space of political protest and activity – that is, safe within the confines of accepted social and patriarchal norms, with no threat of straying into more powerful political positions. The twin exigencies of nationalism and motherhood, from which neither of the Mothers' Fronts disengaged nor which they critiqued, may have been a factor in their disintegration.

The coalition of the MDL, however, was able to avoid the blurring of the private and public arenas of struggle. It did, as in the case of the

Mothers' Fronts, use the gendered concept of motherhood as a tactic of protest and organizing when politically more traditional strategies could not be used. However, its autonomous nature, highly decentralized forms of organizing, and continuous challenge to patriarchal power structures of both state and non-state entities allowed it to survive the political crisis of the 1980s.

Independent from party politics, WAC, and later on MDL, could concentrate on extra-parliamentary forms of protest and continue to be deeply critical of the state. WAC and MDL, throughout their history, were able to make links with women of all ethnic communities. Their protests and struggles were, therefore, inclusive of the causes of minority communities. As Sunila Abeysekera points out, women need to operate within a wide range of differences and diversity to bring about social change and to challenge the exclusionary inequalities that stem from their diversity. Acknowledging women's activism, she notes the need to reaffirm the fact that "women in our conflict-ridden societies have come forward to challenge the patriarchal norms of war and conflict and to replace them with a humane norm of dialogue, consensus and negotiation."[15]

Fundamental to this coming together, however, has been these women's ability to balance their individual concerns as members of a particular community or group with their interests as women. This has been the experience of coalitions such as WAC and MDL as opposed to single-issue, ethnically segregated groups such as the Mothers' Fronts. As Abeysekera further notes: "It is this experience of transversal politics and coalition building that can shape and inform our interventions in the broader political and conceptual arenas of our activism."[16]

Notes

1 Kumudini Samuel, "War and Survival – Women Heads of Household in the East," *Options* 1 (August 1994). *Options* is published by the Women and Media Collective in Colombo, Sri Lanka.

2 See Maxine Molyneux, "Mobilisation without Emancipation: Women's Interests, the State, and Revolution in Nicaragua," *Feminist Studies* 11,2 (Summer 1985) for a similar argument vis-à-vis Nicaragua.

3 Neloufer de Mel, "Static Signifiers," in Kumari Jayawardena and Malathi de Alwis, eds., *Embodied Violence: Communalising Women's Sexuality in South Asia* (New Delhi: Kali for Women, 1996), pp.168-99.

4 Kumudini Samuel, "Gender Difference in Conflict Resolution: The Case of Sri Lanka," in Inger Skejelsbaek and Dan Smith, eds., *Gender, Peace and Conflict* (London: Sage Publications; Oslo: PRIO, 2001), pp. 184-204.

5 Sarwam Kailasapathy, a leader of the Mothers' Front who participated in the demonstration, was my source for this eyewitness account.

6 See letter of invitation dated 6 February 1991, entitled "National Convention

and Public Rally 19 February 1991," signed by Mangala Samaraweera, MP and Co-ordinator, Mothers' Front. The Front was jointly co-ordinated by two SLFP Members of Parliament, Mangala Samaraweera and Mahinda Rajapakse, and was created in response to many demands received, in particular, by these two MPs from the southern constituencies of Matara and Hambantota, from mothers and family members of the disappeared. Although co-ordinated by the MPs, it was not an official party organization.

7 See "Statement of Dr. (Mrs.) Manorani Saravanamuttu on the Convening of the Mothers' Front in Sri Lanka on 19 February 1991," issued as a press release by the Mothers' Front on 19 February 1991. The statement was delivered by Dr. Saravanamuttu at the National Convention of the Mothers' Front held at the New Town Hall in Colombo on the same day.

8 This statement is based on my informal notes, and those of Krishantha Sri Bhagyadatta, taken at the Mothers' Front Convention.

9 *Kannalauwa* is an invocation to the gods that takes the form of an appeal or lamentation in which the gods are implored to give succour in times of need.

10 Nirmala Nithiyananthan was moved to the Batticaloa jail following the July 1983 massacre of Tamil political prisoners held at Welikada. She subsequently escaped to India following an LTTE jailbreak in 1983.

11 The Kisa Gothami Jathakaya narrates the story of a mother who visits the Buddha and begs for her dead child to be brought back to life. In response, the Buddha asked Kisa Gothami to bring him a mustard seed from a home that had not experienced death; when Kisa Gothami could not find such a home, she was taught the lesson that everyone has to face suffering of some kind.

12 These are stories from the life of Lord Buddha.

13 The MDL appeal was published in the three mainstream Sri Lankan newspapers in all three languages on 1 October 1989.

14 See also de Mel, "Static Signifiers."

15 Sunila Abeysekera, "The Female Citizen," *Pravada* 6,6 (2000).

16 Ibid.

Elissa Helms

Chapter 14

Gender Essentialisms and Women's Activism in Post-War Bosnia-Herzegovina

Violent conflict and its aftermath have drawn women in many parts of the world into various forms of public activism. As the public/ political sphere is most commonly constructed as the sphere of men, women's public activism poses an implicit challenge to the established patriarchal gender regimes. Still, many women activists have organized around their roles as mothers and keepers of the domestic sphere, which reflects their positions in the male-dominated gender regimes. These representations essentialize women, as a group, as nurturing mothers who are tied to domestic roles outside the public/political world of men. Some feminists have argued that the use of these gender essentialisms ultimately reinforces patriarchal values and hierarchies, making it easy for women's initiatives to be co-opted into the dominant male-defined power structures, such as the militarist nationalism that has fuelled conflict in places like the Balkans and Sri Lanka. Others point to the dangers of ignoring the agency of women who choose to embrace gender essentialisms, thus relinquishing women's claim to the meanings of motherhood, ethnic identity, and domestic roles.

In Bosnia, and in the successor states of the former Yugoslavia in general, conservative nationalists have also essentialized women in this way through images of women in domestic roles, especially as mothers reproducing the nation.[1] It has been less noted that such gender essentialisms are also apparent in the discourses of non-nationalist, "civic" politicians, as well as in the discourse of foreign donors which fund women's NGO (non-governmental organizations) activities.[2] It would seem that feminist groups,[3] or any organization favouring the dismantling of established gender hierarchies to improve the status of women, would avoid such constructions. But, as this chapter shows, there are practical reasons women's groups allow themselves to be portrayed as apolitical and as mothers, and even put forth these images themselves.

Local women's NGOs in Bosnia take many different forms, according to the class and ethnic backgrounds of their membership, the political and gender ideologies which they represent, and the activities in which they engage.[4] Their use of essentializing gender rhetoric varies according to the degree to which they challenge gender hierarchies, and the relative importance of what they define as "women's interests" vis-à-vis their other goals. Despite this diversity, however, all of the women's NGOs with which I came into contact in Bosnia used some form of gender essentialisms in representing themselves to their local communities and to (potential and actual) foreign donors. In contrast to dominant political discourses, however, the gender essentialisms used by NGO participants (as well as by some of their foreign donors) stress *positive* roles for women, portraying them as peacemakers and nurturers, and as more non-nationalist and capable of dialogue and reconciliation than are men. Thus, women are essentialized and confined to domestic roles (the nurturing mother) but with a positive spin, or what Richard Fox has called "affirmative essentialisms."[5]

In representing their roles as women and as activists in NGOs, Bosnian women's NGO activists operate in dialogue with local (patriarchal) nationalist discourses, established notions of gender, and the discourses and policies of various foreign donors and officials from the powerful "international community" overseeing post-war reconstruction. While many of these forces directly or indirectly encourage women to stay out of the male-dominated political realm and to remain tied to domestic duties, post-war political and material conditions nevertheless offer women new opportunities and spaces for a redefinition of female gender roles and women's public/political activism. Much of this has come about through the relatively new emphasis on NGOs and "civil society" as a new and still-contested form of relations between the family, the market, the state, and formal politics. Foreign donors, including some Western feminists, have actively encouraged women's involvement in the public/political sphere, although this is frequently accompanied by essentialist views of women.

In addition to these new opportunities, women activists must contend with widespread animosities towards both "politics" and those women who assert themselves in the public sphere (who may be "feminists," a negative label in this region). Bosnian women activists have therefore turned in various ways to gender essentialisms, which uphold the "traditional" association of women with the domestic sphere and nurturing, mothering roles. In short, war and its aftermath have created a space for women's public, even political activism, but in many ways has limited the extent to which women can critique and/or challenge existing male-dominated gender hierarchies (see also Mladjenović in chapter 12).

In what follows I outline some of the ways in which Bosnian women's NGO activists use "traditional" gender essentialisms to advance their goals. I briefly discuss the nature of the political and moral climate in which they operate in order to show how women activists face new opportunities as well as limits on how they are able to represent themselves and their activities in the public realm. I then discuss the discursive strategies of several local women's NGO activists in Bosnia. My analysis is based on two years (1999-2000) of ethnographic fieldwork among women's NGO participants, primarily based in the Bosnian town of Zenica. I conclude by comparing the Bosnian case with theoretical treatments of other examples of women's activism and the use of gender essentialisms in various societies.

Women's NGOs, Political Morality, and the "Third Sector"

The post-war reconstruction of Bosnia-Herzegovina has been dominated by the in-country presence of representatives of the "international community," led by the Office of the High Representative (OHR) and the Organization for Security and Cooperation in Europe (OSCE). These have been charged with the monitoring and implementation of the Dayton Peace Accords, which ended the fighting in December 1995. Numerous other non-governmental, governmental, and supra-governmental agencies operate as donors and policy implementers, and, along with OHR and OSCE, play a dominant role in determining the direction of social and political reconstruction. Although the actors in this group employ a variety of approaches to reconstruction, they nonetheless share the common goal of creating a viable, multi-ethnic Bosnian state organized along Western models of free-market democracy, including a strong civil society. This Western-dominated group is often referred to, by Bosnians and foreigners alike, as "the international community," and can very often be read to mean "the West" or "Western governments."

The goal of building a civil society in Bosnia has meant understanding non-governmental organizations, or the third sector, as a separate sphere from that of the state or the family. In practice, this has resulted in a strong push for the establishment and strengthening of as many local

NGOs as possible.[6] More recently, greater attention has been paid to the functions and makeup of local NGOs – the international community encourages and funds NGOs that are multi-ethnic in membership and/or engage in cross-ethnic activities, especially activities which contribute to ethnic reconciliation and the return of displaced persons to areas from which they were "ethnically cleansed." International policy towards local NGOs is therefore part of the larger project of building a multi-ethnic society and a coherent, democratic state. Furthermore, the focus on NGOs as an arena of political engagement outside the formal political sphere reflects a hope of countering the grip of nationalist political control, which has, until recently, dominated government and formal politics and, to varying degrees, obstructed the establishment of a unified Bosnia.[7]

The third sector is still new and its place in Bosnian social and political life is still very much under contention. Many international actors have stressed the need for this sector, that is, the NGOs, to be politically engaged in order to counter nationalist politics. Such positioning, however, becomes problematic for the NGOs themselves, given that "politics," or "the political" more broadly, is viewed as a sphere of corrupt, self-interested nationalist opportunists. These have, after all, been the ones responsible for fuelling ethnic hostility, waging war, and, in the current period, obstructing the implementation of the peace accords.

Women's NGOs are therefore aided by the fact that formal politics, especially since the demise of socialist Yugoslavia, has been overwhelmingly male dominated and perceived as a male sphere. Additionally, one of the only morally acceptable kinds of identity one can espouse in post-war Bosnia is that of the victim (of the opposing ethnic groups' nationalist forces or a victim of Western interventions), and women in Bosnia have specifically been cast as (passive) victims and symbols of their ethnic group's victimization through rapes, ethnic cleansing, and massacres during the war.[8] This feminization of the victim image, combined with the male gendering of the political sphere, has allowed women activists to claim the moral high ground, as "they" – women as a group – were not among those who could be held accountable for any of the suffering (war, ethnic cleansing, poverty, corruption, unemployment) of the past decade.[9]

Furthermore, the dominant opinion is that women do not belong in the political arena because they are not emotionally tough enough and because their domestic duties do not allow them to devote the proper amount of time and energy to the demands of politics. While they are not usually rejected outright, women face much tougher criticism from the general public when they take on public, and especially political, roles.

Detractors of such women – both women and men – typically express their criticism in decidedly gendered terms, claiming that women have no place in the political realm.[10]

Another morally tainting charge is that politicians are self-interested and do not act for the good of the people. It is common, therefore, for all sorts of public actors to attempt to appear as distant as possible from "politics." Humanitarianism is seen as the opposite of selfless political ambitions and is, therefore, a common ideal that public actors evoke in their self-representations. Women, especially groups (NGOs) organized on the basis of being women, can most easily make the claim of being apolitical. Even though their activities take place outside the domestic sphere, they can be linked to women's domestic roles by casting the activities as humanitarian, undertaken out of concern for the communities in which the women's children and grandchildren live – natural outgrowths of women's roles as mothers and keepers of the family.

Finally, when women's NGOs act *as women* on issues perceived to be solely "women's issues," they commonly encounter the charge that other, more compelling problems merit public attention at the moment.[11] Some of these other problems are, in fact, the most urgent problems for the women themselves. Thus, whether they are concerned with dismantling gender hierarchies or not, many women activists find it more expedient to refrain from loudly challenging dominant patriarchal values in order to achieve their other pressing goals – the return of displaced persons to areas of different ethnic control, the prosecution of war crimes committed against loved ones, economic or psychological independence, ethnic reconciliation, and so on. Indeed, many Bosnian women's NGOs have little desire to change women's association with domestic, nurturing roles. Instead, they work as women for the social and political *validation* of such roles. The use of gender essentialisms is, therefore, often the most practical way for women's NGOs to achieve their goals.

Women's NGOs and Affirmative Essentialisms

Gender essentialisms are not only practical, they also reflect commonly held notions of gender roles for women that identify women with motherhood and domestic roles. These constructions become more powerful for women's organizations when the positive aspects of female gender roles are stressed. As I have stated, positioning oneself outside the male sphere of politics in many ways constitutes a positive approach in the current climate of Bosnia, one which women's NGO participants can embrace with enthusiasm. During my fieldwork, I repeatedly heard Bosnian women (and a few men) proudly assert that "if women had been in power, there wouldn't have been a war." The leader of one local women's NGO addressed a gathering of other women's organizations by saying,

> I wish to convey a message to all women and mothers of BiH [Bosnia-Herzegovina] that they are an important factor in maintaining the peace in this region. We need to bring up children in the spirit of tolerance, in valuing those who think and believe differently and not in the spirit of hatred and intolerance.

Another women's NGO positioned itself in much the same role by printing T-shirts that proclaimed, "World Peace begins right here. I will not raise my child to kill your child."[12] In this way, the activists define women's roles through a uniquely female, universal motherhood.[13]

Motherhood connotes not only the bearing but also the raising of children, a role which includes both moral guidance and the (less desirable) job of cleaning up messes as the "sacrificing mother." As another activist noted, "This is still the expectation of society. Women smooth out what men have messed up," in other words, the aftermath of conflict and war. Local gender constructions place men in the role of warrior and political actor, while women are seen as passive (war) victims, mothers, and nurturers, especially in times of war.[14] Women as a group fall outside the category of potential (armed and aggressive) adversaries, making it easier for them to cross politicized ethnic boundaries and to communicate with those on "the other side," especially with other women.[15]

Although some activists are sceptical of these formulations, they often allow themselves to be categorized in this way because, as "women's organizations" they can expect to win foreign funding more easily.[16] Donors and the "international community" also express and encourage the view that women are better able to engage in inter-ethnic communication and carry out ethnic reconciliation projects – the post-war "clean-up work," which is a main priority for the international community.[17] As one member of a self-described feminist NGO complained of the donors' approach, "The international community goes on the principle of 'men make war, women make peace.'"

One loosely organized group of veteran women's activists, many of whom describe themselves as feminists, has used their common identity as women to forge a strong cross-ethnic network of activists. While most of these women reject gender essentialisms that exclude women from the sphere of the political, they nevertheless rely on common essentialist perceptions to achieve their goals. This group has achieved a significant measure of trust and co-operation, and indeed strong friendships, across ethnic divides,[18] precisely through their perceived common identity and interests *as women* – women who reject the divisive ideologies of ethnic nationalism. Through a process of what one activist termed "strategic avoidance" (*strateško zaobilaženje*), they tread lightly around sensitive issues of ethnic-national identity and the causes of the war in order to work together on what they deem as issues important to women.[19]

Being women, these activists are aware that they are not seen by their communities as (potential or former) combatants or political decision-makers. The underlying assumption they all cling to, and often articulate, is that none of the women wanted the war, that everyone on all sides suffered, and that women were not in a position to stop the war. This gendered position has allowed women to achieve much stronger working relationships across ethnic divides than have groups dominated by men in Bosnia. Indeed, it has allowed them to organize in the first place. However, this position can relegate women to a strictly female sphere, marginalized from formal structures and institutions of power. We might ask, therefore, whether women are rendered powerless in their pursuit of political goals. To address this question, I discuss two local women's NGOs that have successfully wielded gender essentialisms to achieve some decidedly political goals.

Success with Affirmative Gender Essentialisms

Constructions that place women outside the arena of formal political power are familiar ones to women activists, and it is clear that they make conscious use of them. The discursive strategies of two Bosnian women's NGOs, whose leaders I came to know, illustrate this. Both groups are made up of displaced Bosniac[20] women whose primary goal has been to achieve the return of their members to the communities from which they were ethnically cleansed in the war. The first group is from northwest Bosnia (Kozarac near Prijedor) and the other is from the Podrinje region of eastern Bosnia (Srebrenica, Bratunac, Zvornik, Vlasenica). Both areas were sites of some of the most brutal cases of ethnic cleansing of Bosniacs by Serb forces in the war, and are now populated by Serbs and controlled by Serb leaders as part of the Republika Srpska, the Serb political entity that, together with the Bosniac-Croat Federation, constitutes the current Bosnian state.

The women's goal of refugee return is one of the most highly politicized issues in post-war Bosnia as it fundamentally divides those who favour building a multi-ethnic Bosnian state from those who oppose it.[21] While the public pronouncements of women's organizations are not given much attention or held to carry much weight by local officials or community members, these groups have nonetheless drawn much attention to their actions of crossing ethnic (now political) borders and agitating for refugee return. In other words, although women's talk is taken to be of little political consequence, their actions on an issue this politically sensitive are noted. Indeed, both groups have been met with considerable resistance, threats of violence, and, in one case, even the stoning of the women's buses when they tried to visit their old homes or hold meetings in their towns of origin.

Most of the services that these organizations provide focus on displaced and returning women and their families (which are, in many cases, missing their male relations). These include psychological counselling and support for women survivors of war trauma, as well as practical aid such as information and logistical help for initiating the return process, basic clothing and supplies the women need to maintain or re-establish households, and aid for women's income-generating projects (e.g., seeds for planting, farm animals, micro-credit loans). The organizations also engage in more intangible, yet effective, activities that encourage successful return: providing moral support to women returnees and their families; meeting with local community leaders to lobby for conditions for return; arranging round-table discussions and public tribunals, which bring together Serb and Bosniac women to discuss issues of return; and various kinds of small, everyday gestures.

It is significant that these women frame their activities not as political but as humanitarian and, specifically, apolitical. They portray themselves as working within women's circles rather than "meddling" into the male world of politics. When I asked the leader of the Podrinje women's NGO why her group only worked with women, she looked at me as if I was asking the obvious. "We *have* to work with women," she explained, "because we're women. If we tried to talk to the men there [in our towns], then it would be political." Male activity is, by her definition, political, while female activity is not.

The Kozarac NGO began distributing aid, organizing income-generating projects, and offering therapeutic support to women recovering from war trauma to the refugees in Zagreb, Croatia. It has continued to offer these services to refugees as they first moved into Bosniac-controlled areas of Bosnia, and more recently into Serb-controlled areas, where members of the NGO are returning to their former homes. Although this group has been active in campaigns to increase women's participation in politics and lobbying those in political offices, its leader describes the activities as strictly "humanitarian" and compares this with the "political" activities of other NGOs in the area with whom she is in conflict. She thus shores up the moral superiority of her cause by distancing herself from the dirty, corrupt realm of the political, which includes her rival NGOs by association. She also stresses that motherhood is at the core of her group's identity and the main motivation for its activism. On one visit to the group's office, I was shown some newly printed certificates of appreciation the group had created. The message of appreciation was printed atop an image of a woman with a small child on her lap. When another visitor questioned the relevance of this image, group members who were present insisted that the message of "a mother at peace with her child" was precisely the public image they wanted to project.

This approach is essentialist and gender-conservative, placing women outside the male sphere of politics. It is also effective to some extent because women are seen as less threatening or as politically inconsequential since they actually lack any power in the formal political realm. The women can quietly circumvent the spotlight without putting the public reputation of (male) officials directly on the line. In fact, since 1998, the Kozarac women have been instrumental in bringing a substantial number of Bosniac returnees back to their homes, which now lie in Serb territory. Ethnic relations there are far from smooth, yet their goal was achieved against strong odds and they continue to push successfully for improvements in their community. Interestingly, the group leader's husband is quite active in these return activities, yet the group still benefits from its image as a women's NGO.

At the end of 2000, after several years of effort, the Podrinje women succeeded in holding a cross-ethnic meeting in Bratunac, one of the towns most politically resistant to returning ethnic minorities and the place where stones had been hurled at them to prevent them from entering a few months before. The Podrinje NGO's leader now lives and works in the town (though she hasn't returned to her old house) and has made a Serb woman living in Bratunac co-leader of the group. Together, they are working to achieve the return of Bosniacs and to improve communication with the current Serb residents.[22]

This quiet circumvention of political channels may also rest on the popular Bosnian notion of hidden female power.[23] Such female power is usually limited to the sphere of the household and family, yet these women activists are using this channel to accomplish very political and public goals. In several conversations with the Podrinje and Kozarac NGOs, the leaders insisted on the apolitical nature of their activities, making it amply clear through sarcastic tones and winks of the eye that they were perfectly aware of the political nature of their activities and goals. The leader of the Podrinje NGO was even quite explicit about it when she explained that it was easier for her group to achieve its goals working through an NGO rather than from within formal political structures:

> An NGO is also easier for men but precisely because we're women no one expects anything clever from us. . . . It was a huge effort to [organize a meeting in] Bratunac. They said, "Well hey, they're only women, let them in, what can they do?" And then they saw what "they" could do, what we would do!

Despite this awareness, however, their strategies rest on their *public* presentation as apolitical.

In spite of the considerable power this strategy holds for women's NGOs, in most cases there is little guarantee that it will be successful by itself, largely because many decisions crucial to the return process are still made by men in the formal political sphere. The Podrinje NGO therefore used another channel to circumvent the world of local male politicians: the international officials and donors who had been encouraging the NGO's multi-ethnic activities for some time.

Indeed, none of these successes by women's NGOs could have been achieved without the support of and pressure from international institutions whose goal is to assist organizations, regardless of their views on gender, with the return of refugees. Return to Kozarac was allowed, it seems, as a concession by the Republika Srpska leadership in exchange for international funds for the economically depressed territory. The Bratunac meeting was achieved through persistent pressuring of local Serb leaders by international officials who held out the promise of donor funds being given to local (Serb) NGOs in desperate need of assistance to help an even more desperate local population. In other words, significant changes were achieved through the formal male-dominated political structures.

Beyond Bosnia: Implications of the Use of Gender Essentialisms

The material I have presented here begs several questions, especially for feminist researchers and activists interested in how women's involvement in conflict situations can contribute not only to peace but also to improving the lives of women. Does the use of gender essentialisms only reaffirm patriarchal gender hierarchies or can one extract a positive message for women from such representations? If the women activists using "traditional" essentialisms and motherhood images are not themselves critical of patriarchal gender hierarchies, should feminists condemn their activities? Are the successes women do achieve through essentializing strategies doomed to eventual failure because positioning women outside the sphere of formal politics and power ultimately marginalizes them? Or, do such strategies make women vulnerable to being co-opted by larger patriarchal power structures such as nationalist and militarist states?

These questions have been central to research on women's political activism in many historical, cultural, and political contexts,[24] including those addressed by the essays in this volume.[25] As the essays on Sri Lanka demonstrate, feminists have long grappled with issues of how to represent and mobilize women without reinforcing patriarchal value systems. Tension has revolved around whether feminists should embrace and acknowledge the agency of women who find meaning and power in gender essentialisms that privilege patriarchally defined female roles – as mothers, nurturers, widows, wives, and passive, apolitical dependents of men. Some point to the positive traits women are able to express in these contexts.[26] Indeed, in Bosnia, this approach has produced a healthy focus on the positive traits normally associated with women in this kind of patriarchal gender regime: willingness to listen and engage in dialogue, caring for the well-being of others, and attention to important social issues such as education and health.

Positive traits aside, many researchers have nevertheless been critical of such essentialisms for reinforcing patriarchal values.[27] Essentialisms, they point out, not only restrict females but also males, whose roles are thereby limited to those of aggressors, power-hungry careerists, and uncaring parents – roles in which men are incapable of dialogue or compromise. For Bosnia, I would agree that this approach does little to further the implementation of peaceful solutions among the men who wield power in the political and public spheres. Furthermore, this portrayal obscures women's roles in the production and reproduction of chauvinistic nationalisms and patriarchal gender constructions. As the Serbian feminist sociologist Marina Blagojević writes, "Releasing women of any blame for the war and 'crises' would be another trap of patriarchal narcissism. Where there is no guilt, there is no complicity and therefore no subjectivity."[28] This lack of subjectivity means that women are not readily taken seriously as political actors.

However, others argue that while affirmative essentialisms may at first reinforce patriarchal hierarchies, they in fact provide women with unique opportunities to be recognized and active in the public male sphere. As Fox points out, in late-colonial India, these portrayals mobilized women to become involved in the first place. Once involved, women's actions actually "superceded the original gender stereotypes."[29] Norma Stoltz Chinchilla, writing about revolutionary women in Central America, argues that taking part in national processes put women in a position in which they could become conscious of gender hierarchies and women's inferior status – in short, by some definitions, to develop a feminist critique of society.[30] These are the experiences that lead to organic feminist movements and ultimately, though not necessarily, to change from within a society. In the case of Bosnia, it is already apparent that a core group of women's NGO activists is beginning to engage the rest of society on questions of women's rights and male privilege where such challenges had grown virtually silent before the war and international intervention.[31]

Still others point to the moral power of gender essentialisms, especially of motherhood. Groups of mothers such as the Mothers of the Plaza de Mayo in Argentina and the Mothers' Fronts in Sri Lanka[32] succeeded in publicly shaming the state precisely because they engaged themselves in the public/political sphere as mothers and widows. Their public activist identities were based on their belonging outside the male realm of politics and on their relationships with male kin and the private sphere. In some contexts, this form of women's protest may be the only way possible for women to successfully achieve their goals.[33] Given the current political climate in Bosnia, Bosnian women activists achieve more immediate respect and moral clout by positioning themselves outside the male realm of politics and within the roles of mothers and nurturers. Indeed, groups of women survivors of the massacre at Srebrenica, who stress their traditional roles as mothers and wives, regularly draw public sympathy and feelings of disgust towards the authorities through their public protests demanding their missing male relatives be accounted for and their killers brought to justice.

However, many feminists have charged that movements of mothers and women identifying themselves with domestic roles are too easily co-opted by patriarchal, male-dominated nationalist movements.[34] Because the protesters are women, they are easily dismissed or overtaken by larger national or ethnic movements, and the potential force of their movement is diffused. This has been said of many mothers' movements, including those in Sri Lanka and the former Yugoslavia.[35] But, as several writers have argued, to dismiss all gender-essentializing initiatives as pawns of male ideologies is to dismiss the legitimacy of women's agency.[36] In the Bosnian case, as in others, women activists use gender essentialisms not only because they are practical, but because they also fit into familiar notions of gender relations for the women themselves as well as for members of their communities.

Furthermore, as Dubravka Žarkov has argued, for feminists to dismiss any women's agency that is based on motherhood, or on traditional gender essentialisms, is to "surrender motherhood to nationalism,"[37] a force which, in the Balkans, has notoriously claimed ownership of the power of motherhood.[38] Žarkov's thorough study of Croatian and Serbian discourses in the years leading up to and including the violent disintegration of Yugoslavia reveals a variety of much more intricate meanings attached to motherhood, and to ethnicity, than either nationalist *or feminist* ideologies tend to allow. To wrest motherhood and ethnic identity – elements commonly associated with patriarchal, essentialist roles for women – from the purview of nationalist and patriarchal ideologies is thus a step towards reclaiming what is significant to women in their daily lives, towards understanding the different forms of women's agency, including those which use essentialist discourses. As Patricia Jeffery has written, "only then can we determine what is key to *feminist* agency and imagine how women's agency might translate into feminist political action."[39]

The wars following the disintegration of socialist Yugoslavia brought these issues to the fore for the region's feminists and for the feminists and other women activists who have emerged since, or because of, these conflicts. At this juncture, Balkan feminists, and indeed anyone interested in the gender dynamics of the region, may best learn from the experiences of women and feminists living in areas with even longer histories of violent conflict, such as Sri Lanka. Local political and cultural meanings strongly affect the possibilities of women's activism and how they envision ideal gender roles and relations. Bosnian women activists acknowledge the tension between reproducing established patriarchal values, in order to achieve practical goals, and forcefully initiating a public critique of such power structures. The Bosnian feminists I worked with are keenly aware that they must balance the expectations of their local communities and their foreign donors with their own feminist ideals. They may not always agree with other women activists who openly embrace the gender essentialisms of motherhood and nurturance, but they do not condemn them. Indeed, they often allow themselves to be portrayed in affirmative essentialist terms.

Gender essentialisms are not only meaningful to women and their communities but have also proved practical, especially in the short term, as Kumudini Samuel[40] has also concluded for the Mothers' Fronts of Sri Lanka. Over time, this women's activism, initiated in response to violent conflict and its aftermath, may yet prove to be the foundation for strong, indigenous feminist movements, for a significant increase in women's public participation, and for improving the lives of women and their societies.

Notes

1 See, for example, Wendy Bracewell, "Women, Motherhood, and Contemporary Serbian Nationalism," *Women's Studies International Forum* 19, 1-2 (1996), pp.25-33; Slavenka Drakulić, "Women and the New Democracy in

the Former Yugoslavia," in Nanette Funk and Magda Mueller, eds., *Gender Politics and Post-Communism: Reflections from Eastern Europe and the Former Soviet Union* (New York: Routledge, 1993); Elissa Helms, "Representations of Wartime Rape in Bosnia-Herzegovina: Nationalism, Feminism, and International Law" (M.A. thesis, University of Pittsburgh, 1998); Vesna Kesić, "From Reverence to Rape: An Anthropology of Ethnic and Genderized Violence," in Marguerite R. Waller and Jennifer Rycenga, eds., *Frontline Feminisms: Women, War, and Resistance* (New York: Routledge, 2001); Žarana Papić, "How to Become a 'Real' Serbian Woman?" *War Report* 36 (September 1995), pp. 40-1; Renata Salecl, *The Spoils of Freedom: Psychoanalysis and Feminism after the Fall of Socialism* (London: Routledge, 1994); and Dubravka Žarkov, "From Media War to Ethnic War: The Female Body and Nationalist Processes in the Former Yugoslavia, 1986-1994" (Ph.D. diss., Center for Women's Studies, University of Nijmegen, 1999).

2 Much of the ethnographic content of this chapter appears in a longer analysis of the discourses of Bosnian women's NGO participants and their donors in Elissa Helms, "Women as Agents of Ethnic Reconciliation? Women's NGOs and International Intervention in Post-war Bosnia-Herzegovina," *Women's Studies International Forum* 26,1 (Jan./Feb. 2003) pp.15-33.

3 Very few women's organizations describe themselves as "feminist" or are comfortable using the term publicly in Bosnia, though some do embrace it privately (see Cynthia Cockburn, *The Space Between Us: Negotiating Gender and National Identities in Conflict* [London: Zed Books, 1998], pp.189-92). This is due to the negative associations with the term common in the whole region of post-socialist Central and Eastern Europe. See, for example, articles in Funk and Mueller, eds., *Gender, Politics and Post-Communism*; Susan Gal and Gail Kligman, *The Politics of Gender after Socialism: A Comparative-Historical Essay* (Princeton, NJ: Princeton University Press, 2000), pp.103-5; Laura Grunberg, "Women's NGOs in Romania," in Gal and Kligman, eds., *Reproducing Gender*, p.307; and Eva V. Huseby-Darvas, "'Feminism the Murderer of Mothers': The Rise and Fall of Neo-Nationalist Reconstruction of Gender in Hungary," in Brackette F. Williams, ed., *Women out of Place: The Gender of Agency and the Race of Nationality* (New York: Routledge, 1997), p.161.

4 See Cynthia Cockburn with Rada Stakić-Domuz and Meliha Hubić, *Women Organizing for Change: A Study of Local Integrative Organizations and the Pursuit of Democracy in Bosnia-Herzegovina* (Zenica, Bosnia-Herzegovina: Medica Zenica, 2001); Martha Walsh, "Aftermath: The Role of Women's Organizations in Postconflict Bosnia and Herzegovina," Working Paper No. 308 (Washington, DC: U.S. Agency for International Development, Center for Development Information and Evaluation, July 2000); and Martha Walsh, "Mind the Gap: Where Feminist Theory Failed to Meet Development Practice – A Missed Opportunity in Bosnia and Herzegovina," *European Journal of Women's Studies* 5 (1998), pp. 329-43.

5 Richard G. Fox, "Gandhi and Feminized Nationalism in India," in Williams, *Women out of Place*, p.37.

6 See Ian Smillie, *Service Delivery or Civil Society? Non-Governmental Organizations in Bosnia and Herzegovina* (Zagreb: CARE Canada, 1996); Paul Stubbs, "Nationalisms, Civil Society and Globalisation in Croatia and Slovenia," *Research in Social Movements, Conflict and Change*, 19 (1995), pp.1-26.

7 Nationalist parties sustained substantial losses in the Bosnian elections in 2000, though they continue to wield influence and to obstruct the implementation of the Dayton Peace Accords in many areas and seem poised to regain power in the elections of 2002. (This chapter was written prior to the 2002 elections.) For election details see the Web site of the Organization for Security and Cooperation in Europe, Mission to Bosnia-Herzegovina <http://www.oscebih.org>.

8 Dubravka Žarkov, "War Rapes in Yugoslavia: On Masculinity, Femininity and the Power of Rape Victim Identity," *Tijschrift voor Criminologie* 39,2 (1997), pp.140-51.

9 Women held 17 per cent of parliamentary positions under the quota system of socialist Yugoslavia. This percentage decreased dramatically after multi-party elections in 1990 and remained low until an internationally backed rule (Rule 7.50) was installed in 1998, mandating that one-third of candidates on party lists be "members of the minority gender," that is, women in all cases aside from that of the Women's Party (*Stranka Žena BiH*). As a result, by the 2000 elections the percentage of women in parliamentary bodies had risen to 18 per cent (see OSCE Web site as cited in note 8).

10 Elissa Helms, "'Politics Is a Whore': Women, Morality, and Victimhood in Post-War Bosnia-Herzegovina," in Xavier Bougarel and Ger Duijzings, eds., *Bosnia: Picking up the Pieces* (forthcoming 2003).

11 See Cynthia Enloe, *Bananas, Beaches, and Bases: Making Feminist Sense of International Politics* (Berkeley: University of California Press, 1990).

12 Implicit in this declaration, however, is that *some* (bad) mothers *do* raise their children to kill other people's children, namely, the women belonging to hostile ethnic groups, in this case Serbs. A full exploration of this dynamic is beyond the scope of this chapter but part of a larger dissertation project for which these data were collected. For the purposes of this chapter, however, it is important to note that such moral qualifications made on a supposedly universal, morally pure motherhood identity expose the inaccuracy of affirmative essentialisms, as some women are obviously excluded.

13 See also Kumudini Samuel, "Activism, Motherhood, and the State in Sri Lanka's Ethnic Conflict," chapter 13 in this volume.

14 Julie Mostov, "'Our Women'/'Their Women': Symbolic Boundaries, Territorial Markers, and Violence in the Balkans," *Peace and Change* 20,4 (October 1995), p.515; Žarkov, "From Media War to Ethnic War"; and Katherine Verdery, "From Parent State to Family Patriarchs: Gender and Nation in Contemporary Eastern Europe," *East European Politics and Societies* 8,2 (Spring 1994), pp.225-55.

15 This is not to say that such border-crossing has been easy or without problems, especially for women who experienced traumatic personal tragedies during the war at the hands of members of "other" ethnic groups, but that women as a group are afforded more room to engage in such activities.

16 Nearly all the women's NGO leaders I spoke with, in fact, readily admitted to tailoring their project proposals and organization literature to suit donor demands, especially demands for multi-ethnic membership and for projects involving cross-ethnic communication. Thus, the leader of one women's NGO proudly told me how she advised the leader of another NGO, whose membership was exclusively mono-ethnic and who was having trouble getting outside

funding, to "go with multi-ethnic cooperation. That's what's going now" (Helms, "Women as Agents of Ethnic Reconciliation?" 9).

17 There are, of course, many donors whose project proposals are informed by the ideas of liberal feminism or "Women-in-Development" paradigms and therefore call for the "empowerment" of women or the full participation of women in economic, political, and social processes. Affirmative gender essentialisms still creep in, however, especially in direct presentations made to local women's NGOs. For examples of these see Helms, "Women as Agents of Ethnic Reconciliation?"

18 These women (many of whom are part of the Women in Conflict Zones Network) have been crossing internal ethnic boundaries (within Bosnia between the RS and the Federation, as well as across newly established boundaries in what was Yugoslavia) since the war ended, and in some cases, since the war itself. See Jill Benderly, "Women's Movements in Yugoslavia, 1978-1992," in Melissa K. Borovoy, Jill A. Irvine, Carol S. Lilly, eds., *State-Society Relations in Yugoslavia 1945-1992* (New York: St. Martin's Press, 1997), p.183.

19 See Lepa Mladjenović, "Feminist Politics in the Anti-war Movement in Belgrade," chapter 12 in this volume.

20 "Bosniac" (*Bošnjak*) refers to Bosnian Muslims as an ethnic or national group and has been used in most official discourses in Bosnia since 1993. On the history of designations for Bosnian Muslims see Ivo Banac, *The National Question in Yugoslavia: Origins, History, Politics* (Ithaca, NY: Cornell University Press, 1984), pp.360-2; Tone Bringa, *Being Muslim the Bosnian Way: Identity and Community in a Central Bosnian Village* (Princeton, NJ: Princeton University Press, 1995); Steven L. Burg, "The Political Integration of Yugoslavia's Muslims: Determinants of Success and Failure," *Carl Beck Papers in Russian and East European Studies* 203 (1983); Dennison I. Rusinow, "Yugoslavia's Muslim Nation," *University Field Staff International Reports* 8 (1982).

21 Resistance by nationalist leaders to the return of displaced persons of a different ethnicity is a continuation, by political means, of wartime ethnic cleansing of territory (see Robert M. Hayden, "Imagined Communities and Real Victims: Self-Determination and Ethnic Cleansing in Yugoslavia," *American Ethnologist* 23,4 [November 1996], pp.783-801). Local nationalist leaders, especially in Serb- and Croat-controlled areas, do not want their control of these now ethnically homogeneous territories to be threatened by the return of ethnic "others," be they women, children, or men. Bosniac leaders differ in their goals from Serb and Croat nationalists, in that they have no neighbouring state of ethnic kin to look to for help. Rather, their best option is seen to lie in the creation of a viable Bosnian state (see Steven L. Burg and Paul S. Shoup, *The War in Bosnia-Herzegovina: Ethnic Conflict and International Intervention* [Armonk, NY: M.E. Sharpe, 1999]). Bosniac nationalist leaders, therefore, while perhaps eager to maintain Bosniac majorities in the smaller political units they control, want to encourage the return of ethnically different refugees to areas of Serb and Croat control so as to facilitate the construction of a multi-ethnic state.

22 Neither of these cases is without serious problems and there is some question as to whether refugee return will foster or complicate ethnic reconciliation. Indeed, as in the Kozarac case, return to many areas has been easier because the villages in these areas were ethnically homogeneous before the war. Return to urban

areas, which were ethnically mixed before the war, is much more problematic and has, for this and other reasons, been much slower to realize.

23 Andrei Simić, in describing the power women wield through their sons in Balkan patrilineal and patrilocal family structures, has called this "cryptomatriarchy" (Andrei Simić, "Machismo and Cryptomatriarchy: Power, Affect, and Authority in the Contemporary Yugoslav Family," *Ethos* 11,1-2 [Spring/Summer 1983], pp.66-86). See also Eugene Hammel, "The Jewish Mother in Serbia or les Structures Alimentaires de la Parente," in William G. Lockwood, ed., *Essays in Balkan Ethnology* (Berkeley: Kroeber Anthropological Society Papers, Special Publications, No. 1, 1967)

24 See, for example, Partha Chatterjee, "Colonialism, Nationalism, and Colonialized Women: The Contest in India," *American Ethnologist* 16,4 (1989), pp.622-33; Malathi de Alwis, "Motherhood as a Space of Protest: Women's Political Participation in Contemporary Sri Lanka," in Patricia Jeffery and Amrita Basu, eds., *Appropriating Gender: Women's Activism and Politicized Religion in South Asia* (New York: Routledge, 1998); Fox, "Gandhi and Feminized Nationalism in India"; Patricia Jeffery, "Agency, Activism, and Agendas," in Jeffery and Basu, *Appropriating Gender*; and Diana Taylor, "Performing Gender: Las Madres de la Plaza de Mayo," in Diana Taylor and Juan Villegas, eds., *Negotiating Performance: Gender, Sexuality, and Theatricality in Latin/o America* (Durham, NC: Duke University Press, 1994).

25 Malathi de Alwis, "Reflections on Gender and Ethnicity in Sri Lanka," and Samuel, "Activism, Motherhood, and the State in Sri Lanka's Ethnic Conflict," both in this volume.

26 See, for example, Sarah Ruddick, *Maternal Thinking: Toward a Politics of Peace* (Boston: Beacon Press, 1989).

27 See, for example, Marina Blagojević, "War and Everyday Life: Deconstruction of Self-Sacrifice," *Sociologija* (October/December 1994), pp.469-82; Chatterjee, "Colonialism, Nationalism, and Colonialized Women"; Drakulić, "Women and the New Democracy in the Former Yugoslavia."

28 Blagojević, "War and Everyday Life," p.475.

29 Fox, "Gandhi and Feminized Nationalism in India," p.48. See also Chatterjee, "Colonialism, Nationalism, and Colonialized Women"; Norma Stoltz Chinchilla, "Nationalism, Feminism, and Revolution in Central America," in Lois A. West, ed., *Feminist Nationalism* (New York: Routledge, 1997), p.201; Barbara Jancar-Webster, *Women and Revolution in Yugoslavia, 1941-1945* (Denver: Arden Press, 1990); Leda Maria Vieira Machado, "'We Learned to Think Politically': The Influence of the Catholic Church and the Feminist Movement on the Emergence of the Health Movement of the Jardim Nordeste Area in Sao Paulo, Brazil," in Sarah A. Radcliffe and Sallie Westwood, eds., *"Viva": Women and Popular Protest in Latin America* (New York: Routledge, 1993); Taylor, "Performing Gender."

30 While women were welcomed by socialist revolutionary movements into the military as fighters, they were nonetheless expected to carry out traditionally prescribed roles during and after the revolution such as caring for war orphans, cooking and cleaning for male soldiers, and providing sexual "comfort" to male soldiers. See Chinchilla, "Nationalism, Feminism, and Revolution in Central America," and Jancar-Webster, *Women and Revolution in Yugoslavia*.

31 "Second wave" feminists began organizing in Yugoslavia as early as 1978 but were concentrated in Zagreb, Ljubljana, and Belgrade and were not active in Bosnia. For historical overviews of women's movements in socialist Yugoslavia and before, see Benderly, "Women's Movements in Yugoslavia"; Barbara Jancar-Webster, "Women in the Yugoslav National Liberation Movement," in Sabina P. Ramet, ed., *Gender Politics in the Western Balkans: Women and Society in Yugoslavia and the Yugoslav Successor States* (University Park, PA: Pennsylvania State University Press, 1999), p.67; Sabrina P. Ramet, "In Tito's Time," in Ramet, *Gender Politics in the Western Balkans*, 89.

32 Taylor, "Performing Gender"; de Alwis, "Motherhood as a Space of Protest," and "Reflections on Gender and Ethnicity in Sri Lanka'"; Samuel, "Activism, Motherhood, and the State in Sri Lanka's Ethnic Conflict."

33 Samuel, "Activism, Motherhood, and the State in Sri Lanka's Ethnic Conflict."

34 De Alwis, "Reflections on Gender and Ethnicity in Sri Lanka"; Samuel, "Activism, Motherhood, and the State in Sri Lanka's Ethnic Conflict."

35 In 1991, mothers from all over the former Yugoslavia protested, demanding the return of their sons from the Yugoslav People's Army (JNA). Several feminists writing about the break-up of the former Yugoslavia have charged that various movements of mothers were made to be pawns of male nationalist politicians, for example, Drakulić, "Women and the New Democracy in the Former Yugoslavia"; Daša Duhaček, "Women's Time in the Former Yugoslavia," in Funk and Mueller, *Gender, Politics and Post-Communism,* 131. See Žarkov, "From Media War to Ethnic War," for a critical analysis of such charges.

36 de Alwis, "Motherhood as a Space of Protest"; Jeffery, "Agency, Activism, and Agendas"; Žarkov, "From Media War to Ethnic War."

37 Žarkov, "From Media War to Ethnic War," p.171.

38 See Bracewell, "Women, Motherhood, and Contemporary Serbian Nationalism."

39 Jeffery, "Agency, Activism, and Agendas," p.223.

40 Samuel, "Activism, Motherhood, and the State in Sri Lanka's Ethnic Conflict."

Chapter 15

The Women's Movement in Sri Lanka: An Interview with Kumari Jayawardena

Colombo, 6 May 2002

Wenona Giles: We have discussed women's movements and activism extensively in the Women in Conflict Zones Network. With your depth and breadth of knowledge of, as well as participation in, feminist activism for many years in Sri Lanka and in other countries, can you comment on the women's movement here?

Kumari Jayawardena: I think it is important to realize that there was not only a women's movement in twentieth-century Sri Lanka, but there was also a consciousness about women's issues in the nineteenth century. Women writers and poets raised issues that dealt with women's subordination, and also challenged patriarchal structures. Women's education expanded along with opportunities for employment, including the emergence of the first women doctors in the 1890s. But it was in the early twentieth century – perhaps also inspired by talk about suffragettes and women's rights in the West and in India – that Sri Lankan women started campaigning for the right to vote, which was obtained in 1931. By 1932, there were two women members in the legislature. So that was quite a dramatic start! But women of today do not know about those debates. It is just something we read in one line in textbooks. Recently, Malathi de Alwis and I wrote on this issue and we researched the Sinhala, Tamil, and English newspapers and journals in which the franchise issue of the 1920s was hotly debated.[1]

Those of us who came into the women's movement in the latter part of the twentieth century had not realized that, in a sense, the grandmothers of this generation were already in the women's movement in the 1920s. We have now discovered that the women's movement was ongoing from the 1930s to the 1990s. For example, in the 1940s and 1950s, liberal middle-class women's groups were active. One of their inspirations was a Canadian, Dr. Mary Irvin Rutnam, from Toronto, a pioneer doctor of the period who married a Sri Lankan and came to the island in 1896.[2] She brought with her a lot of the experience of early women's struggles in Canada, including the suffrage struggle. In 1930-31, she inspired the Lanka Mahila Samiti, a rural women's organization, which spread to the whole of Sri Lanka. As a doctor she was able to start women's and children's education programs for health, hygiene, sanitation, and child care. When I recently read her school texts on health, I saw that there were also underlying social messages against the caste system and child servants and in favour of women speaking out for their rights and being active in public affairs. Women of the Left were also active from the 1930s onwards and, in 1948, formed a short-lived socialist women's organization that was autonomous. Women from Left parties were active in parliamentary politics from the 1950s onwards.

There were quite a number of middle-class women in the Women's Political Union of the 1930s and 1940s, and in the All Ceylon Women's Conference, which organized seven regional women's conferences in Colombo in the 1950s and 1960s. Actually, my mother was in these organizations, which took up many issues including equal pay, women on the jury, and the right to enter professions. I remember her travelling throughout Sri Lanka on women's issues and going abroad for international meetings.

So by the mid-1970s, when the United Nations International Decade for Women was declared, there was already a history of women's activity, which some of us had been aware of through our mothers. While it was a continuation of the earlier movement, in another sense the 1970s marked a new phase in which we got to talk about feminism, patriarchy, and violence against women – issues that had not been debated earlier. In the post-1970s phase, a whole new feminist agenda arose, and some of us women academics were asked to speak on trade union and political party platforms about the UN Decade for Women.

I wrote an article in 1976 entitled "Women of Sri Lanka, Oppressed or Emancipated?" There was a question mark in my article because I was not sure. When I looked at one area I thought women were emancipated. For example, women in Sri Lanka had good quality of life indices as demonstrated in infant and maternal mortality, literacy, and life expectancy statistics. I remember when it suddenly dawned on me (it was in the middle of one of these speeches to a trade union group of men) that women were oppressed! Where were the women in the trade union leadership? How many women were in politics? Wasn't there male domination in the home, in the workplace, and in all institutions? So the research agenda also evolved, including both research and action. And, of course, by the 1980s we were in the middle of a civil war, which gave a new dimension to the women's movement.

WG: In what ways do you think that the current peace process in Sri Lanka has affected or been affected by the women's movement here?

KJ: Women were already organizing and agitating for peace by the 1980s when the war began. We started making links with women in the conflict zones of Sri Lanka. The women's groups gave the peace movement a big push because they had networks already in place. Women were already networking here and abroad on other issues and meeting each other at conferences in Sri Lanka, in the region, and internationally. South Asian women's solidarity was there from the beginning of the war and throughout it. Women have always been part of the peace movement, but we have to remind the public not to forget that during the darkest days, it was the women who held up the peace banners. The peace movement often led us to work with women in India and Pakistan. We travelled a lot, speaking on platforms that often included Sinhalese and Tamil women together. In India, Pakistan, and Sri Lanka women would come together, irrespective of what their governments were doing. We have often openly opposed the policies of our own governments, and were always critical of their warmongering.

A group called Women for Peace, which started in the 1980s in Sri Lanka, took out a half-page advertisement in the newspaper with a hundred prominent women in Sri Lanka signing for peace. Other peace activists went into schools, talking about the need for ethnic harmony and peace, and distributed our material. Activities included contacts with women's groups throughout Sri Lanka in spite of criticisms that we were "unpatriotic." Today, everybody is talking peace, and there is a lot of renewed activity after the ceasefire and peace initiatives. There are visits between women from the south, north, and northeast of the island. The state is also interested in publicizing this networking. We have been transformed from "suspicious characters" into "good citizens" and are asked, "Why don't you do more?" It is amazing how attitudes change! In the early days of the war – in the 1980s – participants in marches would be charged by the police. It was illegal to hold meetings or to participate in processions and demonstrations, even on International Women's Day!

WG: Can you comment on transnational feminism, that is, the recognition of difference, or working across or with difference, towards achieving an international women's movement?

KJ: With our South Asian friends, we have taken up issues on peace and democracy, human rights, and women's rights. Also, many feminists have travelled widely, more frequently than they were able to do in the past. In the early twentieth century, many Indian women in the independence movement and suffrage campaigns – most notably Sarojini Naidu and Kamaladevi Chattopadyaya – visited Sri Lanka. Western women campaigners for women's causes also travelled in Asia, among them Margaret Fawcett, Marie Stopes, and Margaret Sanger, and a few South Asian women spoke on platforms in the West. After the 1970s, we had more contact with women in Asia, Africa, the Middle East, Europe, North America, and Latin America. An important visitor to Sri Lanka was Nawal El Saadawi who, in the late 1970s, inspired us with her lectures on women's rights.

The international links with both Western and other feminists have been very useful for us. I believe that women raise issues based on their own history, experiences, and current problems. These may or may not be applicable in other countries, but we are interested in seeing how women have tackled such issues. However, I also believe that we have to get away from the idea that there is a serious Third World – First World division between feminists. Feminism was not imposed on the Third World by Westerners. Each country has had its own history of feminism.[3] Also, if you say "First World – Third World," you aren't taking into account the fact that Europe and North America have a history of dissent, into which we have tapped. Indians and Sri Lankans have been in contact with many of these dissidents over the decades, and have had links with anti-colonial movements, free-thought, theosophy, socialism, and feminism in the West. Such subverters of their own societies were well known in India and Sri Lanka, but if you mention their names in Britain or North America they are unheard of!

Personal acquaintance with such dissidents – often through my parents – led me to write *The White Woman's Other Burden*,[4] in which I explore the way foreign women in South Asia were not only those "Women of the Raj," whom we see depicted in films as the wives of bureaucrats, but were also women with their own agendas, which had nothing to do with their own governments and which sometimes went against colonial policies of their own countries. They included Annie Besant, Helena Blavatsky, and Margaret Cousins, who spearheaded the women suffrage campaign in India in the 1920s and 1930s. Even some of the missionary women in South Asia had a "feminist" agenda against their own patriarchal bishops and clergy.

Many famous Indian "gurus" had foreign women soulmates. Gandhi had the English woman Madeline Slade, the daughter of a British admiral, as his disciple, secretary, guide, philosopher, and friend. When she went to London with him, she caused a huge stir, wearing a sari, washing Gandhi's feet, giving him his breakfast, and doing his correspondence. The British found this to be a very strange thing, but in India she was honoured. Similarly, Sister Nivedita, an Irish woman (Margaret Noble), was a disciple of a famous Indian reformist leader Swami Vivekananda at the beginning of the twentieth century. She was a revolutionary and a friend of many socialists and anarchists in Britain, and was very influential in Bengal. Another such figure was the "Mother" of Pondicherry, spiritual partner of the Indian savant Aurobindo. The "Mother" – Mira Rachel Alfassa of Sephardic Jewish origin from Egypt and France – was a great modernizer and reformist and is revered even today, thirty years after her death.

Many European and American socialist and communist women married Indian and Sri Lankan nationalists and Left leaders, and lived and worked for these causes in South Asia. Their "foreignness" was not at issue, since they were not only serving local causes but were also opposing the colonialism of their countries of origin, and even the politics of South Asian governments in the post-independence phase. These women were accepted; a few of them even becoming elected members of the legislature.

WG: Perhaps this consistent political involvement of women in Sri Lanka is related to the view expressed by the Sri Lankan participants in the Women in Conflict Zones Network. They always said, "We are both academic and activist at the same time and we don't want to be identified as one or the other."

KJ: In many Third World countries, that is indeed the case – you can't avoid activism, because there is always something going on which calls for intervention and protest on both social and political issues in one's own country, or in another country. So, it is difficult to isolate yourself from action in the streets, drafting resolutions, collecting signatures, and lobbying. Also in normal everyday life, if you are in any movement, there is no big dichotomy between action and research. As Sri Lankan academics, that has been our social practice for a long time. And a lot of the inspiration did come from both university women and from the struggles of working-class women. Peace was one issue that brought us all together irrespective of ethnicity, religion, and class.

WG: What is your view of comparative approaches to research and activism?

KJ: These are crucial debates for the women's movement. One criticism has been that Western feminists do the theory and we do the action. This is, of course, not strictly true and not a serious allegation. But in Pakistan, India, and Sri Lanka, many feminists come from another political tradition – namely, a socialist and anti-colonial one. You don't tell a socialist, "Hey, that is a white man/woman." Instead you ask, "What are his/her politics, which class is she/he working for?" and other such questions. Similarly, Western feminists have a political approach to people that is not based on race. Maybe Third World women living abroad where racism prevails are more sensitive about such issues and have raised issues of race, because of the societies they are living in.

Another important point is that problems affecting women – such as dowry, caste, and so forth – may be part of a more feudal society. And that is where politics becomes important. Many of us are against cultural relativism that argues, "Our culture is the best; we don't need to change, and local women who come and say how terrible child marriage is, say so because they are Westernized and don't understand their own cultures." Here we fall into a trap, trying to defend ourselves and our cultures.

WG: In your view, what are some of the difficulties of working across academic-activist boundaries? Does working across such boundaries enhance research and activism?

KJ: I know it is not easy because both academics and activists sometimes feel awkward in the presence of the other. The academic always feels guilty that she/he is not activist enough, and the activist is always apologizing by saying, "I am not an academic, but. . . . " So there is a certain uneasiness, but nevertheless, I think the experience of the Women in Conflict Zones Network has shown that it can work. When I met some of the Yugoslav women in Colombo, I couldn't tell the difference between activists and academics. The activists talk in a way that academics understand and the academics are constantly referring to various actions that are taking place and the progress made by women through struggles. Perhaps it is in the feminist movement that the boundaries are crossed more easily, and awkwardness is not a major problem; it is just the predicament of being slightly apologetic – "I am sorry, I'm only an activist," "I'm sorry, I'm an academic." But it is not really a serious problem because feminists can't avoid being both. A certain humility is also needed; it is not that some women are just pushing their way in, saying they are academics. They are actually learning from the others, who are more activist than they are.

If you are doing cross-country research, you cannot leave out activists and only bring a few university people together. And I am not so sure about this word "activist." I don't know whether we should have another word for activist-cum-researcher. Academics of course have more time to think and read, but they can also be directly in touch with working women, peasant and plantation women, and women in conflict situations, including women displaced by war. In addition, when academics go to a village or a plantation, organize meetings and give speeches – then what are they? They are speakers, political speakers with commitment – so no one asks, "Which caste are you, activist caste or research caste?"

WG: Are we then challenging another boundary when we do comparative research – the so-called activist-academic caste divide?

KJ: Yes. It is like finding the third way. However, once you start labelling people, you are getting into unnecessary debates and arguments. The same women can be sometimes activists sometimes researchers, and sometimes writers and participants in political debates – so who are they then?

Perhaps the dichotomy drawn between "academic" and "activist" is a false one. First, what is the definition of "academic"? Is an academic only a person teaching at a university? At a high school? Does conducting "research" place one solely in the "academic" category? Clearly not, for research spans the "activist-academic" spectrum. Is writing and research not activism? Are well-researched publications put out by "activist" organizations "academic" in nature? In the end, use of such terminology can serve to strengthen stereotypes, and thus divide individuals and groups. Whose purpose does this serve? In Sri Lanka, and mostly likely everywhere, the use of this dichotomy is entrenched and plays out in negative and positive stereotypes. Part of the agenda of women's groups should be to counter this thinking and to reclaim the use of language, and to value contributions of all sorts equally.

WG: How do we deal with a cultural politics versus a human rights approach in a comparative research project such as ours? Does comparative work push us to challenge more cultural relativist kinds of perspectives?

KJ: I strongly believe in a human rights approach. I am not so geared to cultural relativism or culture and religion based on diversity and customary laws. I think, as women, we had better look at what the constitution of the country says about fundamental rights, what the International Conventions (especially CEDAW) say, and then uphold them. I and many others would not uphold anything customary if it is oppressive to women. Of course this does not mean denying diversity.

But also when you undertake comparative research, I think you group together those who are fairly like-minded. You know, there is a kind of a middle-of-the road agenda, where we may have differences but we all agree on women's rights and human rights and can adopt the guideline "universality in diversity," which Nira Yuval-Davis argues should be the inspiration.

WG: Can you discuss why comparisons between Sri Lanka and the post-Yugoslav states may be useful and important?

KJ: I think Sri Lanka and the post-Yugoslav countries are a good choice of countries for comparison. Countries that have been through a socialist experiment recognize that there can be a social system which is not feudal or capitalist, but rather aims at some kind of socialist model. When you talk about Yugoslavs of a certain generation, trying another pattern, but not totally subservient to Stalin or the Soviet Union, it rings a bell here in Sri Lanka. There are many people here who went to socialist Yugoslavia. In fact, at this conference, I met a Sri Lankan woman who told me that her father, as a young man in a Left political group, went to build railways in Yugoslavia.

There was also the non-aligned movement that presented an alternative to the two superpowers of the time. Yugoslav experience and history thus resonates with the Sri Lankan experience; we unsuccessfully tried a form of socialism and then we watched those experiments collapse. But other movements continue, including the women's movement! There is also a basis for comparison insofar as both Sri Lanka and Yugoslavia have been through civil war, ethnic pogroms, and turmoil in recent years.

WG: Could you comment on the importance of research on class inequities in post-conflict and conflict research? Do you think we have adequately addressed class in the WICZNET project? I am concerned about this because it is often difficult to ask questions about class when discussing ethnicity and nationalism.

KJ: That is very much a generational question, because when I was young, class was all we talked about. And we would not only refer to "working-class women" and "upper-class woman" but we would also ask, irrespective of their social origins, which class they claimed to represent? This question arises all the time in the Third World in situations where political leaders from other classes represent workers and peasants. For example, trade union leaders may not be from the classes they are fighting for, namely, from working-class or peasant origin.

When you first come to the feminist movement, there is a slight contradiction that you have to face. Feminism problematizes class issues, because if you go among the working-class in a trade union group and you talk about feminism, they say you are dividing the class into men and women. If you go among women, they may not want to hear about class issues. They say there is only one class and that is women. So our task of bringing class issues into women's groups and bringing women's issues into political party or trade union groups could make feminists unpopular. But, actually, that is why feminism is challenging and interesting – from an intellectual perspective. It is not simply a kind of dogma that you hang around your neck. It really is a very live issue.

Context is very necessary, and those of us who have a certain line of thinking believe that we should give as much of the total picture as possible. I do not mean that one has to write a book on the history of Yugoslavia, but we need to know a bit about the country, the class structure, and the background of the society. Then we can better understand the issues. Recently, when I asked a woman these questions, she said, "It is not relevant which class these people belong to, because I am talking about Islamicism." But you can't just say a bunch of women are Islamicists, without saying whether they were peasants in the fields or women in their golf clubs. So my reaction is then twofold. First, I would like to know the society and class a woman is coming from, the country of origin, who she is, and what her political agenda is; and second, who are the people she is studying?

WG: What is the relationship between globalization, international corporate investment, and conflict in Sri Lanka?

KJ: The business community in Sri Lanka and abroad would welcome prospects of peace, and they visualize rapid economic development linked to global markets. In formulating projects, new issues do come up pertaining to globalization. I don't think it is a bad word – in fact, it has been good for women in some respects. Particularly pertaining to the contact women can have with others and the immediate action that is possible. You can press a button and reach women around the world to begin a protest. As Amartya Sen says, globalization is not new; it has been here for some time. But within open-market and globalized structures it is important to understand the nature of the exploitation between rich and poor, between the powerful and the less powerful, between some strong multinationals and those with fewer resources. How do the policies determined by these structures, including those of the International Monetary Fund and the World Bank, affect women? These are our serious concerns.

WG: What about the relationship between patriarchy and post-conflict situations?

KJ: I certainly think that it is in post-conflict times that we have to be really vigilant. In conflict situations and anti-colonial struggles, patriarchy breaks down a bit, sometimes quite a lot. Women are in battle dress, carrying bombs, and are even suicide bombers. They also do a host of "unwomanly" things and even become empowered as heads of the households. Some huge social changes take place in the attitudes of men towards women, and this is reflected in times when women are in the armed forces and guerrilla movements, as in Sri Lanka where there are women in the army, navy, airforce, and police. We see them at checkpoints, in fatigues and boots, and carrying guns. During times of war and revolution, such changes are accepted. But afterwards patriarchy says, "Thank you very much, now you can go back home." People don't want to hear about them let alone marry them, and that is where patriarchy enters and says, "women must be chaste," and "these girls have been in the army and we can't vouch for them," and "they have been carrying guns and will be a menace."

Many countries including Colombia, Vietnam, and Mozambique have encountered this problem of stigma. And now it has come here. Traditionalists in the east of Sri Lanka are saying that women should be traditional in dress and behaviour, should wear the sari and put flowers in their hair, and so forth. Feminists are warning against the Talibanization that is possible with regard to women and dress codes. Thus this post-conflict period can be a defining moment for women. It is also among the best of moments, because when peace prevails, women's sons and daughters are not going to get killed. But it is a time for greater vigilance, since the patriarchs will now assert their authority and will tell you how to behave, what to wear and whom your daughter should marry. So you have to watch out for patriarchal backlash, and monitor the way in which it tries to come back into the lives of women and girls. That is an interesting issue.

WG: What are some future directions for research that have arisen from this Women in Conflict Zones project, in your view?

KJ: The post-conflict situation has many problems – the treatment of displaced women, women in the army, women and girl guerrillas, and war widows. Here a comparison of the situation in the former Yugoslavia and in Sri Lanka on the "comeback" of patriarchy would be revealing. Further, the political economy of peace brings with it problems of rehabilitation and transformation. Marie Aimée Lucas, of the organization Women Living Under Muslim Law, has analysed the Algerian experience to show that although the bitter anti-colonial war may have occurred a long time ago, the practices of war continue in various ways, especially in ultramacho attitudes – for example, in the use of violence against women and children.

But also, what does "rehabilitation" really mean? Does it signal a mythic going back to "home sweet home," doing what your grandmother did, reconstructing the old patriarchal society? Rebuild it like it used to be and you will feel secure and forget the war? That is one danger. But there is also a chance for "transformation," and we have to think about what kind of transformation we would like. Often the fighting groups haven't thought about an economic plan, nor have they visualized the new society. They have been too busy fighting and sometimes do not even have a political wing that thinks through policies. Transformation is often a question that neither side has thought too much about. On occasion, foreign agencies and the governments give money that nobody knows how to use because they haven't thought it through.

WG: I would like to end by asking you to say a few final words on something that has been a central concern for the WICZNET and that you have been touching on throughout this interview – how would you define conflict zone?

KJ: In Sri Lanka, there were periods of ceasefire, but in those times, we never said there wasn't a conflict. In fact, the conflict could even extend into the capital city, with its five-star hotels. We were in a country at war, where even one checkpoint near a big hotel meant life was not "normal." So one can't say that there wasn't any part of the country that was not affected. The war was at the back of everyone's mind. It is true that some places were more dangerous than others and there are some areas that we haven't visited for twenty years because they were in "conflict zones."

Now that there is a ceasefire, huge crowds and middle-class tourists are going to places in the north and east that they have not seen for a long time – Sri Lankans are filling up all the hotels. Even poor people want to go. One person said to me, "Oh, I want to go to Jaffna!" and I asked him, "What for?" and he replied, "Just to see!" Today a conflict zone also means that you are conscious that there have been tremendous restrictions on the spaces where you could previously go. When that is lifted, everyone wants to fill the space, and to see the devastation caused by war. The last time there was a ceasefire in Sri Lanka in 1995, everybody wanted to rush on a train to Jaffna – trade unions, women's groups, the Girl Guides, and the Federation of University Women. They wanted to revive their organization's branches in the conflict zones. Such attempts to return to normalcy prevail today. So we can only be cautiously optimistic and at the same time vigilant about issues of women's rights, children's rights, and democracy, in this difficult period of our history.

Notes

1 Malathi de Alwis and Kumari Jayawardena, *Casting Pearls: The Women's Franchise Movement in Sri Lanka* (Colombo: Social Scientists' Association, 2000).
2 Kumari Jayawardena, *Dr. Mary Rutnam: A Canadian Pioneer for Women's Rights in Sri Lanka* (Colombo: Social Scientists' Association, 1993).
3 Kumari Jayawardena, *Feminism and Nationalism in the Third World* (London: Zed Books, 1986).
4 Kumari Jayawardena, *The White Woman's Other Burden* (London: Routledge, 1995).

Malathi de Alwis, Wenona Giles, and Edith Klein

Future Directions:
Sri Lanka and the Post-Yugoslav States

We go to press just as the government of Sri Lanka and the Tamil militant group, the Liberation Tigers of Tamil Eelam (LTTE), with the facilitation of the Norwegian government, have successfully concluded the first round of peace talks in Sattahip, Thailand. The eight-month-long ceasefire continues to hold, resulting in increased travel and interaction between the previously isolated regions of the north, east, and south of the island. While the mood in the south of Sri Lanka as well as among the international community is optimistic, we remain more cautious in light of the thoughtful analysis provided in the most recent report issued by the extraordinarily courageous members of the University Teachers for Human Rights (Jaffna) – many of whom have remained in hiding for several years because their lives were threatened by the LTTE.[1] In their report, "In the Shadows of Sattahip: The Many Faces of Peace," they warn against placing too much confidence in the Sattahip agreement:

> We have a government quite willing to ditch the Tamil opposition and its ministers shamefully performing the gratuitous service of exonerating the LTTE from charges of child conscription, extortion and planned attacks on Muslims. We moreover have reports, the undignified fallout from which surfaces in media gossip, of rival groups of ministers falling over and undercutting each other to cultivate advantageous relationships with the LTTE, presumably with an eye to the millions of dollars expected as rehabilitation aid. According to sources close to the LTTE in Vavuniya, Poovannan, an important LTTE figure there who deals with NGOs, had visited Colombo twice recently. First as a guest of one minister, and then of a minister in the rival camp.

We are seeing today a strange arrangement where the Tigers claim to be moving towards Eelam, while the Government congratulates itself before the Sinhalese claiming to have saved the Unitary State. In the meantime we are hearing the same old UNP [United National Party] claim that the country is moving towards becoming an El Dorado, and would get there but for the Opposition. Hence a demand for absolute control over Parliament, clipping the President's wings etc. There are also strong indications that the Government is preparing for repression in the South.

The "effective administration," the LTTE hopes, will continue to run [by] sponging [upon] a titanic injection of US dollars from the International Community. The LTTE has no intention of taking on formal responsibilities that would make them answerable for human rights violations and oblige them to respect a democratic opposition.

This means life would become increasingly dangerous in the North-East. Whether any injection of cash could perform the miracle of development in a political climate where committed persons, whom the community needs badly, are killed, beaten, intimidated and expelled is highly questionable. The North-East has potentially the intellectual and professional skills to lift itself up without a massive injection of cash. What it needs is democracy, security and dignity. The more fundamental question for peace activists is whether the people want the kind of order envisaged at Sattahip.[2]

In the post-Yugoslav states, recent developments indicate that the status quo still holds in Bosnia-Herzegovina, that a similar pattern of international care-taking (i.e., overseeing and/or supervising in the post-conflict stage) is emerging in post-war Kosovo/a, and that Serbia appears to be embarking on a new political path in the post-Milošević era, perhaps in the direction of a new (quasi-) democratic order. While openly violent conflict has been contained, the problems of hypernationalism have not yet been directly addressed, and the transition to a post-communist, post-Milošević, and post-Dayton political order will not likely be a smooth one. The election in Serbia in October 2000 of a coalition of democratic opposition parties marked the beginning of a new era; but along with the positive developments brought by this change in government, there are negative consequences, to be sure. For example, campaigns for privatization in many sectors threaten to off-load a number of services from government into private hands – a move that usually takes the harshest toll on women, as they struggle to provide family care and other services that would normally have been provided by state agencies. All successor states of the former Yugoslavia have seen a diminution in the percentage of lawmakers who are women and, as a result, women's voices are not heard as loudly. Deeply entrenched patriarchal values remain relatively unchanged by shifts in governments, and as long as they are present – even in a dormant state – the threat of a resurgence of virulent nationalism can never be discounted. It will be some time before communities broken by a decade of war can begin the process of healing and reconciliation, and indeed the legacy of violence, rape, and destruction is most certainly a permanent one.

Against these dominant indicators there are, nevertheless, fledgling efforts to rebuild bridges and forge new links. In 2002, government officials from the successor states met each other publicly to discuss common matters of concern – trade, travel, and visa requirements – a move that would have been unthinkable a mere few years earlier. With the sustained support of international organizations, families dispersed and separated by war now find it slightly easier to visit one another and perhaps even be reunited, if not with their property at least with each other. The forces for peace, it seems, may gradually overtake the forces for nationalism and war. The assassination in March 2003 of Serbian Prime Minister Zoran Djindjić unleashed a wave of reprisals against the remnants of Milošević supporters and launched an effort – more determined than ever – to return society to the rule of law.

Many of the WICZNET members who participated in this comparative analysis in Sri Lanka and the post-Yugoslav states have gone on to projects in other parts of the world, building on the knowledge gained from the WICZNET in their continuing activism and research. Some of the questions they raised as this project came to a conclusion are outlined below.

Future Directions: Research on Gender and Conflict Zones

Debates at our workshops indicated the need for co-operation but also revealed a necessity for better and more context-sensitive understanding of the situation and/or locations of actors involved in such co-operation. Workshop participants stressed the importance of an information-sharing process where all the actors are regarded as equal partners in a mutual effort to end the victimization of women in conflict and enable their involvement in peace negotiations, as well as their participation in the political reconstruction of post-conflict situations. Better co-operation of international NGOs and international agencies with local women's, human rights, and peace groups in order to protect and strengthen women's position and political power in conflict and post-conflict situations was highlighted. While there was a critique of international humanitarian aid

organizations for the paternalism and cultural insensitivity they sometimes express (see Elissa Helms in chapter 14), it was also agreed that
NGOs and feminist organizations face accusations and harassment from
nationalist organizations that perceived them as being traitors and moral
degenerates (see Žarana Papić in chapter 4), and especially in Sri Lanka,
as the harbingers of a neo-Christian imperialism.

Network members made a number of important interventions regarding violence and resistance in a comparative perspective. First of all, patterns of violence against women in war zones cannot be generalized, but
the forms of violence against women in war are similar – for example,
rape is a specific violation and has always been a part of war strategy.
However, it has taken a long time to achieve the current public recognition of rape as a war crime. Indeed, the resolutions of The Hague Tribunal following the recent wars in the region of the former Yugoslavia,
seem arbitrary and are stronger on paper than in the prosecution of perpetrators (see Radhika Coomaraswamy in chapter 7). Second, the problem of blaming the victim for the crime against her has not been resolved,
and this is an intrinsic part of the fact that conflict-torn societies tend to
see an increase in all types of civilian violence. Third, the fact that rape in
war is also an embodiment of the hatred of ethnic location is hidden, or
else is subject to manipulation by governmental propagandists who mis-
use the fact of war rape to emphasize women's nationality rather than to
condemn the incidence of violence against women per se. Finally, feminist
activists must themselves be self-critical about the challenges they face in
dealing with victims of violence; it is essential to remember the contradiction between the need to talk about violence against women in war, and
the importance of doing so in an enabling way. Participants pointed out
that in both Sri Lanka and the region of the former Yugoslavia women's
groups are wholly inadequate to the task that confronts them, since there
are no existing shelters, nor a history of SOS Hotlines and similar
resources.

The Network project participants defined women's peace initiatives as
crucial for future study. Our discussions indicated a discrepancy between
women's political activism for peace and their role and involvement in
peace negotiations as well as in post-conflict situations. As Kumudini
Samuel (in chapter 13) has observed, "Women's aspirations for peace,
and their activism within the peace movement, have not been translated
into the determination of either the content or the direction of the peace
process" in Sri Lanka. It was also noted that while women's activism at
the grassroots level has been frequently appropriated by both traditional
party politicians as well as militant movements, women themselves have

rarely been invested with any concrete powers within the political process. Even those women who have managed to gain representation in local and national governing and legislative bodies have almost always achieved such positions on the backs of their male kin – the best examples being the president and prime minister of Sri Lanka, both of whom entered politics after the death of their husbands. It was emphasized by the WICZNET that it is critical to address these issues in light of the debate on the empowerment of women resulting from armed conflict.

Participants in this comparative project were also careful to point out that it is incorrect to assume that women are intrinsically oriented towards peace (women's increasing involvement in violent, right-wing organizations and militant groups effectively contradicts this) or that by merely having women in leadership roles, women's concerns will be addressed (see Elissa Helms in chapter 14 and Djurdja Knežević in chapter 6). They concluded that it is imperative that women be politicized and conscientized about their marginalized status within society, especially at a time when many younger women perceive themselves to be already liberated.

Some of the participants raised the fact that women's groups can't sustain the message of peace for long, particularly because certain external forces can always influence the peace agenda (i.e., women's groups have no control over the military state). In Sri Lanka, the Women's Coalition for Peace (WCP) could not prosper because of the complex question of the WCP's "mass involvement" – historically, the WCP has had no mass base and therefore has had no mass support. Thus, the class/nationalism contradiction was recognized as a universal problem requiring extensive critical evaluation. There was a general debate about the issue of ignoring class in nationalist rhetoric. It was agreed that where class has not been sufficiently recognized, opportunities are missed to build a mass peace movement which is sustainable.[3] As well, discussions about "mass movements" pointed out that war affects different sectors of society differently and in order to understand the international dimensions of war, we must recognize that regional and global politics can sometimes overdetermine national mass movements. In summary, while we have begun to address the political economy of armed conflict, this should not supersede attention to the political economy of peace, which should be a significant area for future consideration.

Participants raised the issue that one's multiple identities as a member of a suppressor group or of a suppressed group are not lessened by being a feminist (see Lepa Mladjenović in chapter 3). Nor should it be forgotten that most peace movements are not deeply informed by feminism, which further complicates struggles for peace. One question that resonated throughout the workshops was: How do we create a working knowledge of difference? Theories of ethnic-national identity which probe this area are emerging. Through them, we can examine the perennial problem of the relationship between how we constitute organizations and how we constitute ourselves. Class, guilt, and relative position become important as one works through the often disparate identities that constitute the self. Women in Black was offered as one site where these questions are being practically resolved, and the example was given of women in Northern Ireland and Palestine who faced their fears of talking about nationalist divisions through allowing periods of silence that permitted the creation of safe spaces wherein the debate could begin again.[4]

It was argued that we need multi-level peace education for leaders, and in school curricula, and that these need to be established before conflict ever erupts. As well, future research should focus more closely on the role of the media in worldwide conflict. Participants concluded that feminist peace politics has to conceptualize and define ways for feminists to deal with the state, to address the question of whether and how to be engaged with state politics in a way that is strategic and productive. This is a long process, and one with which feminism has been insufficiently engaged to date. We hope that this collection will contribute towards continuing these crucial debates and to building a more democratic, transversal, and peaceful politics.

Notes

1 One of their founding members as well as a leading feminist activist and scholar, Dr. Rajini Thiranagama, was brutally assassinated by the LTTE in 1989, as the UTHR(J) was preparing their first human rights report for publication.

2 Extracted from "In the Shadows of Sattahip: The Many Faces of Peace." *University Teachers for Human Rights (Jaffna), Sri Lanka.* <http://www.uthr.org/SpecialReports/spreport15.htm>, 4 October 2002.

3 It may be that only in countries with a strong pro-feminist presence at leadership levels, such as in South Africa, that the peace process can be expected to challenge patriarchal assumptions about the reconstruction of society.

4 Cynthia Cockburn, *The Space Between Us: Negotiating Gender and National Identities in Conflict* (London: Zed Books, 1998).

Selected Bibliography

Abeysekera, Charles, and Newton Gunasinghe, eds. *Facets of Ethnicity in Sri Lanka*. Colombo: Social Scientists' Association, 1987.

Aleksov, D., ed. *Deserters from the War in Former Yugoslavia*. Belgrade: Women in Black, 1994.

Alexander, M. Jacqui, and Chandra Mohanty, eds. *Feminist Genealogies, Colonial Legacies, Democratic Futures*. London: Routledge, 1997.

Anderson, B. *Imagined Communities: Reflections on the Origins and Spread of Nationalism*. London: Verso, 1983.

Anthias, Floya, and Nira Yuval-Davis, in association with Harriet Cain. *Racialized Boundaries*. New York: Routledge, 1992.

Bandaranayake, Senake. "The Peopling of Sri Lanka: The National Question and some Problems of History and Ethnicity." In Charles Abeysekera, and Newton Gunasinghe, eds. *Facets of Ethnicity in Sri Lanka*. Colombo: Social Scientists' Association, 1987.

Bhavnani, Kum-Kum. "Towards a Multicultural Europe: Race, Nation and Identity in 1992 and Beyond." *Feminist Review* 45 (1993), pp.30-45.

Boehmer, Elleke. "Motherlands, Mothers and Nationalist Sons: Representations of Nationalism and Women in African Literature." In A. Rutherford, ed. *From Commonwealth to Post-Colonial*. Aarhus: Dangaroo Press, 1992.

Brownmiller, Susan. "Making Female Bodies the Battlefield." In A. Stiglmayer, ed. *Mass Rape: The War against Women in Bosnia-Herzegovina*. Lincoln: University of Nebraska Press, 1994.

Busfield, J. *Men, Women and Madness: Understanding Gender and Mental Disorder*. London: MacMillian Press, 1996.

Ćetković, N. "Feministicka alternativa nacionalizmu i ratu" (Feminist Alternative to Nationalism and War). *S.O.S. Bulletin*, No. 6-7. Belgrade: S.O.S. Hotline for Women and Children Victims of Violence, 1993.

CHA Newsletter. *Listening to the Displaced* 2,3 (July/August 1997). Colombo: Consortium of Humanitarian Agencies.

217

Chatterjee, P. *The Nation and Its Fragments: Colonial and Post-Colonial Histories.* Princeton, NJ: Princeton University Press, 1993.

Chhachhi, Amrita. "Identity Politics, Secularism and Women: A South Asian Perspective." In Zoya Hasan, ed. *Forging Identities: Gender, Communities and the State.* New Delhi: Kali for Women, 1994.

Cockburn, Cynthia. *The Space Between Us: Negotiating Gender and National Identities in Conflict.* London: Zed Books, 1998.

Coomaraswamy, Radhika. "'Through the Looking Glass Darkly': Politics of Ethnicity." In Committee for Rational Development, ed. *Sri Lanka. The Ethnic Conflict: Myths, Realities and Perspectives.* New Delhi: Navrang, 1984.

_____. "Myths Without Conscience: Tamil and Sinhalese Nationalist Writings of the 1980s." In Charles Abeysekera and Newton Gunasinghe, eds. *Facets of Ethnicity in Sri Lanka.* Colombo: Social Scientists' Association, 1987.

Corrin, Chris, ed. *Super Women and the Double Burden: Women's Experience of Change in Central and Eastern Europe and the Former Soviet Union.* Toronto: Second Story Press, 1992. Now available from Sumach Press, Toronto.

De Alwis, Malathi. "The 'Purity' of Displacement and the Re-territorialization of Longing." In Wenona Giles and Jennifer Hyndman eds. *Sites of Violence: Gender and Conflict Zones.* Berkeley: University of California Press, forthcoming.

De Mel, Neloufer. *Women and the Nation's Narrative: Gender and Nationalism in Twentieth-Century Sri Lanka.* New Delhi: Kali for Women, 2001.

Desjarlais, Robert, et al. *World Mental Health: Problems and Priorities in Low Income Countries.* New Delhi: Oxford University Press, 1995.

Djebar, Assia. *Women of Algiers in their Apartment.* Charlottesville, VA: Caraf Books, 1992.

Drakulić, S. "Women and the New Democracy in the Former Yugoslavia." In N. Funk and M. Mueller, eds. *Gender Policy and Post-Communism.* New York: Routledge, 1993.

Einhorn, B. *Cinderella Goes to Market: Citizenship, Gender and Women's Movements in East and Central Europe.* London: Verso, 1993.

Eisenstein, Z. *Hatreds: Racialized and Sexualized Conflicts in the Twenty-first Century.* New York: Routledge, 1996.

Foucault, Michel. *History of Sexuality.* Volume 1. Translated by Robert Hurley. London: Penguin, 1981.

Friedman, M.J., and A.J. Marsella. "Post Traumatic Stress Disorder: An Overview of the Concept." In A.J. Marsella, M.J. Friedman, E.T. Gerrity, and R.M. Scurfield, eds. *Ethnocultural Aspects of Posttraumatic Stress Disorder.* Washington, DC: American Psychological Association, 1996.

Gandhi, Nandita, and Nandita Shah. *The Issues at Stake: Theory and Practice in the Contemporary Women's Movement in India.* New Delhi: Kali for Women, 1996.

Giles, Wenona, and Jennifer Hyndman. "New Directions for Feminist Research and Politics in Conflict Zones." In Wenona Giles and Jennifer Hyndman, eds. *Sites of Violence: Gender and Conflict Zones.* Berkeley: University of California Press, forthcoming.

Grewal, I., and C. Kaplan. "Introduction: Transnational Feminist Practices and Questions of Postmodernity." In by I. Grewal and C. Kaplan, eds. *Scattered*

Hegemonies: Postmodernity and Transnational Feminist Practices. Minneapolis: University of Minnesota Press, 1994.

Gunawardena, R.A.L.H. "The People of the Lion: Sinhala Consciousness in History and Historiography." In Charles Abeysekera and Newton Gunasinghe, eds. *Facets of Ethnicity in Sri Lanka*. Colombo: Social Scientists' Association, 1987.

Hasan, Zoya, ed. *Forging Identities: Gender, Communities and the State*. New Delhi: Kali for Women, 1994.

Hauser, Monika. "The War against Women and How They Are Defending Themselves." *Medica Bulletin* (January 1996).

Helms, Elissa. "Women as Agents of Ethnic Reconciliation? Women's NGOs and International Intervention in Post-war Bosnia-Herzegovina." *Women's Studies International Forum* 26,1 (Jan./Feb. 2003), pp.15-33.

Hoole, Rajan, Daya Somasunderam, K. Sritharan, and Rajani Thiranagama. *The Broken Palmyra: The Tamil Crisis in Sri Lanka – An Inside Account*. Claremont: The Sri Lanka Studies Institute, 1992.

Hyndman, Jennifer. "Refugee Camps as Conflict Zones: The Politics of Gender." In Wenona Giles and Jennifer Hyndman, eds. *Sites of Violence: Gender and Conflict Zones*. Berkeley: University of California Press, forthcoming.

Jayawardena, Kumari. "Ethnic Consciousness in Sri Lanka: Continuity and Change." In Committee for Rational Development, ed. *Sri Lanka. The Ethnic Conflict: Myths, Realities and Perspectives*. New Delhi: Navrang, 1984.

_____. *Feminism and Nationalism in the Third World*. London: Zed Books, 1986.

_____. "The National Question and the Left Movement in Sri Lanka." In Charles Abeysekera and Newton Gunasinghe, eds. *Facets of Ethnicity in Sri Lanka*. Colombo: Social Scientists' Association, 1987.

_____. "Some Aspects of Religious and Cultural Identity and the Construction of Sinhala Buddhist Womanhood." In Douglas Allen, ed. *Religion and Political Conflict in South Asia*. New Delhi: Oxford University Press, 1993.

Jayawardena, Kumari, and Malathi de Alwis, eds. *Embodied Violence: Communalising Women's Sexuality in South Asia*. New Delhi: Kali for Women, 1996.

Jeganathan, Pradeep. "Violence as an Anthropological Problem." *Nethra: Journal of the International Centre for Ethnic Studies* 2,2 (1998), pp.7-47.

Joseph, Stephen, Ruth Williams, and William Yule. *Understanding Post-traumatic Stress: A Psychosocial Perspective on PTSD and Treatment*. New York: John Wiley and Sons Ltd., 1997.

Kandiyoti, D. "Identity and Its Discontents: Women and the Nation." In P. Williams and L. Chrisman, eds. *Colonial Discourse and Post-Colonial Theory*. London: Harvester Wheatsheaf, 1993.

Klein, Edith. "Multilateralism and Its Consequences for Women in the Balkans: Intervention, Reconstruction, and Globalization." In Wenona Giles and Jennifer Hyndman, eds. *Sites of Violence: Gender and Conflict Zones*. Berkeley: University of California Press, forthcoming.

Kleinman, Arthur. *Writing at the Margin: Discourse between Anthropology and Medicine*. Berkeley: University of California Press, 1995.

Korač, Maja. *Linking Arms: Women and War in Post-Yugoslav States*. Uppsala: Women and Non-violence Series, No. 6, Life and Peace Institute, 1998.

Menon, Ritu, and Kamla Bhasin. *Borders and Boundaries: Women in India's Partition*. New Delhi: Kali for Women, 1998.

Muzychka, Martha, Carmen Poulin, Barbara Cottrell, Baukje Miedema, and Barbara Roberts. *Feminist Research Ethics: A Process*. 2d ed. Ottawa: The Canadian Research Institute for the Advancement of Women, 1996.

O' Brien, L. Stephen. *Traumatic Events and Mental Health*. Cambridge: Cambridge University Press, 1998.

Papić, Žarana. "From State Socialism to State Nationalism: The Case of Serbia in Gender Perspective." In Rada Iveković and Neda Pagon, eds. *Otherhood and Nation*. Ljubljana: Institutum Studiorum Humanitatisana, and Paris: Éditions de la Maison des Sciences de L'Homme, 1998.

_____. "Women in Serbia: Post-Communism, War, and Nationalist Mutations." In Sabrina Petra Ramet, ed. *Gender Politics in the Western Balkans: Women and Society in Yugoslavia and Yugoslav Successor States*. University Park: Pennsylvania State University Press, 1999.

Pandey, Gyanendra. *Constructing Communalism*. New Delhi: Oxford University Press, 1996.

Pickering, Natalie. "Cartographies of the Body and Being: Deconstructing the Biology of Identity." In *Introduction to Social Theory*. New Delhi: Konark Publishers, 1994.

Robin, Robert W., Barbara Chester, and David Goldman. "Cumulative Trauma and PTSD in American Indian Communities." In A.J. Marsella, M.J. Friedman, E.T. Gerrity, and R.M. Scurfield, eds. *Ethnocultural Aspects of Posttraumatic Stress Disorder*. Washington, DC: American Psychological Association, 1996.

Rubin, Gayle. "Thinking Sex: Notes for a Radical Theory of the Politics of Sexuality." In Carole S. Vance, ed. *Pleasure and Danger: Exploring Female Sexuality*. London: Routledge and Kegan Paul, 1984.

Sangari, Kumkum, and Sudesh Vaid, eds. *Recasting Women: Essays in Colonial History*. New Delhi: Kali for Women, 1989.

Scott, Joan Wallach. "Women's History and the Rewriting of History." In Christie Farnham, ed. *Impact of Feminist Research in the Academy*. Bloomington: Indiana University Press, 1987.

Silva, Neluka. *The Hybrid Island: Culture Crossings and the Invention of Identity in Sri Lanka*. Colombo: SSP, and London: Zed Press, 2002.

Silva, Neluka, and Rajiva Wijesinha, eds. *Across Cultures: Issues of Identity in Contemporary British and Sri Lankan Writing*. Colombo: British Council, 2001.

Smith, Dorothy E., and Sara J. David. *Women Look at Psychiatry*. Vancouver: Press Gang Publishers, 1975.

Tennekoon, Serena. "Symbolic Refractions of the Ethnic Crisis: The *Divaina* Debates on Sinhala Identity." In Charles Abeysekera and Newton Gunasinghe, eds. *Facets of Ethnicity in Sri Lanka*. Colombo: Social Scientists' Association, 1987.

Thiruchandran, Selvy. *The Other Victims of War: Emergence of Female-Headed Households in Eastern Sri Lanka*. New Delhi: Vikas Publishing House Pvt. Ltd., 1999.

Walby, Sylvia. "Woman and Nation." *Journal of Comparative Sociology* (September 1990).

Young, Allan. *The Harmony of Illusions: Inventing Post-Traumatic Stress Disorder*. Princeton, NJ: Princeton University Press, 1995.

Yuval-Davis, Nira. "Women, Ethnicity and Empowerment." *Feminist Psychology* 4,1 (1994), pp.179-97.

————. "Identity Politics and Women's Ethnicity." In Valentine Moghadam, ed. *Identity Politics and Women: Cultural Reassertations and Feminisms in International Perspective*. Boulder, CO: Westview Press, 1994.

Yuval-Davis, Nira, and Floya Anthias, eds. *Women-Nation-State*. London: Macmillan Press, 1989.

Contributors

Duška Andrić-Ružičić has studied economics and is the co-ordinator of the Infoteka project of Medica Zenica, Bosnia-Herzegovina, a community-based women's NGO established in 1993 to offer medical, psychological, and practical assistance to women survivors of war violence. Medica has continued to address issues of violence against women in the post-war period. The Infoteka project carries out research and publication, public advocacy, alternative education for other NGOs and local institutions, and networks with local, regional, and international activists. Duška Andrić-Ružičić has been active in Medica's work since the organization's beginnings and is committed to its growth as a leader in the effort to combat violence and discrimination against women in all its forms.

Malathi de Alwis is a Senior Research Fellow at the International Centre for Ethnic Studies, Colombo, and at present is a Visiting Professor of Anthropology at the New School for Social Research, in New York City. She received her Ph.D. in Socio-Cultural Anthropology from the University of Chicago, and is the co-editor, with Kumari Jayawardena, of *Embodied Violence: Communalising Women's Sexuality in South Asia*. Many of her articles, which focus on feminist/peace movements in South Asia as well as on issues of gender, nationalism, militarism, and humanitarianism, have been published in various parts of the globe both in English and in translations. She is a founding member of the National Women's NGO Forum and the Women's Coalition for Peace, Sri Lanka, and a regular contributor to "Cat's Eye" – a feminist column on contemporary issues – in the *Island Newspaper*.

Radhika Coomaraswamy is the United Nations Special Rapporteur on Violence Against Women. She received her B.A. from Yale University, her J.D. from Columbia University, and her LL.M. from Harvard University. She is the Director of the International Centre for Ethnic Studies Colombo and has published books and articles in the area of constitutional law, ethnic studies, and women's human rights.

Neloufer de Mel is Director of Studies, Faculty of Arts, and a senior lecturer at the Department of English, University of Colombo, Sri Lanka. She is also a faculty member of the M.A. in Women's Studies Program at the University of Colombo and a member of the Social Science Research Council's Regional Advisory Panel for South Asia. Her essays and research interests cover gender studies, post-colonial literature, nationalism, film, militarism, and popular culture. Her most recent book is *Women and the Nation's Narrative: Gender and Nationalism in Twentieth-Century Sri Lanka*. She is co-editor of the forthcoming anthology *Writing an Inheritance: Women's Writing in Sri Lanka 1860-1948*.

Ananda Galappatti is involved in human resource development, service provision, policy formulation, and research related to armed conflict and psychosocial distress in Sri Lanka.

Wenona Giles is an Associate Professor and Chair of the School of Social Sciences, Atkinson Faculty of Liberal and Professional Studies at York University, Toronto. She teaches and publishes in the areas of gender, migration, ethnicity, nationalism, work, globalization, and war. Her publications include *Maid in the Market: Women's Paid Domestic Labour*; *Development and Diaspora: Gender and the Refugee Experience*; *Portuguese Women in Toronto: Gender, Immigration, and Nationalism*; a special two-volume issue of *Refuge* on Gender Relations and Refugee Issues (1995); special issues of the *Canadian Woman Studies Journal* on Immigrant Women (1999) and Women in Conflict Zones (2000); and is co-editor with Jennifer Hyndman of *Sites of Violence: Gender and Conflict Zones*. With Maja Korač, she co-ordinated the international Women in Conflict Zones Research Network and the project "A Comparative Study of the Issues Faced by Women as a Result of Armed Conflict: Sri Lanka and the Post-Yugoslav States" at York University.

Elissa Helms is a Ph.D. candidate in Cultural Anthropology at the University of Pittsburgh. She is currently working on her dissertation entitled "Gendered Visions of the Bosnian Future: Women's Activism and National Identity in Post-war Bosnia-Herzegovina," which is based on ethnographic field work in Bosnia among women participants in NGOs and politics (1997, 1999-2000). She has been engaged in the region since 1993, working in various capacities with refugees, youth, and women in Bosnia, Croatia, and the U.S.

Kumari Jayawardena, a long-time activist and academic in Sri Lanka, is a member of the Social Scientists' Association in Colombo, Sri Lanka. She is the author of *Feminism and Nationalism in the Third World,* and co-editor with Malathi de Alwis of *Embodied Violence: Communalising Women's Sexuality in South Asia.*

Edith S. Klein is a Resident Fellow (Political Science) at the Centre for Russian and East European Studies at the Munk Centre for International Studies, University of Toronto. She is also the Programme Manager for European Studies, the Joint Initiative in German and European Studies, and the York - U of T Institute of European Studies at the Munk Centre. She holds degrees from the University of Michigan and the University of Toronto, and has published articles on conflict resolution in the territories of the former Yugoslavia. Her research interests are in the politics of the post-Yugoslav successor states, specifically on issues of political culture, gender relations, conflict transformation, social policy, local government, and community-based reconciliation and reconstruction.

Djurdja Knežević is the founder and director of the Women's Resource Centre, Ženska infoteka (established in 1992), in Zagreb, Croatia. She is also editor-in-chief of the feminist magazine *Kruh i ruže* (Bread and Roses). For the past four years, through her work with Ženska infoteka, Knežević has organized an annual international seminar, Women and Politics, that focuses on the political participation of women in Eastern European countries and that takes place in Dubrovnik, Croatia. She has published many articles, essays, reviews, and interviews on the topics of women's issues and feminist politics, women's history, problems of nationalism, and peace processes in the former Yugoslavia. Her research interests include contemporary women's history in former Yugoslavia/ Croatia, feminist politics, and women and nationalism.

Maja Korač gained her Ph.D. at the Graduate Program in Sociology, York University, Toronto, in 1998. From 1996 until 1999 she was a Research Consultant and one of the co-founders of the Women in Conflict Zones Network Project initiated and housed at York University. Her research and academic work relate to the field of forced migration as it pertains to gender as well as to the situation faced by women in zones of armed conflict involving ethnic divisions. From 1999-2001, Korač was the "Lisa Gilad" Senior Research Officer at the Refugee Studies Centre (RSC), University of Oxford. At present she is a Lecturer at the School of Cultural and Innovation Studies at the University of East London and a Research Associate at the RSC, University of Oxford. Her publications include the book *Linking Arms: Women and War in Post-Yugoslav States*, as well as chapters in edited volumes and academic journals, including *Identities*, *Women's Studies International Forum*, the *Journal of International Migration and Integration*, and *Sociology*.

Lepa Mladjenović is a feminist counsellor at the Autonomous Women's Centre, Belgrade, a co-founder of the women's peace group Women in Black against War, and a lecturer in the Centre for Women's Studies. In the last ten years of wars in the region of the former Yugoslavia, she has been a feminist activist in the movements for peace, anti-violence, lesbian rights, and anti-fascism of the Serbian regime.

Žarana Papić was an Assistant Professor at the Faculty of Philosophy, University of Belgrade, co-founder and Professor at the Belgrade Women's Studies Centre, and at the Alternative Academic Educational Centre (AAEN) in Belgrade. She was also an Associate Researcher with the Laboratoire d'Anthropologie Sociale (Collège de France) Paris and a feminist activist/supporter of Women in Black, Women's Political Action, and other women's initiatives in the region of the former Yugoslavia. Before her death in 2002, she had been working in the field of gender studies, cultural studies, and socio-political theory, the construction and representation of bodies, violence, and gender, and on an ethnography of nationalism in Serbia, and the constitution of the social sphere in the area of discourse analysis. Her articles have been published in academic journals and edited volumes in English, French, and German, which include "From State Socialism to State Nationalism: The Case of Serbia in Gender Perspective," in Rada Iveković and Neda Pagon, eds., *Otherhood and Nation*, and "Women in Serbia: Post-Communism, War, and Nationalist Mutations," in Sabrina Petra Ramet, ed., *Gender Politics in the Western Balkans: Women and Society in Yugoslavia and Yugoslav Successor States*.

Kumudini Samuel is the current Joint Co-ordinator of the Women and Media Collective, Sri Lanka. She is also a founding member and serves on the Executive Committee of the Sri Lanka Women's NGO Forum (SLWNGOF) and is a member of the Women's Coalition for Peace, Sri Lanka. She has worked as a women's rights and human rights activist since 1980, and has published on gender, peace, human rights, activism, and violence against women.

Neluka Silva is a Senior Lecturer in and Head of the Department of English, University of Colombo. She has published articles on issues of nationalism, gender, and identity in cultural production in South Asia. She works on issues of representation of gender, identity, and peace in Sri Lankan teledrama. She has edited *The Hybrid Island: Culture Crossings and the Invention of Identity in Sri Lanka*, and co-edited with Rajiva Wijesinha, *Across Cultures: Issues of Identity in Contemporary British and Sri Lankan Writing*.

Selvy Thiruchandran holds a Ph.D. in Socio-Cultural Studies and is at present the Executive Director of the Women's Education and Research Centre (WERC), Colombo. She is the Editor of *Nivedini* (English and Tamil editions), a feminist journal published bi-annually by her organization. She has edited *Images*, a collection of research papers of the multi-lingual media-monitoring project conducted by WERC, and *Women, Narration and Nation: Collective Images and Multiple Identities*. She is the author of a number of books, including *Ideology, Caste, Class and Gender: The Spectrum of Feminity; The Politics of Gender and Women's Agency in Post Colonial Sri Lanka; The Other Victims of War: Emergence of Female-Headed Households in Eastern Sri Lanka; Feminine Speech Transmissions: An Exploration into the Lullabies and Dirges of Women*, as well as a number of books in Tamil on Gender Studies.

Index

229